RINGS
AROUND
LONDON

To the driver stuck in a traffic jam on the M25.
In case he or she wonders why.

RINGS AROUND LONDON

Wayne Asher

CAPITAL HISTORY

Acknowledgements

Many people helped me with this study. In first place must be the librarians and archivists who are the custodians of our history and who dug items out for me. Without them there is no history and without history we have no present.

They include London Metropolitan Archives in Clerkenwell, where the files of the London County Council and Greater London Council were deposited, and the National Archives at Kew, where Whitehall's vast files on road building and policy may be consulted, along with the documents relating to the Layfield Panel. The collection of Guildhall Library on London's history is an essential resource, as are various local authority archives. I also benefited greatly from access to the libraries at University College London.

Carol Morgan at the Institution of Civil Engineers kindly arranged access to the archives of the British Road Federation, which were deposited there when the BRF ceased operations in 2000. The papers of Roland Moyle MP at Lewisham borough archives provide an archive of both the London Motorway Action Group and a decade of anti-motorway campaigning in Blackheath. The papers of Dave Wetzel and Paul Moore are at Bishopsgate Institute in the City. The archives of the Hampstead and Camden Town Motorway Action Groups are at Camden borough archives. Much material relating to motorway construction for the south-east and eastern regions has been deposited at the Surrey and Northampton County Archives

Among the people who gave generously of their time, recollections and loan of documents I must thank, in no particular order. Mary Jay, Tim Pharoah, Sara Neill, Terence Bendixson, Stephen Plowden, Stephen Joseph, Michael Ward, Andrew Warren, Terry Hill, Jonathan Bray, Stephen Norris, Edmund King, John Stewart, John Adams, Paul Moore, Dave Wetzel, Tony Belton, David Quarmby, Steve Chambers, David Lawrence and Jonathan Roberts. Especial thanks are due to Mary Jay who arranged access to Douglas Jay's papers, deposited at the Bodliean Library in Oxford, and which are normally unavailable to researchers pending cataloguing and to Jonathan Bray, who lent me his vast archive of anti-motorway activism in the 1980s and 1990s.

Any errors which remain are naturally mine alone.

Front cover image: Builders carve the Westway through North Kensington, late 1960s. (PA Photos)

First published 2018

ISBN 978-1-85414-421-8

Published by Capital History Publishing

www.capitalhistory.com

Printed by Parksons Graphics

© Wayne Asher

Contents

Abbreviations	6
Introduction	7
1 – Genesis of an idea	9
2 – Lobbyists and councillors	25
3 – Green light for the ringways	43
4 – Rage against the concrete	58
5 – Defeat into victory	95
6 – Round and round the M25	112
7 – Ghosts	135
Epilogue	157
Appendix – Was your home at risk?	160
Notes	170
Bibliography and image credits	181
Index	182

Contexts

We are not going to do without a great car economy
  – Margaret Thatcher, prime minister, 1979-1990[1]

The private motorist wants the independence and status of his motor car. He wants the chance to live a life that gives him a new dimension of freedom—freedom to go where he wants, when he wants, and for as long as he wants.
  – Nicholas Ridley, secretary of state for transport and secretary of state for the environment 1983-1987[2]

We have to face the fact that whether we like it or not, the way we have built our towns is entirely the wrong way for motor traffic. We want an entirely different type of town.
  – Ernest Marples, minister of transport, 1959-1964[3]

By 1960, the great fear was upon us. how much longer could we go on? When would traffic come to a total standstill? When would we suffocate in our own fumes?
  – Greater London Council, 1970[4]

Abbreviations

ALARM	All London Against Road Menace	Campaign group which fought road building plans in the 1980s
AA	Automobile Association	
BRF	British Road Federation	The main road lobby group, financed by oil, construction and car interests
COBA	COmputerised cost Benefit Analysis	Controversial government method for appraising the financial value of road building in the 1980s and 1990s
DoE	Department of the Environment	Absorbed the MoT from 1970 to 1976
DoT	Department of Transport	1976–1997
ELRC	East London River Crossing	1980s successor to Ringway 2 in east London
GLDP	Greater London Development Plan	The formal plan which contained the motorway proposals of the 1960s
GLC	Greater London Council	The strategic planning authority for London from 1965 to its abolition in 1986
HBR	Homes Before Roads	Anti-motorway group which contested the 1970 GLC elections
LATA	London Amenity and Transport Association	Umbrella group for local amenity societies which fought against the London ringways
LTS	London Traffic Survey	Three volumes of traffic studies and analysis which were used to justify building the London ringways
LCC	London County Council	The county council for the inner London boroughs which was merged into the GLC in 1965
LMAG	London Motorway Action Group	Umbrella group which coordinated the fight against the London Ringways
MHLG	Ministry of Housing and Local Government	
MoT	Ministry of Transport	1919–1970
PARC	People Against the River Crossing	Community group in south-east London which led the battle against the East London River Crossing
RAC	Royal Automobile Club	
RCC	Roads Campaign Council	Road lobby group, set up in 1955
TGB	Thames Gateway Bridge	Successor to the East London River Crossing
SACTRA	Standing Advisory Committee on Trunk Road Assessment	Government committee which advised on road building in the 1980s and 1990s
TfL	Transport for London	In charge of London transport since 2000

Introduction

London does not look like Los Angeles. Even if the sun and the palm trees were added in, London would still look – and feel – very different. But it is surprisingly little-known that London could have become very much more like Los Angeles, (or Houston, Atlanta or indeed most US cities).

In the 1960s and 1970s plans were made to build a network of vast urban motorways – the ringways and the Motorway Box – across the capital. The plans were deadly serious and highly detailed. Parts were actually implemented – one became the M25, others exist today in the East End and North Kensington.

The full network was never built, and we enjoy the London of today in part precisely because they were never built. They would have transformed the cityscape, been the largest public works project in Britain since the Second World War, and made London a very different city. Building them would have cost billions of pounds, made thousands homeless, wreaked enormous environmental damage and, by making the capital a car dominated city, changed the way we live for the worse. The 21st century renaissance in public transport could never have happened.

This book explores what the ringways were, where the idea came from, and where they would have gone. It looks at the campaigns and protests which prevented most of them from being built, and which – subsequently – blocked a determined attempt to revive them in the 1980s.

In so doing, (historian's bias declared here), they did a great and lasting favour for all present day Londoners.

The London motorway plans of the 1960s. COLOUR CODING: Black – radial motorways; Red – Ringway 1 (the Motorway Box); Green – Ringway 2; Blue – Ringway 3; Orange – North and South Orbital Routes; Purple – Parkway E; Turquoise – linking sections built to complete M25.

Solid lines show motorways actually built (even if built to sub-motorway standards), hatched lines ones which were planned

1 – Genesis of an idea

The year is 1943. The place is County Hall on London's South Bank. The context is war; east London, Coventry, Southampton, Devonport all lay in ruins after German bombings. D-day was still a year away. Yet after Stalingrad and the US entry into the war, final victory over the Nazi menace was certain. The sense of optimism in Britain was palpable. The Beveridge report into the future welfare state had been published to acclaim, and in London, two men had already been tasked to look at what the bombed and battered capital would be like when peace and prosperity were finally restored.

The two were Patrick Abercrombie, a 64 year old architect and unchallenged doyen of the town planning movement, and 48 year old John Forshaw, architect to the London County Council. Their taskmaster was Lord Reith of the BBC, the wartime minister of works. Their 188 page report was called the *County of London Plan*.[5] Its appearance, as a well-produced hardback at a time when paper was strictly rationed, indicated the importance attached to it, and it went on to sell 10,000 copies, with abridged versions produced for schools and the armed forces.

In it, Abercrombie and Forshaw took an all-round view of a set of interlocking problems and the damage they had done to the pre-war, chaotic, city which had grown incrementally over the centuries, with no attempt at central planning. It was implicit that planning and organisation would offer a brighter future than the free markets and private interests which millions now held responsible for the horrors of the 1930s. Planning, it was universally believed, could help put us in control of our environment, instead of the other way around.

Abercrombie and Forshaw blamed London's ills on a combination of;
- Traffic congestion ('the most obvious and ubiquitous defect in pre-war London')
- Overcrowded and insanitary housing, which was a risk to health, public welfare and the general quality of life
- Inadequate and inequitable distribution of open spaces – which were scarcest just where they were most needed, in the poor and over-crowded East End
- The mixing together of houses and industries, which was a prime cause of pollution and poor quality of life

Abercrombie and Forshaw offered a way out of all this – a utopian vision of a future London, replanned from the ground up in the best interests of the citizens. They were influenced by the precinct-like natures of the university quarter in Bloomsbury, and the Inns of Court, and they discussed how devastated inner London communities should be rebuilt, with much of the Victorian housing stock, overcrowded, unsanitary and run down, being replaced by new housing. In future, homes would be segregated from the pollution and noise of industry. Green open space would be provided for the first time and Londoners would enjoy 'their dwellings grouped around their social and shopping centres, inter-spersed with open spaces, their schools spaced according to the new population requirements and their industries collected into more compact areas.' Children would play in parks – not in the streets.

The County of London then encompassed what as we know today as inner London.[6] Today's outer boroughs mainly classed as urban districts with varying powers, and formed parts of five counties; Middlesex, Surrey, Essex, Kent and

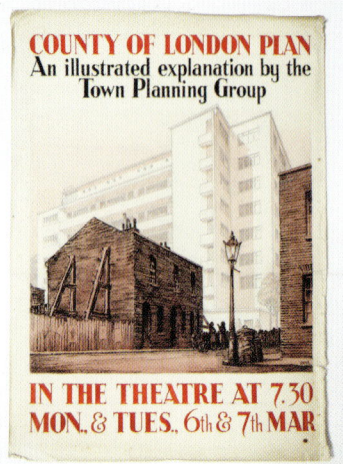

PoWs in Germany discuss the Abercrombie Plan

Hertfordshire. Only West Ham, East Ham and Croydon ranked as county boroughs with the full powers of a county council.

Many of these outlying areas had grown spectacularly in the 1920s and 1930 as London suburbanised itself on a raft of cheap credit. Two examples will suffice; Edgware grew from 1,516 people in 1921 to 88,002 in 1952; Ruislip from 9,112 in 1921 to 16,035 in 1931 and 68,288 by 1951. So strategic planning for London as a whole was impossible if it were limited to the County. So in 1944, the ministry of works asked Abercrombie to repeat the exercise, but this time for the London conurbation as a whole. The result was the 1944 Greater London Plan.[7]

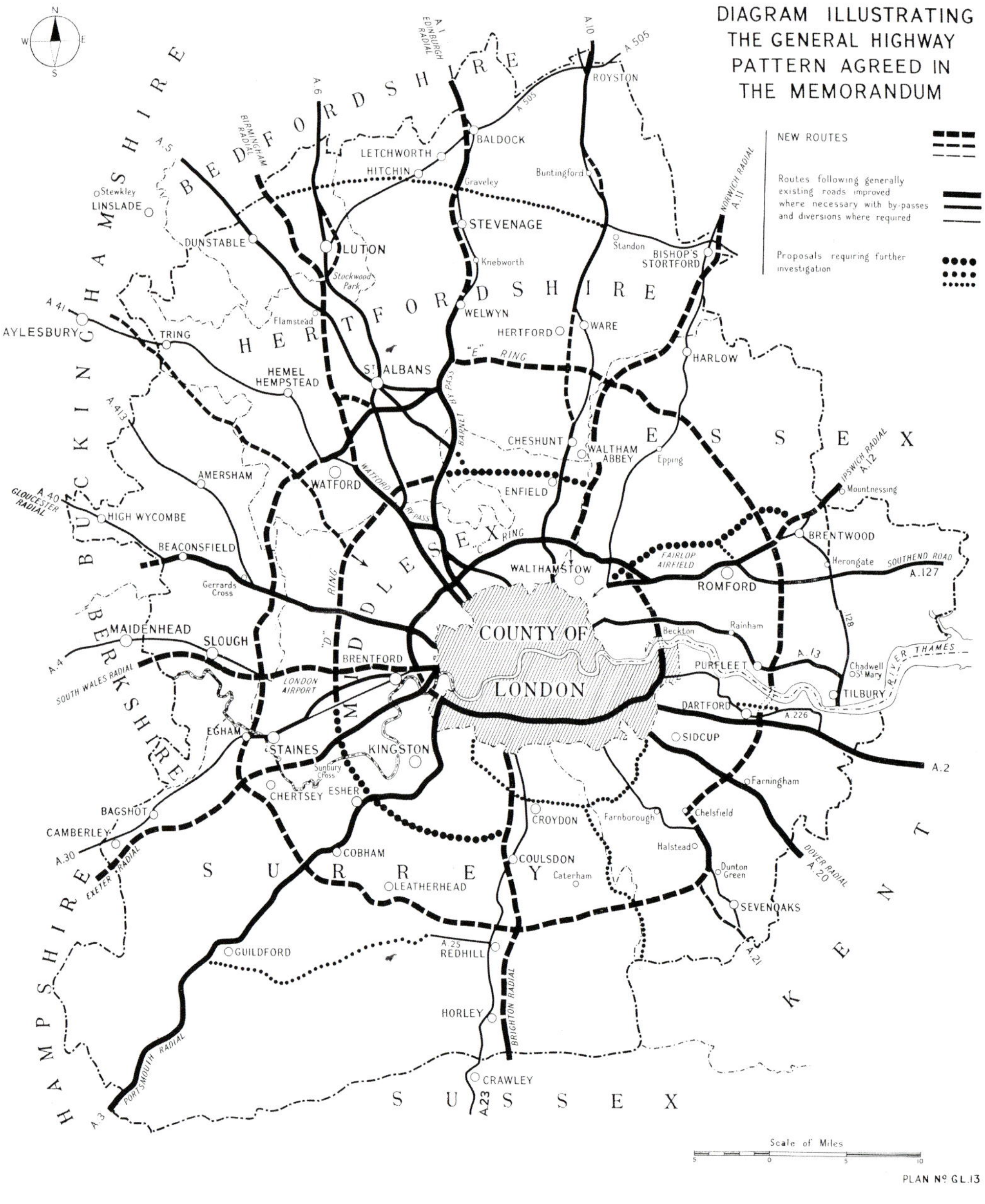

Abercrombie's ring and radial network of 1944. What became the motorways of today are clearly visible, as are the Ringway plans of the 1960s and 1970s.

Like many observers, Abercrombie looked with horror at the ugly, unplanned, suburbanisation of the 1920s and 30s. He wanted to control this unplanned expansion by enforcing a green belt around the built up area where development would be prohibited. The population (London was still the world's largest city) would be managed by decanting residents to a group of planned New Towns in the home counties, which were influenced by the Garden City movement of the 1920s. Existing towns such as Ashford, Luton and Basingstoke would be expanded to take more of London's surplus population.

London's history is, of course, that of its transport systems, and Abercrombie promised a revolution here also. All suburban train services would be electrified, and to ensure the green space would be protected from traffic, cross-London road traffic, that 'most obvious and ubiquitous defect,' would be directed away from the centre by a network of five ring roads built at increasing distances from the centre. These would link with a network of new radial routes connecting London with major provincial cities.

Abercrombie's report was a grand vision by Britain's leading town planner. It was produced at exactly the right time; in Greater London, 110,000 houses had been completely destroyed while over two million properties had suffered some bomb damage. There would never be a better time to implement such a vision. Indeed, in its vast scale the report looks back to the plans drawn up the last time huge areas of London needed to be redeveloped, after the Great Fire of 1666, when John Evelyn and Christopher Wren were among those who proposed a brand new City featuring a set of long, wide, straight roads linking new urban space.

This vision of a new world had tremendous resonance; 75,000 people visited the exhibition at County Hall and it was even discussed by RAF prisoners of war at Stalag Luft III in Germany, where a poster was made to advertise a discussion about it in the camp theatre.[8]

Yet Abercrombie was not the first expert to call for massive road building programmes, and his report drew explicitly on the work of others before him. And that means that we must first look backwards, before returning to Abercrombie and what was to follow.

Londoners, it turns out, had been complaining about traffic since the 17th century. A commons select committee sat in 1836, when London's present suburbs were detached villages, 'to consider the most effectual plan for raising of money to carry into effect the necessary improvements required in the cities of London and Westminster, borough of Southwark and counties of Middlesex and Surrey, etc.' Further select committees were appointed in 1838, 1839, 1840 and 1841 to carry out similar duties, and in 1842 a royal commission was established to inquire into and consider 'the most effectual means of improving the metropolis and of providing means of communication within the same.'

Another Royal Commission on London Transport was appointed in 1903 and presented eight volumes of reports during the following two years.[9] It concentrated mainly on railways, buses and trams, but it did consider a circular ring road around London, on a route very similar to today's North and South Circular roads. The argument made was that London's roads would be quieter and less congested if through traffic which did not actually want to be there could take a detour around.

The man behind this proposal was William Rees Jeffreys, leader of the AA as well as a lobby group called the Road Improvement Association, and subse-

Patrick (later Lord) Abercrombie

Staples Corner 1944: where the North Circular crosses the A5. No flyover and No M1 either. See page 104 for a current view

quently secretary of the government's Road Fund.[10] He called it a 'disgrace that no road existed which encircled the English capital city'. He added that while tram, railway and road communications should all be considered together, 'the most urgent need was for this orbital road.'

For several years before the First World War, the board of trade tried to grapple with London's traffic problems, and following a deputation from local councils to the prime minister, Herbert Asquith, a series of Greater London arterial roads conferences took place between 1913 and 1916. These brought together all local authorities in greater London, and they prepared plans for 255 miles of new roads.[11]

Unlike most road projects proposed for London, the arterial roads conferences actually led to things being done. It was, in fact, the most impressive and successful road building programme ever carried out in the capital, and with the coming of peace, 214 miles of new roads were built. The central reason for the success is instructive when we look at events in subsequent decades. It was that the newly-formed transport ministry was willing and able to throw money at road schemes to relieve unemployment, and that the government as a whole was scared enough that dole queues bred Bolshevism to go along with it.

The result of this spending included the North Circular Road from Gants Hill (A12) in the east to Hanger Lane on the A40 in the west, Western Avenue from White City to Greenford, and its eastern analogue, Eastern Avenue, from Romford to Wanstead. The Great West Road was built through Brentford, a new route to the Royal Docks built, and a whole series of suburban bypasses put in place, including those at Kingston, Croydon, Watford and Barnet.

All were designed to provide fast routes for through traffic; they would intentionally duplicate existing routes through established town centres.

Planners often underestimated how popular these roads would become; even on the North Circular, the most important for the continuing story, only four miles were built with dual carriageway from the outset and 12 miles had carriageways no wider than 30 feet.

Most of the North Circular was built and opened in stages by Middlesex County, acting as agent for Whitehall. It would be a government trunk road due to the fragmented nature of local government in the suburbs. In return for its contribution, Middlesex was guaranteed its share of jobs on the new project. The official opening ceremony took place on 25 April 1933, and the last section was named Pinkham Way after alderman Sir Charles Pinkham, chair of the Middlesex highways committee.

The road was a key factor – along with tube extensions – in the urbanisation of Middlesex and was seen as a spine linking the western and northern zones of the county more closely together.

Although much of the land traversed was still open country, building the North Circular still involved some heavy engineering works; at Stonebridge Park an aqueduct had to be built so the road could pass under the Grand Union Canal. Another highlight was the 600-yard viaduct carrying the road over the Lea Valley at Edmonton, where there were three waterways. It featured huge gateway-type pylons designed specifically to make an architectural statement. *The Times'* architectural correspondent thought the viaduct stood out for 'a frank use of concrete as a material capable of architectural treatment, and a statement of scale.'[12] The total cost of the project – the first attempt at building a London ring road – was £1.25 million (£76 million in today's money).[13]

Although there was no opposition to this huge building programme, the North Circular could be alarming once open; in 1936, Willesden's mayor led a demonstration demanding that a 30mph speed limit be imposed,[14] and *The Times* recorded that 'a procession of motor vehicles, cyclists and pedestrians traversed the road in both directions, holding up the traffic on what was formerly regarded as an arterial road but now had many houses on each side of it.'[15]

The North Circular – numbered the A406 – was a misnomer – it did not form a complete link north of the river. True, a route could be traced from Hanger Lane to join the A4 at Chiswick, and in the east to the Woolwich ferry, but these were normal urban roads with their own designation and not technically part of the North Circular.

Buoyed by the momentum, local councils and the ministry met in 1924 to plan another route – the 70 mile long North Orbital. This would be built around 20 miles from the centre and run from the A4 at Colnbrook to Tilbury, via Uxbridge, Watford, Hatfield, Hoddesdon, and Ongar. Most of it would consist of upgraded existing roads, although some new stretches would be needed.

The ministry, which led the project, would pay half of the cost. But building would be in the hands of county councils, which would pay the other half. Their

Sir Charles Bressey

enthusiasm for the road therefore hung on the 'what's in it for me' question. Hertford County built the A405 from Hatfield to near Watford as part of the North Orbital because it provided a useful bypass for St Albans. But Essex saw no local benefit, and so did almost nothing. The ministry's chief road engineer, Sir Charles Bressey, complained that 'there is not the least sign of any willingness on their part to undertake works, such as the long and (locally) unremunerative stretch across the Lea Valley.'[16]

In the meantime, traffic congestion increased relentlessly, driven by the rise in the number of cars, which had leapt from less than 250,000 in 1912 to 2.4 million by 1934.[17] Everyone expected this figure to keep on increasing exponentially and as usual, experts looked to the US for a vision of our own future.

The US experience was ominous; there was already one car for four people by 1937 – in Britain it was only one for 20 people. In US trendsetter regions such as southern California, the density was greater still – there was one car for each 1.6 people as early as 1925, a ratio the rest of the US did not reach until the late 1950s.[18] No-one saw any reason why car ownership in the UK should not increase just as sharply, and if it did, it followed that more and bigger roads would be needed.[19]

Lines on a map – Bressey's plans for London. Lines in red are the three priority routes

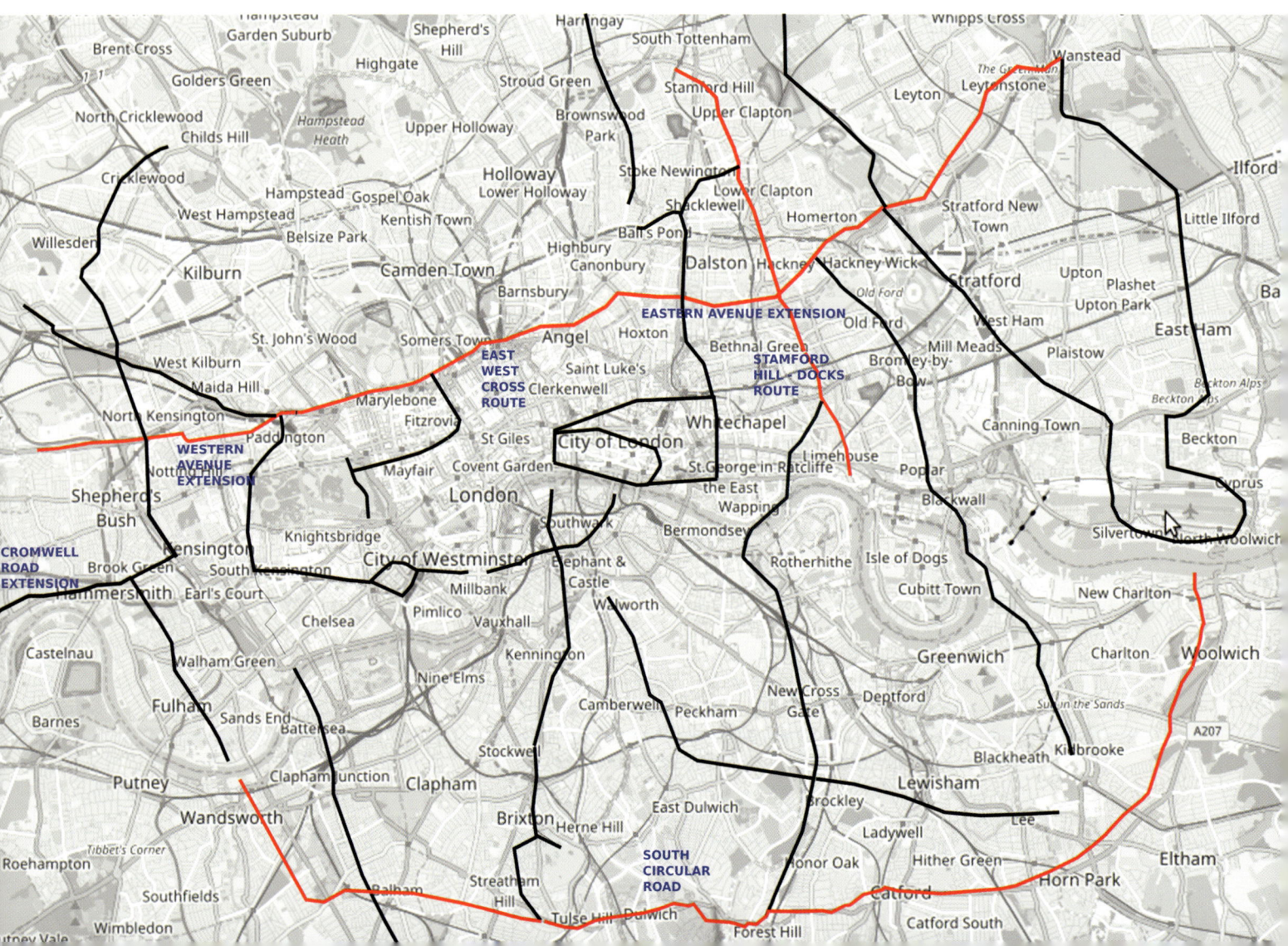

In 1934, the then transport minister, Leslie Hore-Belisha (of beacon fame) decided on a new approach. Instead of further committees, he gave one man a free hand to come up with a definitive plan to fix London's road transport needs right up to the 1960s. That man was Sir Charles Bressey. Hore-Belisha accepted that road building and bridges had 'an important bearing upon the general development and amenities of Greater London'. So he appointed the architect, Sir Edwin Lutyens, to act as consultant to Bressey. As planning for the County of London alone was already understood to be a meaningless activity, they were told to consider an area roughly 25 miles from Charing Cross.

In May 1938 the transport ministry published Bressey and Lutyens' work as the *Highways Development Survey*.[20]

Bressey recommended a monster roads programme with 66 separate schemes and improved junctions at key congestion points. Central to his proposals was the outer North Orbital route as discussed since 1924, and a counterpart in the south through Surrey and Kent. They would be built as US-style parkways[21] – wide, landscaped roads with limited access and grade-separated junctions – road engineer-ese for flyovers and underpasses designed to boost fast through traffic, with no roundabouts or traffic lights to halt progress. There was a clear influence from the German autobahnen which a UK delegation had viewed with awe the previous year.

In London itself the key proposals included a south circular route, and a 12 mile east – west route from East Acton to Wanstead. It would involve two motorways being built, linking Western Avenue and Eastern Avenue, via Pentonville and Marylebone Roads, which would be widened with roundabouts installed to help speed through traffic, with a tunnel built near King's Cross. The extension to Eastern Avenue would pass to the north of Victoria Park in Hackney, providing what Bressey called 'an attractive route' for the road.

In central London there would be tunnels under Hyde Park and Mayfair. The map shows some of the Bressey proposals in inner London.

Some of Bressey's projects would be widening and improvement of existing routes, others would be brand new highways which would have been hugely destructive to property, Bressey did mention this slight drawback, but took it no further, and he had no compunction about planning new roads right through established communities which would be sliced in two.

The South Circular would be a particular headache – it had been recommended by the Arterial Roads Conferences but never built, instead, it had been 'declared' in 1935 by the simple expedient of stitching existing streets together to make a route. This subterfuge was instructive; most roads built after the conference era passed through what was still open country. But the area where a proper South Circular route could run was already built up, and work here would be hugely expensive. Although some existing roads could be used, Bressey warned that 'improvements' at Forest Hill, Tulse Hill and Catford Bridge 'would have to take a far more drastic form' to boost through traffic.

So Bressey had thought big; the word 'ambitious' seems inadequate to describe the scope of his proposals – an Australian newspaper correspondent in London was awe-struck by their scale and cost; 'one hesitates to think of the millions the new roads would cost, for they traverse the most expensive tract of land in the world. But sooner or later the expense must be faced.'[22]

Bressey looked for evidence to back his ideas, So he carried out traffic surveys which showed that on three radial routes, the average speed was only 12.5 mph, while speeds on the new North Circular averaged 23.6 mph. So new, planned, roads could speed up traffic and loosen congestion.

To get the data, the routes were 'traversed continuously by a 16 HP Austin Light Six Touring car during a six day working week. From Monday to Friday inclusive, the car ran driven by a steady and competent professional chauffeur, who had no inducement to attempt to break records or take risks. His pace may be assumed to be that of the punctilious, cautious, and considerate driver who presumably constitutes the bulk of the British motoring community.'[23]

Bressey's report was typical of its time, produced when the great engineering achievements of the Victorian era were not ancient history but things in recent memory; things to be proud of – and if possible – to emulate. It was a report based on a simple logic understandable to everyone; if existing roads were congested then we obviously needed to build more of them. Yet an astonishing point was made, carefully justified with respect to the evidence – and then passed over.

Referring to the new arterial roads, Bressey said 'one could hardly conceive the degree of congestion which would now prevail on the older highways – however much widened and improved – but for the relief afforded by the arterial roads.' He looked at the Great West Road which had opened in 1925 and offered the following traffic data for the number of vehicles a day;

Table One – Traffic on Great West Road compared with the old route

Year	Old route	New route
1922	1,404	Not open
1925	1,435	6,440
1928	1,887	9,404
1931	2,238	12,610
1935	3,826	16,993

So the new route, almost as soon as it was opened, carried 4.5 times as many vehicles as the old route through Brentford town centre. So far, so good, and entirely to be expected. But Bressey added; 'no diminution however, occurred in the flow of traffic along the old route, and from that day to this the number of vehicles on both routes has steadily increased.'

Bressey did not put this counter-intuitive result down to the greater number of cars. Quite remarkably, in view of later arguments about the futility of road building, he said; 'these figures serve to exemplify the remarkable manner in which new roads create new traffic.'

Unfortunately Bressey left it there. He did not pursue an absolutely central point which would lie dormant until taken up by anti-motorway campaigners 30 years later. Possibly he thought traffic generation was actually a good thing. Alternatively, as a leading road engineer, he found himself in a difficult position – he had been mandated to specify what roads were needed to solve London's traffic problems and had he followed the logic of his own evidence, he would have had to conclude that building new roads could never solve traffic congestion as they merely stimulated new traffic. It followed that London's traffic jams could not be solved simply by building more roads, but required a holistic approach with a major investment in public transport.[24]

Unfortunately, the 1930s were a decade of lost opportunity for public transport, at least for inner and central London. While money *was* invested in the tube under the New Works Programme, it went mainly to extending existing tube lines to outer suburbs, often by projecting tube trains over main line suburban tracks, as in the case of the Central and Northern Line extensions. There is an argument that some of these extensions were misconceived, actually leading to longer journey times, from, for example, the Central Line stations in Essex.

Many central London stations were comprehensively rebuilt, which massively improved capacity, and new trains were built for the Bakerloo and Northern Lines.

But no new lines serving central and inner London were built.

The government accepted Bressey's plans in principle, although approval was hedged about with the usual caveats about money. In June 1939, the transport minister, Captain Euan Wallace, gave an update on progress,[25] for those outer zones where the minister was the highway authority. These included the Cromwell Road extension, which he hoped would be completed 'within a year or so,' bypasses for Crawley, Staines and Maidenhead, and a new road from Coulsdon to Crawley, where the route had been safeguarded against development. Other schemes which were either in progress or about to begin were the Dartford Tunnel and approaches, the second Blackwall Tunnel, and Wandsworth Bridge and its southern approach.

But progress was complicated by the divided responsibility for roads. Trunk roads, well signposted and where through traffic had priority over local traffic, were everywhere the responsibility of the transport ministry, while local roads, designed for local needs, belonged to local councils.

But in London County, there were no trunk roads at all, only local roads, so the minister's writ only ran in Middlesex and the other suburban counties. So when Captain Wallace was quizzed about progress on the Western Avenue extension, he could only sidestep the issue, saying 'I am always ready to press the London County Council as far as I can.'

In fact, LCC engineers and Bressey had been talking in detail even as his report was being prepared. There was broad agreement between them on the roads to be built, and disagreements were only on points of detail;. Pierson Frank, the LCC's chief engineer, didn't want a tunnel at King's Cross for example.

The LCC actually preferred that the Eastern Avenue extension cross part of London Fields, today a gentrified part of Hackney, but in those days an absolutely vital lung for a poor and overcrowded part of the capital. This route would have been shorter, and therefore cheaper. From an engineering point of view, Bressey was happy to sever London Fields but he wrote to the ministry urging caution. He thought the LCC was 'underestimating the strength of the protests which would be voiced. In this very same neighbourhood the LCC certainly misjudged the force of public opinion when they put forward proposals for building a housing estate on Hackney Marshes.'[26]

Bressey thought Frank's views on the King's Cross tunnel 'timid and commonplace' and in a fine piece of engineering machismo, warned that the ministry would be condemned for 'want of virility and enterprise if new routes contemplated are a mere replica of schemes constructed immediately after the war.'[27]

But all this was detail. The real disagreement was over who was going to pay for it all. The government would only pay half the cost, leaving London's ratepayers to find the rest. The ministry was prepared to offer a little help; it agreed to up the grant to 60 per cent on three top priority schemes, the east-west cross route, the South Circular, and the road from Stamford Hill to the docks.

But it wasn't enough for London – even 60 per cent grant left an awful lot of money to be found at a time when the LCC was heavily committed to a major house building programme. And progress was inevitably slow where new roads meant extensive demolition works in densely-populated areas.

In February that year, the council wrote to the minister, regretting that even with 60 per cent grant, London could not carry out the three priority schemes quickly. It even refused to safeguard the routes against development until the question of who would pay up was settled to its satisfaction.

Months later it became an academic point; Britain was at war. Transport in wartime was necessarily concerned with making the best of existing networks – there were no resources for vast new transport projects – everything needed to go into winning the war.

Which brings us neatly back to Abercrombie, 1944, and the optimism of a better Britain which marked the latter part of the war.

It was the Bressey/Lutyens thinking which Abercrombie took over and incorporated in his report, while some of Bressey's ideas can be traced back to the arterial roads programme and the 1903 Royal Commission.

Abercrombie noted that 'the move for arterial road improvement, begun during the last war and energetically pursued, had resulted in some better radial routes, in the carrying out of the North Circular Road and the plotting of a South Circular Road.'[28]

But he pointed to the way the benefits had been eroded by unplanned and chaotic ribbon development along the sides of these roads, many of which now had housing alongside them. This meant they carried a lot of local traffic to the detriment of the fast through traffic which was their original purpose.

The arterial roads had already become one of the images of 1930s London – and not usually a positive one either. The historian of suburban London, Alan Jackson, defined the combination of new roads lined with factories, speculative housing, petrol stations and 'garish public houses in mock Tudor style' as one of 'haphazard and restless ugliness.'[29] Other observers too, were repelled by the dreariness of London's suburbs, the cartoonist Osbert Lancaster damming them as being full of 'bypass-varigated' and 'stockbrokers' Tudor'.

Yet there was some gold among the dross; the Great West Road through Brentford still boasts one of London's best collection of art deco factories, despite the controversial demolition of the Firestone plant during August Bank Holiday 1980 – days before it was due to be listed.

Abercrombie pointed to the little difficulties over money which had stymied new road building in inner London. 'Any hope of a really comprehensive programme of road construction has hitherto always been stultified by the lack of government assistance. The idea that money spent on wisely-planned roads will save human lives and economic waste is not yet fully realised, and successive ministries of transport still beg for funds.'[30]

Abercrombie's 1944 report gave almost 10 pages to roads and only 2.5 to public transport improvements, but he still regarded commuting to central London as the key transport problem, and he called for the electrification of all suburban services which were still steam operated.

With London still lacking a completed ring road, the core of his proposals was a set of five concentric rings which would link 10 fast radial roads to the major provincial cities. However Abercrombie didn't just want faster traffic, the point of his ring roads was to minimise the effect of through traffic on residential areas. Segregating traffic would solve both traffic congestion and the need to protect open space. London's citizens could walk along quiet, tree-lined avenues without fear of being hit by long distance traffic, which would be moved out of the way to high-level roads. The new, fast, roads would be provided with service roads to handle local traffic and shopping centres would be located in precincts and not by the side of major roads. Abercrombie's road plans have to be seen as part of his integrated vision for a planned future London.

The idea of segregating different types of traffic is a seductive one. It had already been raised in the Alness report into road safety in 1939.[31] This suggested that cyclists be provided with wide, well-surfaced cycle tracks they would be compelled to use, so leaving the roads open for faster moving vehicles.

Abercrombie's ring roads came in two types, arterial, and sub-arterial. For Abercrombie, a sub-arterial road meant a main road where frontage development on the road was allowed, but where service roads for local facilities were provided wherever possible and side streets blocked off. An arterial road, however, would be a true motorway; there would be limited access, no footpaths for pedestrians, underpasses to cross the road, and no frontages for shops or access to side streets. The five rings were as follows

- **A Ring:** a sub-arterial route encircling an extended central area. It mainly followed Marylebone, Pentonville and City Roads towards the City, then across the Thames in a new tunnel east of the Tower. From here it would cross Southwark and Lambeth to reach Vauxhall Bridge, before following Chelsea Embankment, cutting north and tunnelling under Hyde Park to reach Paddington and Marylebone Road
- **B Ring;** an arterial for fast through traffic. It would run from Chelsea, where it followed the West London railway up to Notting Hill. It then picked up the Western Avenue extension near Paddington, before cutting through Maida Vale, running just north of Regent's Park to Camden and Highbury. From here, it turned south-east across Canonbury, De Beauvoir Town and Limehouse. It then went through the Isle of Dogs before going under the river by a new tunnel to Deptford and Peckham, it then followed the South London railway via Brixton, Clapham Junction, a new river bridge at Battersea and so to back to the start
- **C Ring:** a sub-arterial formed of the existing north and planned south circular roads
- **D Ring:** an express arterial just outside the built up area; it would start from a new cross river tunnel at Dartford, before running via Swanley, Sanderstead, Croydon, Esher, Walton-on-Thames and Sunbury to reach Ruislip, Pinner and Barnet, It would then go via Waltham Cross, pass across Epping Forest to reach Chigwell and then heading back to Dartford
- **E Ring:** a sub-arterial made up of Bressey's north and south orbitals and running slightly further out from the D ring

That then was the plan, produced at a time when the physical environment, with London devastated by bombing, would have been most favourable for its execution, when there was greatest faith in the power of planning, and when optimism that a brighter future in a very different capital was at its highest. It

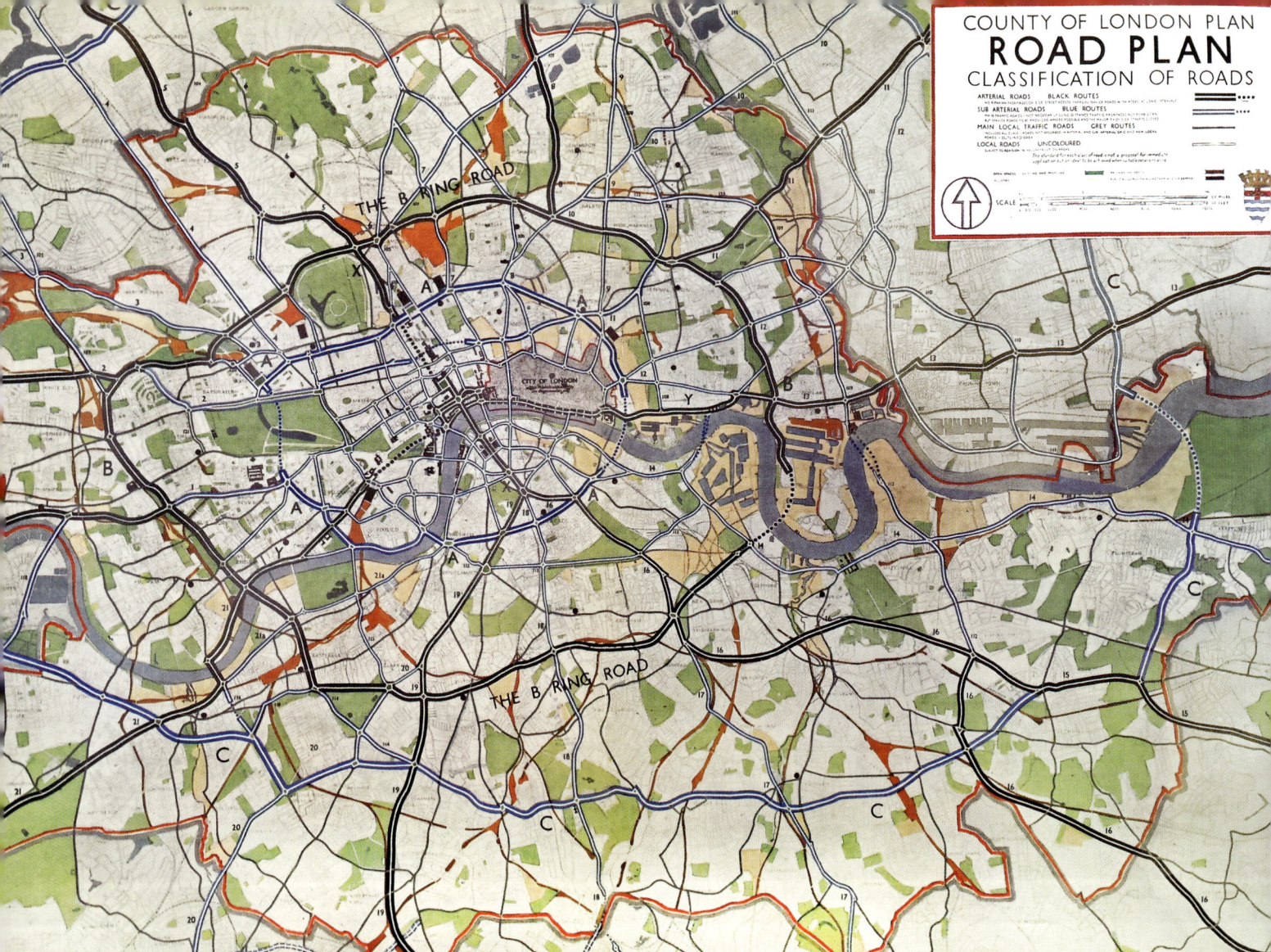

The inner London road plan from the 1943 Abercrombie report

was not – unlike Bressey – just a plan for building more roads, it was a holistic vision of a totally different capital, one built for its people, and the just reward for all those years of blood, sweat and tears.

Officialdom received Abercrombie's report as a clarion call to action, and the minister of town and country planning set up a committee of all the affected local councils to study the proposals – the Clement Davies committee. This reported two years later; the minister accepted the plan's general structure and told councils to stick to it, as modified by the Clement Davies report.[32]

Ministers backed much of Abercrombie's road strategy, including the C and E ring roads. The D ring road was approved around north and west London to link the radial routes to Exeter and Norwich. But it was thought unnecessary south of the river and removed from the plan. The A and B rings, entirely within London County, were, of course, a matter for the LCC and not the minister.

Parts of the Abercrombie plan were implemented, and a properly protected London Green Belt and the New Towns indeed owe their very existence to him. But the ambitious road plans proceeded painfully slowly. Abercrombie seems to have suspected that something of the kind might happen – the 1943 *County of*

London Plan noted; 'the cost of the plan, presented as a whole, is apt to be alarming.'

The reality was that Britain had been bankrupted by the war, and, the first need was to rebuild housing and transport as soon as possible, not to leave open space for the construction of hugely expensive roads which would inevitably take years to build. Unlike the aftermath of the First World War, there was no money to spare for major road projects, and no need to spend it to soak up unemployment in any case. The same lack of money defeated plans for new railways and electrification of old ones.

Still, the Abercrombie plan had tremendous power and prestige; in July 1945, with Nazi Germany defeated but the war in Asia continuing, the LCC agreed that London's road plan should indeed consist of a mixture of radial roads linked by concentric rings.[33] Abercrombie's ideas would resonate right into the 1970s.

In 1948 a start was finally made on planning it. A joint technical committee of LCC and MoT officials was set up to consider an inner ring motorway based on an upgraded version of Abercrombie's A Ring. It would be 11 miles long and have three lanes in each direction. But instead of following Abercrombie's plan to upgrade existing roads to the north of central London, it would be built on a new alignment to the south of the Marylebone Road – Euston Road – City Road line connecting with the M1 at Montagu Square and an Eastern Area Extension at Angel, cutting right through established neighbourhoods. North of the river, the road would be mainly in cuttings below street level, and south of it on viaduct.

There were, however, some small drawbacks. The cost was claimed to be £88 million (£2.3 billion in today's money), but because of the post-war rehousing problem, which had to take priority, construction could not start for a decade. That meant that the A Ring had to form part of a 30-year programme which would, in turn, cost £180 million. The technical committee wanted to go ahead regardless. They reckoned the A Ring was completely justified on traffic and economic grounds and far better than any other plan to reduce traffic congestion. The conclusion was based on assumptions as to

- The extent to which the A Ring would reduce traffic in the centre of London
- Time savings for traffic both on the ring and in the centre
- The value of being able to support additional traffic

Then, in May 1950, the Labour government killed the A Ring on cost grounds. The paper cost was bad enough, but it was clear that the road engineers planning the scheme had substantially underestimated the real cost of their project.

- It might be necessary to acquire more land in the area surrounding the road, and that cost had to be considered when calculating the economic benefits
- The A Ring would displace 5,300 families – this was more than the entire 20-year, £120 million rehousing programme. Taking into account the extra land required, almost another entire New Town would be needed

These costs were on top of the environmental losses. The route would devastate some of London's finest areas – Belgravia, Marylebone, Bloomsbury; ones which had survived the war mainly unscathed, while the viaduct across inner south London would have a depressing effect on those who had to live near it. It would mean vast areas would have to be sterilised until the road was built, so holding up reconstruction and enshrining war damage in the cityscape. The idea of a

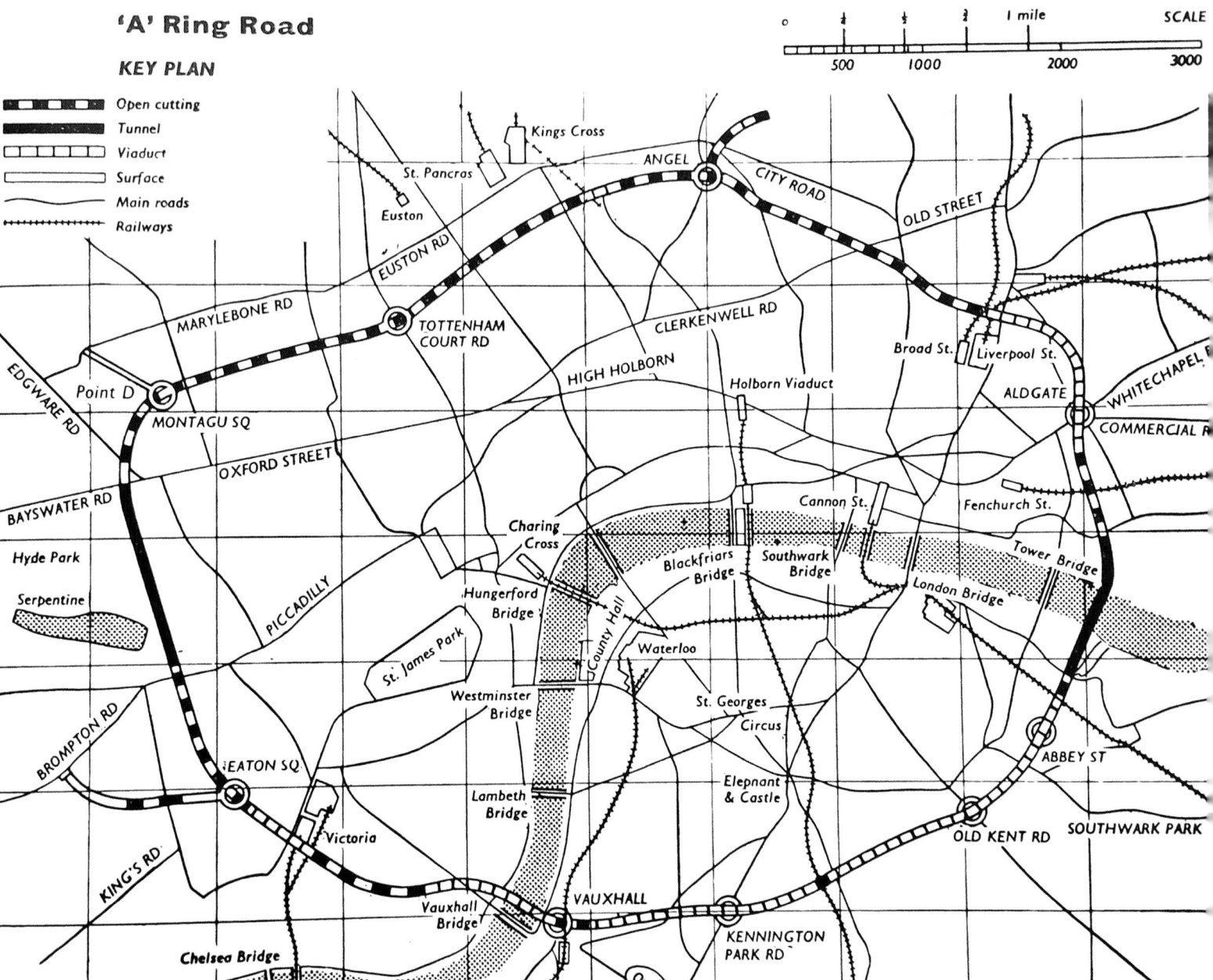

The A Ring across central London – showing the proposal to extend the M1 almost to Marble Arch at Point D (Montagu Square). The link away from the Angel would have led to the Eastern Avenue Extension

motorway at Eaton Square, home of bankers and industrialists, and through the well-preserved De Walden estate in Marylebone and through Bloomsbury, seems inconceivable today.

The men who killed it were Alf Barnes, the transport minister, and Hugh Dalton, the town and country planning minister. Barnes told a key meeting of the civil servants that he had 'never been enamoured' of the A Ring. Dalton added that he was against it 'because of the disturbance it would create and he felt that a decision now to embark on such a costly scheme was impracticable, would be thrown out by the cabinet, and would not in fact be built for 50 years.'[34]

A year later, Lewis Silkin, Dalton's predecessor as town and country planning minster, reflected on his own role in killing the A Ring. He told the Lords that there could be no benefit for 50 years, even if work had started immediately. He said 'It seemed to me that any scheme which required 50 years for its completion was not one which I thought it was in the interests of the community to embark upon without a much clearer conception of what conditions might be like at the end of the period. Moreover, the cost was enormous, and I am not at all satisfied that the cost of the A Ring, with all the interference with transport that it would involve in the meantime, would be justified at the present time.'[35]

The ministers' decision was convened to the LCC; it meant the end as there would be no government grant to build it. And so the LCC decided against safeguarding the route so reconstruction could start and future development would not be blocked.

This practical inability to build a central London motorway was an eerie throwback to the aftermath of the Great Fire. Ambitious redevelopment plans never happened in 1667 because of the need to start rebuilding as soon as possible in an environment where neither the king nor the City had the money to buy up all the property rights in the devastated zone. The result was a compromise, the old road plan was by and large kept, but roads were widened and better building codes enforced.

With the death of the A Ring, the 1951 development plan for the County of London was based on improving the existing network rather than building dramatic new urban motorways.[36]

Late wartime optimism had rapidly given way to a grey and exhausting austerity. Not only had Britain been bankrupted by the war, it was now having to fight a hugely expensive cold war – defence was still top priority and in 1952, defence spending as a percentage of GNP peaked at 9.8 per cent. In this world, roads – and transport in general – had a low priority.

So the LCC plumped for a scaled-down, step-by-step approach to road building. It thought that scarce money would be better spent on a large but coordinated group of smaller schemes rather than risking all on a few major schemes where the full benefit needed the entire programme to be completed.

The LCC 20 year plan focussed on just four of Bressey's 1938 schemes; the Eastern and Western Avenue extensions, the Cromwell Road extension, and a new Blackwall Tunnel and approach roads.

County Hall was well aware these projects meant peoples' homes would be demolished and their occupants would need to be rehoused. The worst offender would be the Eastern Avenue extension which would displace an estimated 2,224 people in densely-populated Hackney and Islington. There would be another 1,700 displaced by the Cromwell Road extension, and 1,300 by the new Blackwall Tunnel and its associated works.

On top of brand new roads, some of the most congested interchanges and junctions would be widened to speed up traffic. But the result of these 'improvements' was often a bleak and soulless cityscape which has not dated well, as at Finchley Road, where the road was widened to provide three lanes in each direction. Cars had total priority here with metal railings preventing pedestrians from crossing except at approved points. Similar projects at Holloway Road, Notting Hill Gate, and Euston Road/Marylebone Road all date from this period, as does the conversion of Park Lane into a dual carriageway, which effectively severed Mayfair from Hyde Park.

Most of London's local one-way schemes are also of this era – as, for example those at Tottenham Court Road/Gower Street, Baker Street/Gloucester Place, Camden Town, Earl's Court, Shoreditch and Kings Cross; all designed explicitly to speed up through traffic. At Elephant & Castle, developers built a shopping centre by the side of huge new roads and found it unpopular because shoppers had to use dingy and ill-lit underpasses to reach it.

Today, one-way schemes have fallen from favour as they created a very pedestrian and cyclist-hostile environment. Hackney council scrapped the Shoreditch one-way in 2002 after a long campaign by residents and cycling groups. The re-civilising effect surely helped Shoreditch's transformation into the cooler-than-cool area of today.

The route from Stamford Hill to the docks was left out of the LCC priority list. In hindsight this was fortunate – it would have become a white elephant within 20 years as the docks started to close in 1969, something which would have seemed inconceivable in 1951.

The 20 year plan was seen as a stepping to stone to an 'ultimate' road plan, which included part of Abercrombie's B Ring – the West Cross Route from Western Avenue to the Embankment.

It can now be revealed however, that the A Ring – apparently dead since 1951 – needed more than a mere decision by elected politicians to kill it off. It continued to live – undead-like – in the dreams of the transport department civil servants and road engineers, and behind the scenes, with the Conservatives back in power, there was a determined attempt to resurrect it in 1953-54.

Behind the lobbying was Alex Samuels, of the London and Home Counties Traffic Advisory Committee, who wrote to transport minister Alan Lennox-Boyd. calling for its revival. Lennox-Boyd replied that he was indeed 'sympathetic' to the idea, Samuels then suggested that Lennox-Boyd discuss the idea with the housing and local government minister, saying that 'the bringing back to life of the A Ring road is one of the most important things which can be done to keep traffic out of the centre of London.'

Samuels' campaign was solidly backed by the transport civil servants, who had vainly urged Barnes and Dalton to keep the scheme in 1951. A minute of 22 April 1954 noted that 'this department has always been solidly in favour of the A Ring Road,' but it regretted that ministers were not likely to resurrect it. They had received 'a most discouraging reply' when they raised the issue with the housing ministry civil servants, who told them that it was useless to try to reopen the project and that their minister agreed with this view.[37]

Only then was the stake finally driven through the dark heart of the A Ring, and so Bloomsbury, Fitzrovia and Marylebone were definitively saved.

2 – Lobbyists and councillors

Ah, the wonderful 1950s. The golden age of British motoring when people could first realistically aspire to owning their first car.

All the lights really were green for what would be called – years later – the great car economy; petrol rationing went in 1950, roads were, by today's standards, relatively uncluttered, there were few parking restrictions; seat belts weren't compulsory, there was easy credit for car purchase, no breathalyser, no speed cameras, and even the MoT was only introduced in 1956.

A whole new lifestyle became available to the millions – who rapidly bought into the dream, boosted by post-war full employment and all the overtime you could eat. HP agreements on cars increased by 20 times in 10 years. UK car making doubled in the years between 1953 and 1960 and Britain still accounted for an astonishing 25 per cent of world car production. Those Ford Prefects and Anglias, Hillman Minxes, and the Austin A50 Cambridge became icons of an era. To crown the great era of British car manufacture, in August 1959, the very first Mini rolled off the assembly track at BMC Cowley.

Your own transport became a potent icon of aspiration, individual freedom and individual rights. In 2009, a BBC documentary called *Ford's Dagenham Dream*[38] documented the rise and fall of the iconic factory, yet its most memorable footage turned out to be evocative interviews with people who spent their weekends polishing and shining their proud possession, and with other Ford owners who went for a spin as a pure leisure activity and had a picnic lunch in a lay-by. It portrayed a different, more innocent, world.

Yet once behind the wheel, there turned out to be unexpected annoyances, and the lure of the open road turned out to be deceptive – others had the same idea too. The new motorists were often condemned to drive in towns and cities whose roads had been designed for horse traffic, which had not changed for decades, and which rapidly became congested. in the 1950s, the number of cars had doubled from 4.5 million to 9.4 million. This was not what motoring was about, surely. *Something must be done about it*. The nature of that 'something' was obvious.

Stuck in a traffic jam in a narrow street, it seemed blindingly obvious that if the roads were too congested when car ownership was rapidly increasing, and would surely increase even more in the future, then the solution was to build more roads and improve the ones which already existed, and do it all as soon as possible.

The above paragraph is set in italics deliberately, because it outlines a simple, easily understood, commonsense logic which underlay everything which was to happen in road transport planning over the next 20 years. It took decades for this popular fallacy to be definitively exposed, and it is one of the themes of this book that during those years, immense damage was done not just to Britain's cityscapes but to the overall transport infrastructure and the environment as a whole.

Demands for wholesale road improvements went well beyond the grumpy mutterings in golf club or public bar. Organised and well-financed lobbying for more roads was in full force, orchestrated by lobby groups representing not just motorists themselves, such as the AA and RAC, but the giant industrial corporations who stood to gain from a switch from rail to road transport; oil companies, motor manufacturers, road haulage interests, construction firms, and aggregate suppliers.

The Roads Campaign Council (RCC) was founded by Wilfred Andrews of the RAC in 1955 – it took MPs on freebies to see the German autobahnen, and leafleted motorists in traffic jams saying 'get out of this jam – press your MP for better roads.' The British Road Federation (BRF) had been formed earlier – in the 1930s – ironically by cycling interests. By the 1950s it was the tool of the oil and car companies and the construction and aggregate industries and was to become one of Britain's most powerful lobby groups.[39]

The BRF's core objective was to lobby for new roads to be built to serve big corporate interests and, incidentally of course, the new motorists. And the Conservative government was listening attentively. Transport minister Harold Watkinson said in 1957; 'Bearing in mind that a useful by-product of our present prosperity is the increasing amount of car ownership, it is not surprising that our roads are extremely congested, particularly at weekends. I am not a bit surprised, nor do I wonder at all at the complaints of motorists and 49 motoring associations and other interested parties who say that is high time that something was done about it.'[40]

The roads lobby was well-resourced (no surprise given the wealth of its backers) and it knew its way intimately around the corridors of power. It also provided easy-to-understand arguments and evidence for why road building was required. Journalists writing about transport turned first to its efficient press service. The BRF could produce what seemed to be an intellectually coherent case, supported by detailed facts and statistics, to back up the commonsense approach of the driver-in-a-traffic-jam.

Below and opposite
Two views at Five Ways, Hendon, showing how the M1 was built brutally close to people's homes.

It wasn't just journalists either – Abercrombie's 1944 report acknowledged support from the BRF, while Bressey in 1938 noted that 'suggestions have been sought and received from the various associations, societies and clubs representative of road users and of road interests generally.' In official eyes, the BRF was sometimes regarded not as a self-interested lobby group with its own axe to grind, but rather as an impartial source of technical expertise on all matters concerning road transport.

As the 50s and 60s waxed, the road lobby grew powerful and confident, and politicians knew it. Barbara Castle, who was Labour's transport secretary in the mid 1960s, said 'when I took over as minister of transport the most vociferous lobby in this country was represented by road interests. The propaganda and pressure groups led by the BRF said we must concentrate all our resources on building the first 1,000 miles of motorway. The environment lobby had barely been born and when I tried to suggest that there were other considerations that we should bear in mind, I had an uphill task because the whole of public opinion and the then opposition were against me.'[41]

The power of the roads lobby can perhaps be overstated of course, Its strength came partly from the fact that it seemed to be arguing for the obvious against the supposed lethargy and red tape in Whitehall. Edmund King, today the president of the AA but once a BRF lobbyist in the 1980s, recalls 'People genuinely thought that there was this vast conspiracy with Peter Witt[42] drawing lines on a map which then turned into motorways. It wasn't really like that.'

After the killing of the A Ring in 1950, strategic road planning focused instead on radial motorways linking cities all across the country on the pattern of the German autobahnen. Building through green fields was a much easier and cheaper activity as there were none of the mass demolitions that urban road building required.

Motorways had come into a legal existence with the passing of the Special Roads Act of 1949, which gave the minister authority to build roads which were not open to all traffic. The M1 had been approved in 1955 as the London to Yorkshire motorway; the motorway numbering system had not yet been invented. The M6 linking the M1 with the West Midlands and Lancashire was approved at the same time. Both formed part of a comprehensive plan for motorways linking all of the country's major cities. Two years later, three more routes were announced, the M4, M5, and M2.

The opening of the first section of the M1 – from Rugby to Aldenham near Watford – in November 1959 ushered in a bright new era, and it showed what might be possible. Amazingly it had only taken four years to build. Early images of a semi-deserted M1, and the fact that service stations had waitress service, have a period charm today, but must have struck Britain's drivers as a wonderful vision of a future which really was possible if only the political will were there.

A privatised, individualistic approach to transport planning especially appealed on ideological grounds to the Conservative governments of the 1950s – and to those who voted for them too. 'You've never had it so good' seemed to make great sense if you were the first person in your street to have a car – and perhaps even more so if you aspired to being the second or third.

The Conservatives had very close links with the road transport industry. The relationship stemmed partly from its denationalisation of much of road haulage after 1951, which gave a huge boost to the freight transport industry. Over 70 Tory MPs were linked to firms which were members of the BRF.

The Mini assembly line at Longbridge, Birmingham.

The Macmillan government was re-elected easily at the 1959 general election, making it three Tory election wins on the trot. Its manifesto claimed that the increasing volume of traffic was a yardstick of rising prosperity which must be 'matched by an intensive drive to build better and safer roads.'

At the same time, Macmillan was concerned about rising losses on British Railways and the apparent inability of a tradition-minded management to get to grips with them. The expensive and ill-thought out BR 1955 modernisation plan was a business failure, and it helped shake ministers' confidence in the railways' management. A 17-day strike by drivers in May 1955 led to a state of emergency being declared and to a discernible shift in Whitehall opinion towards building a strategic road network to reduce dependence on the railways and their unions.

Railways began to be seen in Whitehall as a problem to be solved rather than a solution to transport problems. They seemed to belong to the past rather than the future. And they had a poor public image too; worn-out and filthy steam trains still ran almost all London suburban services north of the river.

In 1948, the British Transport Commission had produced a hugely ambitious plan for new tube routes and railway electrification schemes. Route C – which became the Victoria Line – won parliamentary backing in 1954 but was then blocked for lack of cash until 1962. Other routes, such as Route D (the putative Chelsea – Hackney tube), did not even get this far.

Behind the scenes, the traditional influence of the railway unions was beginning to wane in Labour circles. Although the Labour Party was founded at the instigation of the railway unions, the rising star was now the giant Transport & General Workers Union, whose members drove lorries nationwide, and built cars in the huge factories of Birmingham and Coventry, making themselves, through their trades unions, Britain's best paid manual workers in the process.

In October 1959, a raffish accountant named Ernest Marples succeeded Watkinson as transport minister. Marples was a partner in Marples Ridgway, a construction firm which specialised in road projects. (His partner, Reg Ridgway, supplied the engineering skills). The firm was, naturally enough, a member of the BRF. Marples' firm had built the Hammersmith flyover as part of the Cromwell Road extension project and even in the deferential early 1960s, the conflict of interest did not escape comment. Although this was an LCC scheme, not an MoT one, his ministry had to approve it in order that the LCC could get the capital grant. In order to comply with Commons rules, he had to dispose of his shareholding in Marples Ridgway. He duly did so – to his wife.

It was Marples who would appoint Richard Beeching of ICI as chairman of British Railways with a brief to make the railways profitable at whatever cost. The slash and burn of the Beeching plan led to massive capital disinvestment in national infrastructure when there was no way of knowing whether it might be needed in the future. It would decimate the rail network to the great advantage of the road haulage industry and the great disadvantage of the travelling public.

From 1959, Marples' parliamentary secretary was Lord Chesham, a scion of the Cavendish family headed by the Duke of Devonshire. On leaving office in 1964, he became chairman of the BRF and vice chairman of the RAC. The BRF chairman in the late 1950s and early 1960s was Lord Derwent, who split his time between Belgravia and Hackness Hall in Yorkshire. He had been junior opposition whip in the House of Lords in 1950-51, and in 1962, he left the BRF to become minister of state at the board of trade.

But despite the close links between the Conservatives and road transport

This 1966 view shows building work on the Hendon to Staples Corner section of the M1 – still labelled as the London – Yorkshire motorway

interests, more and better roads were seen as a commonsense, cross-party, solution to growing congestion. In London, the Labour-run LCC enthusiastically backed road building as being essential to keep the capital moving; its enthusiasm was tempered only by the fact that money remained in depressingly short supply.

It is easy to see the appeal of big new roads during the 1950s and 1960s. Roads were *modern* in an era desperate to shake off the dirt and greyness and rationing and austerity of the immediate post-war period. Even concrete was something *new*; it had not had time to acquire its current awful reputation. Along with the cars which used them, roads seemed progressive and emblematic of a clean new way of life. Some even found aesthetic joy in the new creations, which were often billed as the modern equivalent of the railways. The architectural writer Ian Nairn said the Hammersmith Flyover had 'the same kind of humanity as Charles Holden's early underground stations', while the section of the M4 west of Chiswick had 'brought back a scale without brutishness that has been missing since the Victorian viaducts.'[43]

Which politician could honestly stand up and say all this was wrong? Residents who lost their homes because of road building put up little protest if they were going to be rehoused in brand-new council accommodation with inside WC and bath.

Better roads, it was argued, made great economic sense too. They would speed Britain's manufacturing exports to the ports, so helping ease the perennial balance of payments problem. It slipped people's minds that better roads could equally well boost imports.

Writing in 2017, it is easy to sneer at all this, to note how historic cityscapes would be sacrificed to roads all over the country, and to remind ourselves that the desperate yearning for modernity was also expressed in the grim, system-built, tower blocks where slum dwellers were rehoused. But that sneering is partly made with the benefit of hindsight. It really didn't look that way in 1959.

Local council and MoT engineers all saw the building of roads as a simple engineering solution to the traffic problem; they lacked the holistic – if utopian – view of the capital contained in Abercrombie's reports. There was no serious opposition to this approach because the building of roads was seen by the mass of the people as representing progress, and the engineers were the men who knew how to deliver it. Bressey's acute observation – for such an early period – that building roads actually generated traffic – was long forgotten.

In 1956, the BRF had staged a hugely influential and well attended conference on urban motorways at Friends' Meeting House in London. The point of the conference was to show that urban motorways were not just desirable but eminently possible – and to push the government to start a programme to build them.

The conference was opened by transport minister Watkinson who said 'I think I have shown support for the policies which you have advocated at this conference.' The delegate list shows how influential this conference really was – 500 people came from 30 countries, from as far afield as Honduras and Uruguay. From the UK, there were 15 MPs, 200 councillors, aldermen and highway engineers from 120 local councils, as well as six senior civil servants. Delegates from the USA detailed their experience of urban road building, proving that in engineering and traffic terms – it could be done.

The keynote paper came from two senior public servants, William Glanville of the Road Research Laboratory (a former collaborator with Barnes Wallis on the bouncing bomb of dambusters fame), and Allan Baker, the transport ministry's chief highways engineer. Baker had been made head of a special motorways team at the ministry, and like many top road engineers, had visited post-war Germany to gawp at the autobahnen.

In the chair was Patrick – now Lord – Abercrombie and the paper was introduced by Frank Rayfield, the LCC's deputy chief engineer. The Glanville / Baker paper purported to show how the M1 motorway could be brought from its planned terminus at Aldenham, via Staples Corner and all the way into central London, to terminate at Montagu Square near Marble Arch. [44]

The subsequent discussion saw Abercrombie warn that 'after planning the A ring we came to the conclusion that it was quite impossible as an urban motorway largely on economic grounds.' But Rayfield insisted that 'the hard core of the traffic problem is lack of road space and better results will be obtained by motorways at less cost than in any other way.' Put another way, the engineers' view was that rising demand necessarily meant that more of the cityscape should be devoted to roads, which by definition, meant less space for other things. Things such as houses for example.

The stress-filled misery of the traffic jam was a new phenomenon in Britain, and they were beginning to hit the news in a big way. The pre-Christmas period in London in 1958 was a particular horror, and referring to it, the *Daily Mirror's* front page asked; 'Traffic – is the real jam in Whitehall?'[45] The *Daily Sketch* referred to 'the awful warning of five million cars......of worse road jams to come which should remove any lingering complacency in Whitehall about the state of our roads.'[46]

In 1959 the BRF held an exhibition on motorways at the Institution of Civil Engineers called 'town roads for today and tomorrow'. It was opened by Marples and attracted 500 visitors daily, often from municipal delegations anxious to know how urban motorways could solve their own traffic problems.

The government had felt the heat. It had set up a commission to study road improvements in London in November 1957. The chairman was Richard Nugent, Tory MP for Guildford and Watkinson's deputy at the transport ministry. Its brief was to consider proposals for improving the road system in the county of London and to suggest possible programmes for the next 20 years.

Its 12 members included Glanville and Baker, plus LCC architect Hubert Bennett. Both parties on the LCC were represented on the committee, Labour by Richard Edmonds, who chaired the town planning committee, and the Tories by Robert Vigars. Both have important roles to play in the unfolding story.

Nugent reported in July 1959, calling for a measured but cautious increase in road building, suggesting two 20-year programmes, based on spending either £6 million or £10 million a year. The Nugent Committee rejected expensive urban motorway proposals, saying 'what may be an ideal answer for traffic may be far from suiting the neighbourhood and the people living and working in it.'[47] This rejection should not have come as a surprise; in March of that year, Nugent had carefully explained the story of Abercrombie's A Ring to the Commons, stressing why it would have cost so much and the environmental damage it would have done.[48]

Nugent's recommendations were, of course, nothing like enough for the BRF, which dismissed the report as 'unimpressive and bitterly disappointing'[49] Some corners of Fleet Street agreed, the *Daily Mail* calling it 'timid and unimaginative. It will cause widespread disappointment.'[50]

And so the road lobby kept up the pressure. The same year as the Nugent report, the RCC organised a competition to find the best design for urban motorways to solve London's traffic congestion. This was a serious, high-profile competition, aimed at attracting high-calibre entries. The first prize was £2,000 – almost £40,000 in today's money – and entries came from as far away as the US and Australia. The entrants were asked to design for three times the actual traffic figure for 1954.

Among the three judges were the engineer, architect and planner[51] Sir Colin Buchanan, and Sir William Holford, who was mainly responsible for drafting the 1947 Town and Country Planning Act which established the principle that planning permission was needed for development. Holford had also been technical adviser to Lord Reith during his spell as minister of works. Buchanan had published, the previous year, *Mixed Blessing*,[52] his own view of the car which contained prescient comments on the damage it would do to the public realm.

The *Architects' Journal,* which covered the competition in detail, said that 'for the first time the talk about motor roads in London has been translated into specific plans.' But it did note that the competitors had been asked to respect historic values but 'not the equally important living values of existing precincts, neighbourhoods, communities or other social groups.'[53]

The winner was J Alan Proudlove, professor of civil engineering at Liverpool University. In second place came an entry from the Polish-born Konrad Smigielski, who then headed the town planning department at Leeds School of Architecture. We will meet him again very shortly.

The competition had shown that urban motorways in the capital were, in engineering and architectural terms, entirely possible to achieve. This fact added massively to the intellectual argument for their construction.

In fact, the fashion for urban road building was a nationwide phenomenon, Most major provincial cities were Labour-controlled and they shared the general view that roads were modern and progressive and central to speeding traffic up so it could go quickly and easily to where it wanted to without clogging up the city centres. If they demolished buildings and devastated the cityscape, the view was often that the buildings concerned were often old and dirty and life expired – new, modern buildings could and would and should replace them.

Birmingham was to become notorious for its brutal concrete collar separating the central city from its surroundings and making it the least pedestrian-friendly city in the country; it was the brainchild of city engineer Sir Herbert Manzoni, another attendee at the BRF's 1956 conference, and from 1960, president of the Institution of Civil Engineers.[54] Although the first scheme in Birmingham was actually proposed as far back as 1918, Manzoni began planning his inner ring road from 1943 in another example of late-war optimism, and a 1946 Act allowed construction to begin. The familiar problems of money held things up and the first section was not actually started until 1957. The completed ring road was opened by the Queen in 1971. Birmingham is now busy trying to undo the damage from its road mania.

Manzoni never made any secret of his opinions on the value of history and cityscape to the public consciousness; 'I have never been very certain as to the value of tangible links with the past. They are often more sentimental than valuable... As to Birmingham's buildings, there is little of real worth in our architecture. Its replacement should be an improvement... As for future generations, I think they will be better occupied in applying their thoughts and energies to forging ahead, rather than looking backward.'[55]

But when the inner ring road was conceived, in a city which made cars and their components for a living, it was doubtless looked upon as progress.

In 1955, Leeds city council decided to build a dual carriageway to the north of the city centre to remove through traffic. In the final stages before construction began in 1963, the road was redesignated as a motorway, without any changes to the design. Construction began with the demolition of 365 homes and 174 other structures. Leeds was so proud of its motorways that it was to proclaim itself 'motorway city of the seventies,' and even persuaded the Post Office to frank outgoing mail with this inspiring slogan.

In Leicester, Konrad Smigielski had, in 1962, become head of the city planning department (only the second in the country) and on his watch the Southgate Underpass was driven right through the Roman and mediaeval core of the city. The capital of the East Midlands is perhaps Britain's least known big city, a fate it doesn't deserve[56] – but visitors will marvel at how such a road could have been constructed. As in Birmingham, it would surely have seemed the inevitable result of progress at the time. Today, the city's directly-elected mayor has launched an ambitious programme called Connecting Leicester – explicitly designed to mitigate the effects of this vandalism.

In Manchester, planners had carried out a similar exercise to Abercrombie in the 1945 City of Manchester Plan, proposing a set of wide roads encircling the centre together with new, with bold modernist buildings. The elevated Mancunian Way, planned since the 1950s, was opened by Harold Wilson in 1967. It ran for two miles, just to the south of the city centre, and was designed to be part of an inner ring defined in the 1962 SELNEC (South East Lancashire and North East Cheshire) Highway Plan. It aimed to provide a fast route from factories in the east of the city to the docks in the west and was known as 'the highway in the sky.' Within 15 years of opening, the road was superfluous for its stated need; Manchester docks closed and the industrial zones to the east of the city centre collapsed, providing the UK with its nearest equivalent to Detroit.

So urban road mania was a national sport, shared by councils in all cities. And exactly the same schemes with the same objectives were planned in major European capitals. The Paris Peripherique was planned in 1940, and formally authorised in 1954. (It opened in 1973, neatly dividing middle-class Paris from its working class suburbs.) The first sections of the Brussels ring road were opened in the late 1950s, Moscow's vast ringroad – the MKAD – was opened in 1961.

Britain's road builders ought to have been taking a closer look at what was happening in New York however. The city's roads and building supremo Robert Moses had successfully built the Cross Bronx Expressway, showing that you really could drive a motorway through a crowed urban area, despite opposition from residents. It opened in 1963, although extra junctions continued to be built until 1972. But it didn't help ease congestion one whit, indeed, it is said to be the most congested stretch of American road outside California. And it was later blamed for the catastrophic urban decline which hit the South Bronx. Moses insisted that 'we live in a motorised civilisation,' but met serious resistance when he tried to force the Lower Manhattan Expressway through SoHo and Little Italy. A campaign grew up led by community activist Jane Jacobs, who in 1961 wrote *The Death and Life of Great American Cities*, one of the first polemics against top-down, vast-scale, planner-knows-best urban renewal schemes of the kind Moses was running in New York. The protests gathered the support of, among others, Eleanor Roosevelt, and in 1962, the city authorities were forced to back down. But in the pre-internet era, this valuable experience was totally lost upon London's road planners.

Meanwhile, the growing traffic congestion in London had plunged the bus service into crisis. London Transport was not controlled by the LCC or any other elected body. It was run as a nationalised industry under tight treasury control, and repeated attempts to run the buses without subsidy meant that fares stayed high and journeys were in freefall; bus passenger miles fell by nearly 45 per cent between 1955 and 1969.

Traffic jams had made buses slower and less reliable, and so passengers drifted away. But the fixed costs of the service remained the same. So fares were raised to cover the gap, and services were cut. That made bus miles operated fall by 22 per cent between 1960 and 1970, something achieved almost entirely by reducing frequency rather than by axing routes entirely. Reducing frequency when congestion made reliability poor naturally hit usage further. Reduced use of the buses was 1.5 times as great as the reduction in miles operated. Fares were then raised again to compensate, and services were cut further and so on and so forth.

Table Two – Passengers entering central London daily, 1961-67

	BR and /or underground	**LT buses and coaches**
1961	883,000	209,000
1962	907,000	215,000
1963	886,000	191,000
1964	889,000	191,000
1965	878,000	180,000
1966	878,000	175,000
1967	885,000	172,000

Source – GLC, Movement in London, table 6.22

Despite the growing congestion, there was little thought given to prioritising bus traffic, which carries far more people efficiently in terms of road space than the same number of passengers in the private car. As late as November 1970, Greater London had just four bus lanes, it was thought at the time that only 20 to 40 such lanes would ever be worth introducing.

After the Nugent report, the BRF demanded the building of an inner motorway ring surrounding the capital.[57] A BRF report – *London Needs......* – argued that motorways carried twice as much traffic twice as fast, that its scheme didn't alter the 1959 Nugent plan but merely developed it, while the experience of other countries was that inter-city motorways couldn't be allowed to just peter out meaninglessly in the suburbs. The BRF added, reasonably enough, that its plan was exactly in line with the Abercrombie report. The BRF's ring road even expanded on one of Abercrombie's innovations; to minimise the disruption to established communities, it was proposed that wherever possible, the motorways would follow railway lines, the North London Line from Hackney Wick via Camden to Willesden, the West London Line down to Clapham Junction, and then the South London Line to the Peckham area. It would cross under the Thames via a new tunnel at Rotherhithe. The proposed road would have 12 to 15 access points.

The BRF reckoned that building this network would cost £260 million, But it was only too aware that the Bressey plans of the 1930s had been thwarted because the LCC couldn't pay 40 per cent of the cost, and it knew that exactly the same issue would arise again, even with 75 per cent of the cost now being met from central funds. So it proposed new financial arrangements, including better borrowing facilities for local authorities, which would remove a key source of municipal resistance to large-scale road building.

A very similar ring road proposal – prompted in fact by the BRF – came from the Association of Metropolitan Borough Engineers and Surveyors.

The BRF clearly thought it was pushing on an open door. It claimed that when *London Needs.....* was published, 'It is understood that the minister has asked his experts to study the scheme and discuss it with the LCC.'

There was certainly some media support; *The Observer* backed the plans, saying a London ring motorway on top of the existing rail tracks would do far more to relieve congestion and reduce traffic accidents than any other emergency measure.[58] The BRF's internal minutes recorded approvingly; 'There can be little doubt that the sequence of actions by the Federation in respect of its London road programme has had the effect of directing attention again towards the question of urban motorways in the capital.'[59]

That same year, the BRF objected to the County of London Plan, then going through its statutory five year revision process,[60] on the grounds that the revision was piecemeal and didn't include a comprehensive roads plan – code for urban motorways. A very similar objection came from the London Liberal Party. The LCC defended the omission, saying that it would keep the possibility in mind. But it argued that the BRF had hugely underestimated the cost – especially by excluding the cost of rehousing those whose homes would need to be demolished. 'At no time has the council had any assurance that the money for a construction of a new road scheme would be forthcoming,' and while Whitehall would expect to pick up 75 per cent of the cost, the LCC's 25 per cent was, frustratingly, nowhere to be found.[61]

But the ministry's inspectors backed the BRF. They said that the case for urban motorways was 'a matter on which there may appear to be little disagreement on principle…..the logic of the objectors' cases in this respect is inescapable, drawing support from eminent experts,[62] from the scale of the problem and the immediate threat to central London.' They recommended that the revised plan include a statement explaining what would be done to formulate a comprehensive road plan.

Soon after the Nugent report, a London Road Programme Committee was set up, comprised of officials from the MoT, the LCC, and later, the Road Research Laboratory. Its very first task was to commission a comprehensive survey of road traffic movements – the London Traffic Survey.

The survey was executed by the UK's Freeman, Fox consultancy, together with US consultants, who, it was thought, were the experts in this kind of work, having pioneered traffic surveys in Detroit and Chicago in 1955. The idea was to get the facts about London's traffic. However from the beginning there was the clear implication that the results would be needed to justify a predetermined decision that London's traffic problems could only be solved by a set of motorway ringroads.

The original terms of reference, put together by the MoT, actually said that

The Grade II Listed southern entrance to the Blackwall Tunnel.

the consultants 'will draw up comprehensive details of the new roads and road improvements which are needed in the LCC area.'

Hubert Bennett, the LCC architect, was 'quite horrified' when he saw this suggestion; 'I never remotely dreamed that this was what was intended until now.'[63] The term was subsequently deleted in the final contract to the consultants, but Idwal Pugh, the MoT mandarin who chaired the committee, said 'the immediate problem was to obtain sufficient information to pass judgements on the various schemes for London roads, for example, those of the BRF, AMBES and the LCC *Quinquennial plan*.' Pugh hinted that more money for roads might be available and that might 'make a comprehensive plan possible which might even consist of several radial roads and a distributor road.'[64]

At County Hall, the Labour majority on the LCC was now coming under pressure from the Tory minority, which had been shouting for more roads more quickly – in 1957, Robert Vigars, who had sat on the Nugent committee, complained about the 'lamentably tardy' rate of road improvements which were already agreed.[65]

His boss as Tory leader on the LCC was 47 year old Desmond Plummer. By profession an estate manager and surveyor who represented Marylebone, he drove around London in a gold-coloured Mini Cooper; his own commitment to modernity. Plummer was a vocal supporter not just of roads, but of the full urban motorway dream. In January 1961 he demanded of the Labour LCC; 'when will it bring forward a planned motorway system for London as a whole?' Next month, he promised that if the Tories won control of the LCC, they would call for the building of an inner motorway ring as demanded by the BRF, and in May, after the expected Labour victory, he was back demanding more resources for roads 'including the investigation of the provision of an inner ring motorway as proposed by the BRF and the Association of Metropolitan Borough Engineers and Surveyors.'

The Labour LCC, was in fact, equally anxious to do something about what it feared was a looming crisis where total gridlock would be a daily occurrence. Richard Edmonds, chair of the newly-formed roads committee, said in early 1960, 'conditions in November and December 1958 show how dangerously near to a total standstill London's traffic had become.'[66]

Their objection to including urban motorways in the revised plan was not at all about the principle – it was essentially that there was no money to pay for them.

The LCC did what it could. It won additional parliamentary powers for road building as a result of a bill it promoted in October 1962. With the bill now law, an assessment of the LCC's roadbuilding schemes in the early 1960s looked like this;

- **The Westway extension**. This was included in the 1951 development plan and was approved by the LCC in 1959. It was originally planned to be built in two stages and would be in every sense a real motorway; however a joint report from the LCC chief engineer and architect said 'it should not necessarily be regarded as part of a comprehensive motorway system.'[67]
- **The West Cross Route**, whose first stage would link up with the Westway and follow the West London railway line to a roundabout with the A402 at Holland Park Avenue. The LCC approved a second stage in March 1963 which would take this route southwards to the Thames.

- **A second Blackwall Tunnel**. The original tunnel was badly congested and sharply curved, and so a new tunnel, to the east of the 1897 bore, was approved by ministers in March 1959. Construction started a year later. A new approach road – dubbed the East Cross Route in the LCC 1955 plan – would be extended to run north through Poplar to the A11 at Bow. Later it was extended to Hackney Wick, where it would terminate with the projected Cambridge motorway (which became the M11).
- **The Cromwell Road extension,** which ministers approved in 1954, saw its first stage open in 1957, the same year the Hammersmith flyover was added. The M4 west from the Chiswick roundabout had been competed in 1959, so a fast route now existed from west of London, including Heathrow Airport, to the border of the central city.

Individual improvements were continuing on the line of Bressey's East-West Cross route, where planning had even continued during the war period, and the eventual effect of this apparently piecemeal construction programme would have been to build a fast route across the north edge of central London. At Angel Islington, an east-west flyover was being planned to stop traffic being delayed by north-south traffic. Engineers considered it 'would be more pleasing in appearance.'[68] Further west, the LCC had – in league with property developers – opened the Euston underpass at the top of Tottenham Court Road in 1961 and work was in hand to widen the Marylebone Road.

The momentum for urban motorways was exploding even as the London Traffic Survey was underway; everyone seemed in favour, at least in principle, and the BRF had demonstrated that it was possible. However, the LCC's schemes would highlight a unlooked-for drawback with urban motorways; as one piece was built, the more obvious and desirable it appeared to build another piece to add on to it and road planning became a self-perpetuating and self-reproducing business. The intersection between the Westway and the West Cross Route illustrates this point, the original junction was in the curious shape of a jug handle and was so referred to in LCC documents. But in March 1963, the LCC decided to change this to a full roundabout, partly on safety grounds, but partly because it was 'considered wise to adopt a design which could be conveniently adapted later for a northward connection should such prove desirable.' [69]

Richard Edmonds had been challenged on ringways (the lack of them, that is) by the Tories at the 1961 LCC elections, and he replied lamely that it would be wrong to move ahead immediately because the results of the traffic survey were not available. But the BRF's leaders subsequently met with Edmonds, and its minutes record that they found him 'much more receptive to the idea of urban motorways.'[70] Later that year, the BRF's publicity committee was impressed by the 'evident wish of Mr Edmonds to have BRF support and approval for the LCC roads programme.'[71]

In November 1963, that is before the first part of the LTS had even been completed, Edmonds jumped the gun. He said that the results of the study 'will surely point to an extension of the urban motorway system.' The LCC itself also said 'when the survey is completed, it will be possible to establish the nature and volume of the complex traffic flows on the main motorways and trunk routes leading into London, to establish *the need for…ring roads*[72] and other new improved roads within the survey area, and to enable their capacity and best location to be decided.'[73]

Indeed local residents might well have been shocked if they realised just how far advanced the planning for the West Cross Route, for example really was, official documents show that the consulting engineers knew exactly where each of the supports for the overhead structures needed to go.

However, the history of the entire London road programme shows that much of the fine detail was consistently kept away from the citizens (see box).

> **Official secrecy: two vignettes**[74]
>
> In January 1965, P J Hosegood, a transport department civil servant, laid down what information should be provided to homeowners worried by the M23 London – Crawley motorway. 'The intention,' he wrote 'is to restrict information on whether any particular property, which lies within or near the area under discussion, would or would not be affected. The reason for this is that we are at present dealing with a suggested broad area of 600 ft width in which a line might be found and not with a definite width of 129 ft plus cutting/embankment allowances……..the general rule should be to say very little to those who may be affected, and in case it is thought that our knowledge is more precise than is in fact the case (information gets around) to say no more to those who may not be affected.'
>
> In May that year, Travers Morgan, a firm of engineering consultants working on the M23, wrote to the men from the ministry. They explained that the GLC had asked for 1/2500 scale plans of the M23 within the GLC area. Copies had been shown to local councils along the route, but they had not been allowed to keep them. 'The main reason for this procedure was to avoid putting the technical officers in the difficult position of knowing the provisional layout for the motorway and having to refuse to show such detail to committee members or members of the public.'
>
> The consultants explained that the detail could be misleading until engineering surveys and consultations were completed. For various reasons, Travers Morgan now proposed to release this diagrams to the GLC on condition that they were
> - Confidential to technical officers in the GLC highways department
> - Not to be shown to any member of the public
> - Not to be used for discussions with committees, which, of course, had elected representatives on them.

And behind the scenes, the LCC engineers were already planning a complete Motorway Box for London – a continuous motorway enclosing central and part of inner London. They worked closely with Whitehall's road engineers to plan the full network they wanted – not just the parts already approved.

In September 1963, an important meeting took place between the LCC, MoT, and R Travers Morgan, the MoT's consultant for the M23 motorway, of which more later. At the meeting Peter Stott, now acting deputy chief engineer at the LCC, said that the point of the meeting was to ensure than the planned radial motorways, such as the London – Crawley M23, 'would be in harmony with *what was now envisaged as the inner urban motorway system.*'[75] (My italics)

In December that year, Stott told Husbands, the consulting engineers working on the West Cross Route, that the southernmost section should be built with four lanes in each direction instead of three.[76] In turned out – after informal talks – that MoT civil servants thought that extra capacity would be needed as the West

Brave New World – the Buchanan vision of cars segregated from people.

Cross Route would be a bypass for west London which would be needed to absorb traffic from the west and could eventually be extended northwards.[77]

This sort of thinking may also have inspired what became the South Cross Route – minutes of a meeting between civil servants, Husbands and the LCC in late 1964 record the suggestion by the divisional road engineer for London about 'an idea we had in mind that the route should form a direct connection on the west side of London between the M1 and the Brighton radial, in which event a new bridge (over the Thames) was almost essential.'[78] So what became the ringways were partly influenced by the traffic to be generated by the ministry's inter-urban motorways.

1963 also saw the publication of Colin Buchanan's monumental study *Traffic in Towns,* commissioned by Marples in 1960.[79] *Traffic in Towns* was one of the first warnings of the environmental damage that cars would do. Given its head, traffic would 'would wreck our towns within a decade... The problems of traffic are crowding in upon us with desperate urgency. Unless steps are taken, the motor vehicle will defeat its own utility and bring about a disastrous degradation of the surroundings for living... either the utility of vehicles in town will decline rapidly, or the pleasantness and safety of surroundings will deteriorate catastrophically – in all probability both will happen.'

There was much more in this vein in a report which sold 18,000 copies and was popular enough for Penguin to publish it as a paperback, a unique feat for a government report. It established Buchanan's reputation as Britain's leading expert on roads, and ensured that traffic became a central town planning issue.

Like Abercrombie, Buchanan argued the case for pedestrianisation and for traffic to be segregated if our cities were not to be destroyed, and his warnings about the environmental consequences of the motor car were well ahead of his time. *Traffic in Towns* provided policy options; he himself warned that his report was a description of the choices open, from the 'do nothing' to the 'whole hog' with the advantages and disadvantages of each set out. Buchanan later said that Marples 'was really hoping for a miracle, for some formula which, applied to London, would soon have the traffic moving as sweetly as could be desired. Instead of which, he got a readable manual on urban planning.'[80]

Buchanan wrote that 'all American experience of sprawl suggests that in our small country we would do well to have no more of it.' That sprawl was a direct consequence of the dominance of the motor car, and roads being planned and provided to cater for predicted future demand. Yet Buchanan himself went on to be a convinced supporter of the London ringways, arguing urban motorways were complementary to the inter-city motorways and it was difficult to picture one without the other.

The summary itself went further than Buchanan himself did; produced by a steering group including Sir Geoffrey Crowther, Sir William Holford, and Newcastle-upon-Tyne city boss T Dan Smith.[81] It said 'without question there will have to be a great deal of urban road building in British cities.... 'some of them indeed in the larger cities will have to be built to motorway standards.' Yet it was tinged with a melancholy despair;

- 'We believe that there is a need for a vigorous programme of urban road building.......but we cannot hold out any hope that this by itself will go very far towards solving the problem.'
- 'To an increasing section of the community the advantages of car commuting outweigh the facts that it may cost more, that it may take longer and that it may end in a tedious search for a place to park.'

Unfortunately, *Traffic in Towns* was capable of very different interpretations. A 50 years on retrospective by Buchanan's consultancy noted that planners saw it as an argument for rolling back the frontiers of the car and saving towns from the road building needed to accommodate it; public transport professionals saw it as requiring better public transport; and highway engineers saw it as making the case for better roads.[82]

The first volume of the London Traffic Survey duly came out in 1964, based on research from two years before. It found that only 38 per cent of people in Greater London actually owned cars, but 6.3 million trips were made by car each day, compared with only 6.5 million by rail. The average household made 1.33 trips of all types per day – but whereas a non car owning house made 0.93 trips per day, car owning ones made 1.87. So the convenience of a car meant you made more journeys if you actually had one, implying that as more people bought cars, the number of journeys made would grow exponentially.[83]

The first volume also said the 'real objective is to predict the future use of main road networks under consideration.'[84] Quite apart from revealing an underlying road bias, this amounted to saying that if new roads are built, then they will be used, and this circular logic became the case for the ringways. (If they were not built, they would not be used and so the demand would not be there...)

This inbuilt road bias was the central failing with the LTS – it was, just as it said, a *traffic* study. Tellingly, although it found that one in four journeys to work were by bicycle or on foot, little attention was paid to this.[85] Instead it focused on a new world of journeys by car, exactly as was the case in the burgeoning suburbs of Chicago or Detroit, and did not deal with the existing London reality of journeys both by car, on foot, and by unsatisfactory public transport.

The second volume, produced in 1966,[86] attempted to forecast trends from the data in Phase One, including a prediction of what the actual patterns of travel would be if demand was 'channelled into the routes that could be foreseen.' These were two possible networks, one made up of roads already committed plus Abercrombie's D Ring, the other made up of the full Abercrombie plan minus the A Ring. The assumption – explicit here – was the 'dramatic surge' that the mere fact of car ownership had on the number of trips. The pattern of travel was calculated from the 1962 base and used 'speeds for the primary roads that might reasonably be expected in uncongested conditions and speeds on secondary roads similar to those observed in 1962.'

Or, put another way, although traffic would grow, congestion was expected to be no worse....there would be none of Bressey's observation that traffic tended to increase to fill available space.

The LTS was central in providing a statistical justification for the ringways and the fact that it was computer-generated – something new and exciting at the time – helped establish its credibility.

Yet a central assumption in the Phase 2 was also fundamentally flawed. Phase 2 showed that cross-London journeys (Greenwich to Hampstead, or Hackney to Acton for example) would be growing much more quickly than journeys to central London. Extrapolated to 1981, journeys to central London would increase by around 13 per cent, but those outside the central area would rise by over 50 per cent. Much of this would be off-peak travel.[87] This extraordinary predicted growth in cross-London traffic became the central argument for building the London ringways. (It was not, incidentally, Abercrombie's justification for them).

In fact, it was another entirely circular argument – this growth simply reflected the fact that such journeys were the ones which it was still possible to make by car. By contrast, Greenwich to Piccadilly Circus by car was an impossible journey due to congestion and parking controls in central London. Hardly surprisingly, journeys of this type showed less growth.

There was another flaw, explicit in the LTS but later ignored, that the predicted growth in orbital traffic assumed that nothing would be done to curb it, in the shape of parking restrictions for example, or that the growing congestion would itself deter traffic from growing beyond a certain point.[88] If something *were* done about it – the growth would not be there, taking away the justification for the ringways.

Volume 3 – now renamed as the London Transportation Study – followed in 1969.[89] and for the first time looked at public transport options too. It considered three assessments of alternative plans, but it seems that these were so detailed, and said one opponent, 'hence time-consuming and unwieldy' that the only significant assessment were done on the so-called Plan 1, essentially The D Ring, 36 miles of radial motorways inside this, and the parts of the Motorway Box already built and committed; and Plan 3, essentially the roads included in the Greater London Development Plan, which were believed to deliver a return on investment of 8.8 per cent.

A vast edifice would be built upon this flawed logic.

3 – Green light for the ringways

In 1964, the LCC moved decisively to kickstart a complete inner motorway system. The scale of the work was so great that its own staff couldn't handle it all. And so huge contracts were given to engineering consultancies to plan the work. The key dates were;

- March – R Travers Morgan was appointed to survey a possible North Cross motorway from Willesden, via Hampstead, and Dalston to Hackney Wick. The work was justified by the purported need to safeguard potential routes from competing development. [90]
- April – Husbands, the engineering consultancy already working on the West Cross Route, was appointed to draw up proposals to extend the route over the Thames to south of the river.[91]
- November – R Travers Morgan was given an expanded brief – to include links from its North Cross Route to the M1 at Staples Corner. It was also asked to plan two extra links, one to Western Avenue and one to the West Cross Route at Westway. Now it became clear why the original West Cross/Westway jug handle junction needed to be replaced by a roundabout.[92]
- December – Husbands was given a further assignment. It was told that the scope of its work 'should also be extended to the east of Clapham Junction to coordinate the investigations being made by the council's officers into the South Cross Route and possible links to the Crawley and Brighton radial route.'[93]

With these four surveys in place, it was perfectly clear that a full-scale Motorway Box encircling inner London was being planned. This grand design was not secret any more; it was public information, logged in the minutes of the London County Council and available to any local journalist who had the LCC beat and to anyone else who cared either. The import of those discussions between Edmonds and the BRF, and between Stott and the civil servants was no longer a secret.

There is no question that the initial planning for the Motorway Box had gone on behind closed doors and away from the public eye. And it would be somehow satisfying to believe that the idea of knocking houses down to cover London with urban motorways was entirely a sinister conspiracy to be revealed only when it was too late to protest.

But the reality is more nuanced. It is quite true that the citizens were not encouraged to be involved, true that large corporations were lobbying for motorway building, and also true that elected politicians and officials proceeded on the basis that they knew best, and to a significant extent allowed the road lobby to make the intellectual running.

But the evidence indicates that any real conspiracy was one which lasted only for a short period – from sometime in 1963 to early 1964. The fundamental issue was that everyone at the time believed that the answer to present and expected traffic congestion was road building on an industrial scale. That was why there had been no public discussion or debate about the alleged need for more roads, or indeed about the nature of transport as a whole, and how buses and trains fitted into the picture. No one thought it was even necessary.

The engaged citizen could find out about what was being planned if she was prepared to put some effort into it – even if she was hardly encouraged to do so. In fact, the public reaction to the Motorway Box was, by and large, a deafening silence.

Meanwhile, the structure of London government was changing to a form which would make building a huge new motorway network more feasible. In 1957, the Conservative government had set up a royal commission on London government under Sir Edwin Herbert. This reported in 1960, recommending a strategically-oriented Greater London Council be set up, covering much of the outer London area considered by Abercrombie. It proposed that 52 new London boroughs[94] be set up, with the LCC absorbed by the GLC, which would have responsibility for public transport, road schemes, housing development and regeneration.

The Herbert commission was scathing about the inability of London's local government to manage the traffic problem. The housing and local government ministry had told the committee that transport congestion was London's greatest problem – a somewhat odd assertion from the ministry responsible for solving the housing crisis in the capital.

Labour opposed the plan. They suspected it was a Tory scheme designed to remove the inbuilt Labour majority on the old LCC by diluting it with Conservative suburban votes. The Tories pressed on – and the London Government Act became law in 1963. However the first GLC elections, held in 1964 advance of its taking power the following year, actually returned a Labour majority. The vote reflected a public mood which was heartily fed up with the Conservative government. The GLC's first leader was Bill Fiske from Havering.

The new GLC started life with responsibility for future roads, it inherited the detailed plans the LCC had put together, and had its own in-house construction capability with a proven delivery record. Its highways and transport department was experienced in road engineering and traffic management. The GLC, in short, could build roads as well as plan them. The GLC would now be the main highway authority for London, but pending the full handover of former trunk roads outside the former London County, responsibility continued to be divided. There were still trunk roads in the GLC area – such as the North Circular – where the minister was the highway authority and met the full cost of improvements.

The GLC, like the LCC before it, had no responsibility for public transport, and so from the very beginning the system had an inbuilt practical bias towards major road projects.

In November of 1964, the new GLC leaders met with Tom Fraser, the former Scottish miner who was transport minister in the Labour government which had come to power a month earlier. They made it clear to him that 'proper emphasis' needed to be given to build ring roads to deflect traffic from the central areas of London.[95]

However not quite everyone was asleep as the ringways were being planned. And the first stirrings of opposition to major road building were heard in the summer of 1962.

The epicentre was Blackheath, the wealthy enclave in working class south-east London. The trigger was transport ministry plans to improve the A2 Dover Road and bring it from the Medway towns to Falconwood, on the border of the LCC area, by 1967. This plan raised the awkward question of where the traffic would go then, and showed how the growth of the radial motorways moving towards London helped push the need for motorways within the capital to handle all the new traffic.

Angry residents had discovered that the LCC wanted to build a new road to link with this – the Dover Radial Road (DRR) – probably paralleling the Bexleyheath railway line via Blackheath and as far west as Lewisham.

The Blackheath Motorway Action Group (BMAG) sprang up in this prosperous area, and held its first public meeting in July 1962. Its chairman was Jim Callaghan MP, who lived locally, and Lewisham's Tory MP, the athlete Chris Chattaway, gave full support. Key members included Roland Moyle, an industrial relations consultant who lived on the Keep Estate, and Ian Hay Davison, a chartered accountant and councillor who eventually dropped politics for a glittering career in finance, becoming the man Margaret Thatcher chose to sort out the scandals at the Lloyd's insurance market in the 1980s.

A BMAG leaflet warned of what the road would mean; 'a path will need to be blasted for it right through Blackheath Park and the centre of the village itself....... many homes in its path will be destroyed, others will find themselves perched on the verge of a roaring maelstrom of traffic. A third of the shopping centre will be torn down. Three years at least of chaos, noise, and disruption will be the consequence of demolition and construction.' [96]

The group thought that the impetus for the scheme was the sudden availability of land on the former RAF station at Kidbrooke which forced 'the issue of motorway policy before the basis for it has been fully investigated.'

The LCC plan carried the new route to Lewisham station mostly in cut-and-cover, a way of tunnelling where a vast trench for the road is dug, the road laid, and then the lid put back on again.[97] Using this technique under Blackheath Park, would make, said BMAG, 'a complete upheaval of their immediate neighbourhood and alteration of the local area..... noise will probably render life in Corner Green difficult, The Keep will be substantially destroyed, about half the houses being pulled down.' [98]

There was an alternative to all this; if the road really was needed, it could be taken under Blackheath in a deep tunnel – but this idea had been rejected on cost grounds.

The Dover Radial Road was bad enough if you lived in Blackheath, but what would happen to the traffic on this road then? Where would it go next? The campaigners seem to have stumbled on some of the behind-the-scenes work by the LCC's engineers who were already planning the Motorway Box. A protest meeting in 1963 was shown copies of a map outlining the DRR west of the St John's area, which showed it continuing to Peckham, Brixton, Clapham Junction, Battersea, and Hammersmith. The map – clearly that of the South Cross Route – was claimed to be a copy of one shown by someone in the LCC's road planning department. [99]

Ian Hay Davison listed the buildings in the way of this route; first of all there was the Elliot Automation plant at Lewisham, then the road would have to cross two lines of railway at Nunhead; 'Camberwell council haven't been told about this – they have built a new housing estate in the way.' In Peckham, the Lyndhurst Grove primary school was in the way and at Denmark Hill 'it would get the Salvation Army college, the Maudesley Hospital and King's College Hospital in one swoop.'[100]

The *Architects' Journal* was scathing, having this to say; 'accused of piecemeal planning, the roads committee say their published scheme fits into their 'long term master plan.' Asked how they were able to produce such a master plan before their traffic survey – surely the basis for road planning – they reply that

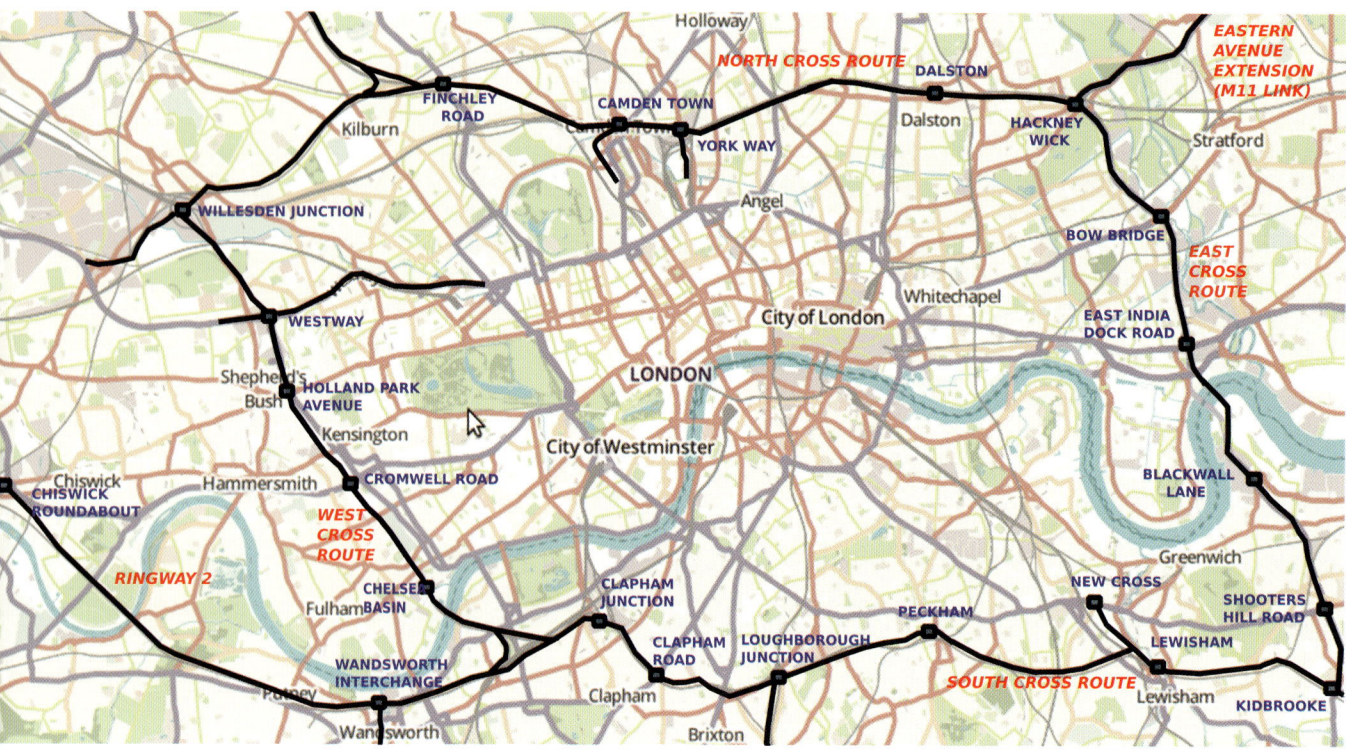

The Motorway Box – later known as Ringway 1 – plus links

the findings of the survey will confirm the rightness of their proposals! Asked if one may see the master plan one hears there is none in existence.'[101]

Ironically, at the same time as the road plans, the LCC town planning committee had developed a four point code to preserve the village-like charm of Blackheath. (In spring 1968, Blackheath Village became London's first conservation area).

The Blackheath protesters had to confront an early myth which was explicitly stated in Abercrombie's plan. It was argued that railway lines already divided communities, and so building a motorway in parallel with a railway would do no further damage to the environment. This wasn't so; for some reason railways seem to fit well into the cityscape, and the Blackheath group insisted that the 'railway line was no barrier – there is no sense of psychological barrier or physical separation raised by the line.'

The protesters in Blackheath went on to form one of the core constituencies in the London-wide fight against the Motorway Box from 1968 onwards.

In April 1965, on the very first day of the Greater London Council's legal existence, its leaders unwrapped the Motorway Box, saying that 'phase two of the traffic survey is expected to show that the urban Motorway Box and links to radial motorways converging on London will be a minimum requirement.'

The Motorway Box was just what it said, a box encircling central, and inner, London with continuous motorways. It looked similar to Abercrombie's B Ring, although some sections would be built somewhat further out, and it would follow more existing railway routes. But it had exactly the same stated objective – to provide environmental relief by diverting through traffic away from central London.

For the first time preferred routes were revealed, based on the work the consultants had been busy on, and all now published in the GLC minutes. These were not necessarily the final routes but it was obvious to the careful observer that very substantial and detailed work had already been undertaken to be able to get this far. The insiders had a very clear of idea of what the Motorway Box would look like and exactly where it would go. The four sides of the Motorway Box were, then;[102]

West Cross Route – from Willesden Junction, following the West London Line via Olympia and crossing the river by a new bridge to terminate in the Battersea area. It would, it was claimed, actually improve the environment because it would serve an area where most roads ran east-west and so for north-south traffic, drivers were rat-running through residential streets.

North Cross Route – from Willesden Junction, following BR's North London Line to Finchley Road and the M1 link, before cutting through Hampstead on the cut-and-cover method as far as Camden, where it would follow the North London Line again to Hackney Wick. There, it would join the Eastern Avenue extension, and the East Cross route.[103]

East Cross Route – from the junction at Hackney Wick, following the industry-choked River Lea down to the duplicated Blackwall Tunnel, and then continuing south of the river through another industrial area to join the South Cross Route at Kidbrooke.

South Cross Route – from the Kidbrooke junction with the East Cross Route, via St Johns, Peckham, and then following the railway to link up with the West Cross Route at Clapham Junction to complete the box. At Loughborough Junction there would be a junction with another of Abercrombie's proposals – Parkway E – which would run south through Tulse Hill, Crystal Palace, and Addiscombe to join the D Ring at New Addington.

Some 60 per cent of the Motorway Box, including many of the junctions, would be elevated above street level. This was the cheapest way of building, but also the one which inflicted the most noise, dust, fumes and gloom on nearby residents. Camden and Battersea would be especially damaged by motorways overhead. Detailed descriptions of what the GLC called 'corridors of opportunity' appear in the Appendix.

The Motorway Box would, said the GLC, encourage through traffic to avoid the central area and would mean quicker journeys within it. 'More important, it would provide for the very many journeys which are not local but which, by their pressure along existing main roads, congest suburban town centres.'

Amazingly, there was no suggestion whatsoever that this vast project would do anything at all to solve London's key transport problem, the overcrowded, unreliable and investment-starved commuter routes into central London. It was accepted cheerfully that the vast majority of commutes would still be on public transport; this, said the GLC, should be 'improved as far as practicable,' but there were no concrete proposals about how it might be done or where the money to do it would come from.'[104] The new GLC, it was clear, was entirely focussed on road transport.

To start with, the borough councils, which were now the planning authorities for London, were told to safeguard all these routes, meaning that no planning permission would be granted for any property on them.

The two key figures fronting the motorway schemes were now Christopher Higgins, chairman of the planning committee, and Jane Phillips, the art connoisseur and patron who chaired the highways and transportation committee. They predicted that road spending in Greater London would rise from £1 million in

1955/56 to £37 million in 1969/70. Standing behind these two were the engineering team who had been planning the Box in detail since at least 1963.

The Motorway Box would form a key part of the Greater London Development Plan (GLDP) which the new authority needed to produce for ministerial approval. The plan would, said the 1963 Act bringing the GLC into being, 'lay down considerations of general policy with respect to the use of land in various parts of Greater London including, in particular, guidance as to the future road system.' Some kind of public hearing would have to be provided to assess the plan and consider objections to it.

Under questioning, the GLC housing chief said that 12,500 families would need to be rehoused as a result of building the Motorway Box. This was a huge number of people whose lives would be turned upside down at vast public expense – and more than twice those who would have been made homeless by the central London A Ring. Officials thought it very difficult to deal with if the work had to be concentrated into 10 years, but it was not reckoned to be a serious problem if the roads were constructed over 20 years.[105]

The coming of the ringways could be personally cruel. In Hampstead, public relations man Peter Brunskill bought his house in Belsize Square in early 1965. His solicitors did the usual checks and found nothing of concern – despite all the LCC's planning work. 'Two months later it was announced that the GLC were planning to drive this motorway through my drawing room.'[106]

1966 seemed the quiet before the storm. Nothing was knocked down on the route of the Box, no compulsory purchase orders were served. But in the background, the consulting engineers and GLC highway engineers were busily turning their 1965 proposals into definite routes; lines on maps had already become engineering drawings; now they became large scale plans that contractors on the ground could work with. There were consultations regarding the M11 London – Cambridge motorway, the proposed route of the Eastern Avenue extension was safeguarded, and the MoT rubber-stamped the northern end of the East Cross Route from Bow to Hackney Wick.

But in the summer of that year, the GLC dropped a bombshell. It warned that there was 'a far more extensive demand' for orbital travel than the Motorway Box alone could serve. So it proposed that along with an improved North Circular, a new South Circular Road was needed from Chiswick right round to Newham via a new river crossing. It would, said the GLC, 'harmonise well with the developing pattern of box and radials.'[107] Once again, detailed planning went on behind closed doors.

The GLC continued to insist that neither peak-hour commuting nor off-peak journeys to the centre would be the key transport headache in the 1980s. Instead it would be 'the very large increase in movement by road outside the centre for all purposes except the journey to and from work, and in particular the increase of 2.5 times the number of non-work journeys made by car.'

Planning professionals were already on the alert, even if the mass of the citizens were not. A packed meeting of the Town and Country Planning Association that April heard an astonishing admission from Tom Widdaker, head of the GLC's policy and general group. He told them that environmentally, the best we could hope for from the motorways was a psychological adjustment to their dominating scale and to its blighting effects on adjoining areas. There was, said Widdaker, 'no room for superficial emotional reactions to the problems ahead.' These problems, thought the acerbic reporter from the *Architects' Journal*, 'included any suggestion that urban motorways were not absolutely necessary or that subsidised public transport with restrictions on car use might provide a more acceptable environmental solution.'[108] This horrifying vision of the future seems to have received no publicity outside of planning and architectural circles.

Meanwhile, in west London, the Westway extension was making progress. Careful acquisition of property on the line of the route had started from 1962 onwards after parliamentary approval for construction; a 'private and confidential' report to LCC members in 1960 reckoned that 3,356 people would need to be rehoused as a result.

The LCC was well aware that the final route, running just to the north of the Metropolitan Line, would bring an urban motorway horribly close to peoples' homes in North Kensington. Hubert Bennett, the LCC architect, had admitted there were cases in Cambridge Gardens and Acklam Road 'where the presence of the viaduct within 20-30 feet of existing houses will make living conditions very unsatisfactory.' The LCC medical officer duly did a noise assessment and concluded that noise on Acklam Road was no worse than to be expected in inner London. The point of this conclusion is unclear – surely the question was how much *additional* noise would be inflicted on residents.[109]

Demolition of the acquired homes began in 1964 and construction began at the western end on 29 September 1966.

Building a motorway across a densely populated area is a devastating business. First property needs to be acquired – by compulsory purchase – well in advance of the construction start date. Enough of it needs to be acquired to allow space for the builders to work in, and hopefully, so that the completed road is not too close to residents. The cynical view is that it can help if the road can be driven through poor communities which are less likely to stand up for themselves or to have their concerns raised in the mass media.[110] Once acquired, such property is either let to short term tenants, so damaging any cohesive community, or is boarded up and abandoned for years, so attracting vagrants and rats. Local businesses close as their customers vanish.

Then the demolition teams move in, creating noise and dust and demanding road space for the building works to commence. Local streets become dominated by noise and pollution from heavy lorries moving spoil away. Local traffic suffers delay and frustration due to the road closures and diversions the building work requires, life for cyclists and pedestrians soon become intolerable.

Only after this stage could the construction actually start, with heavy lorries then needing to move vast quantities of concrete and steel onsite in a residential area. Working with both materials on this scale is a noisy and polluting business. Time is money in construction, so it would make sense to have as long a working day as possible.

Anyone who wanted to understand what urban motorways meant need only visit the Westway site. A *Times* reporter did and found 'spectral rows of empty houses waiting to be demolished, streets full of smashed windows and derelict cars... 'it is worse than the bombs' said an old lady looking out of the gaping windows and smashed doors of the streets opposite....the devastation is such that that hardly any of those I spoke to wanted to stay there any longer. As the shops closed down it became a longer and longer journey to buy food. The neighbours had moved out under the rehousing scheme. One old man, I was told, had committed suicide when told he would have to go.'[111]

The LCC housing director was in the front line of all this, and warned that 'the

Built as planned; the East Cross Route in Tower Hamlets

proposed rehousing of over 2,000 persons for this scheme alone during the four year period 1964-67 in addition to the liability arising in west London from other road improvement schemes (eg the West Cross route), other services of the council, and the slum clearance programme is likely to give rise to considerable difficulty,' or, put less delicately, building motorways would make a bad housing situation even worse.[112]

Twenty years after the war, London's housing situation was a disgrace. Wartime damage had still not been completely repaired, and although slum clearance schemes were powering ahead, council waiting lists were actually growing. A royal commission had been set up to inquire into the crisis – the Milner Holland Commission.[113] It found there was an acute shortage of rented accommodation and that in some areas the shortage was getting worse.

The 1966 census provided housing statistics which seem shocking to us today, revealing a totally different side to the London of the swinging sixties, let alone the booming London of the 21st century

- A quarter of families – over 600,000 – shared accommodation
- Half of these had to share a bathroom
- A third had no access to a bath at all
- 167,000 people lived at more than two people per room

The GLC itself estimated in 1969[114] that there was a shortage of 553,000 satisfactory homes, of which 233,000 represented a crude, absolute shortage with another 320,000 being substandard dwellings. This figure of 553,000 was expected to fall by 1974, but only to 336,000 – London's council home building had begun to fall seriously behind the projected programme from 1969 onwards.

By March 1970, there were 192,000 applicants on London council waiting lists[115] – this figure probably covered over 500,000 people. By 1981, admitted the GLC, there would still be a crude shortage of 95,000 homes by 1981 across the capital.[116]

The housing shortage and overcrowding meant that Londoners had a deficiency of decent housing half as large again as the total stock of housing in Birmingham.

The areas of greatest overcrowding and worst conditions were Islington, Paddington and North Kensington. People rehoused as a result of the Westway extension only piled extra pressure on the housing waiting list. And this was just one road – what would happen if the Motorway Box and the threatened new South Circular route went ahead?

Not everyone was so worried. Colin Buchanan was to tell the public inquiry into the ringways that he was far more concerned about motorways taking up open space then demolishing housing. He said 'when the road goes through housing....there is the chance to replace the housing somewhere.....a good deal of London outside the great historical financial centre, and the housing in particular, is really pretty dreary stuff.'[117]

In the East End, meanwhile, work began on the East Cross Route. Originally it would have two lanes in each direction with limited hard shoulders. Plans for

Bow Flyover in the East End. The East Cross Route here is sunken below ground, running from top left to bottom right.

three lanes (in 1963) were shelved due to fears that it would create a new bottleneck at Blackwall Tunnel. The LCC's road committee noted that it was 'unlikely that full benefit from a six-lane route on the approach roads will be obtained unless a third tunnel is added at Blackwall.'[118] It is three lanes in both directions today.

The East Cross Route was designed by the GLC's in-house engineers and its construction was relatively uncontroversial, apart from the 113 residents of Eastway in Hackney who petitioned the GLC in 1971 about the annoyance and noise from the construction work.[119] Their GLC member complained that these houses would be uninhabitable once the road was completed. She was told that they would be three times as far from the motorway as the homes in Acklam Road and rehousing was not justified.

The overall cost, boosted by land acquisition costs, was £8 million.

North of the Blackwall Tunnel, the route followed the River Lea, whose industrial hinterlands already provided an effective barrier between Tower Hamlets and Newham. A complicated roundabout/underpass was built at Bow – the East Cross route passed underneath the A11 with slip roads allowing access, and a flyover carried the A11 over the roundabout. The result was easy passage for through traffic on both the A11 and the East Cross Route, with a roundabout linking both to the A11.

But there is something profoundly alienating about road junctions of this size; even trying to cross the road can be a major expedition. And yet this interchange was not actually that large, consisting of two carriageways in each direction for both major routes – parts of the Motorway Box would have four lanes in each direction, and so interchanges would have to be exponentially larger. According to urban legend, the Kray twins buried Frank 'mad axeman' Mitchell in the concrete foundations for the flyover. Whether true or not it is an appropriate legend for this grim spot.[120] The East Cross Route finally opened for traffic in 1973.

Ringway 2 plus links to other motorways

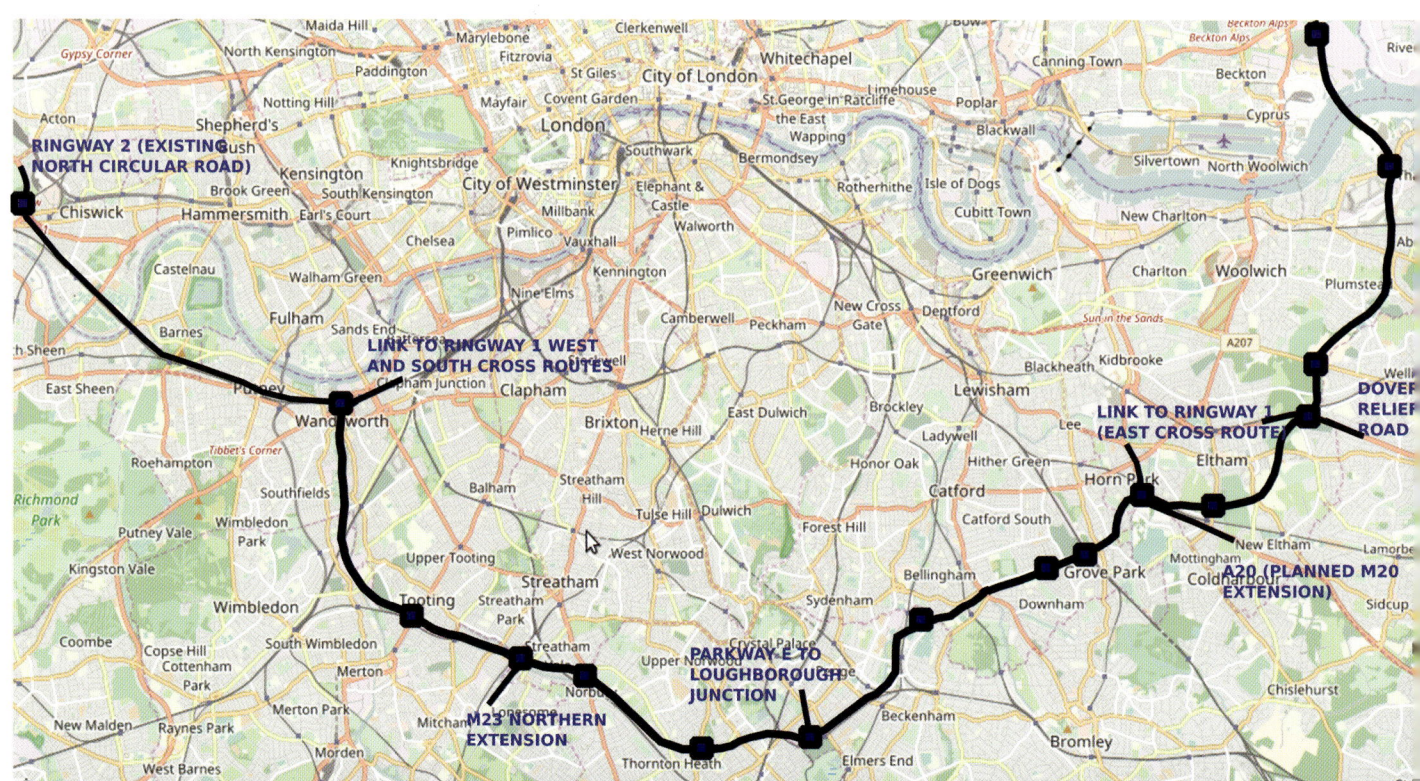

In January 1967, based on the results from the part two of the traffic survey, the GLC firmed up its plans for a new South Circular Road. It revealed that it wanted to resurrect two more of Abercrombie's rings – the C ring and the D ring as full scale motorways.

The existing South Circular Road was still little more than a line on the map; improving it to motorway standard would be an impossibly ambitious task, and building a brand new motorway might even be cheaper. So the C Ring was revived as a brand new urban road running slightly to its south (see map) and requiring a new river tunnel between Newham and the bleak GLC new town at Thamesmead. There were fewer railway routes this road could follow, and although open land could be gobbled up, parts of the C Ring would have to blast a trail of destruction across suburbia, with significant sections built with four lanes in each direction from the start. A detailed description appears in the Appendix.

The C Ring was planned so it would connect with the planned London – Crawley motorway (see below). The combination of the two meant that a whole new class of London's people would be affected by urban motorways – the artisan and lower middle classes of Conservative-voting suburbia.

North of the Thames, Whitehall was already planning to improve the North Circular to near-motorway standards. In 1960, two tunnels carrying the A40 under the North Circular at Hanger Lane were opened, the first major improvement to be made and infamous today as the Hanger Lane Gyratory. The following year, ministry road engineers produced a complete blueprint for upgrading the route to motorway-like status, by widening to three carriageways throughout and building flyovers or underpasses to build a fast route for through traffic.[121]

The *Evening News* billed the project as '£50 million for North Circular – M-road style to end jams.'[122] As this was a national trunk road, Whitehall would pick up the tab for transforming the North Circular into Ringway 2. It would not cost the GLC a penny.

A key project was the three-level flyover at Brent Cross where the North Circular would pass above the A41. This was completed in 1965, just as plans for what became Britain's first out-of-town shopping centre were being worked on.

Hammerson, a leading property developer, first drew up plans to build the Brent Cross centre in 1963 on a former Hendon council sewage farm. This was aimed squarely at motorists, and it was made possible by the improvements to the North Circular. Initially, the GLC persuaded the ministry to refuse planning permission because of its impact on the North Circular; 'it gave rise' it said, 'to conditions prejudicial to the free flow of traffic and general safety on the neighbouring highways.'[123] Only when access roads were ironed out was planning consent granted. It opened in 1976 with 3,500 parking spaces, increased to 5,200 by early 1979 and 8,000 today. [124]

The D Ring would be built much further out, and much of it would be outside the GLC area. As a trunk road it would be a central government project; its engineers would plan the route and pay for it too. Beyond this, in turn, would be the E Ring (Bressey's North and South Orbital roads), entirely outside of Greater London and which did not feature at all in the GLDP. These two outer ringways have a very different history to the inner rings, and their story needs to be deferred to a subsequent chapter.

The three ringways, together with the radial motorways which would terminate on one or other of them, would constitute the primary road plan for London.

In February, the transport sub committee returned to the full GLC with detailed proposals and costings for three key pieces of the jigsaw. The first sample costings actually published were;[125]
- The North Cross Route
- The Camden bypass
- The Eastern Avenue extension

Table three – 1967: first costs revealed

	Miles	Property costs	Cost of works	Rehousing costs	Total cost
North Cross Route and West Cross Route north of Western Avenue	16	61	135	13	209
Camden Town bypass	1	3	4	1	8
Eastern Avenue extension	3.5	12	12	1	31

This is the first we hear of the Camden Town bypass – a truly hair-raising scheme which would have devastated what is now one of London's cultural hotspots. It was actually suggested by the Travers Morgan team and was a knock-on requirement from the North Cross Route – once again, motorways begat motorways. When Travers Morgan engineers were investigating an interchange for the North Cross route it became clear that any junction in the area would worsen the traffic in Camden Town itself, and so Travers Morgan suggested a dual three-lane, north-south bypass terminating on Hampstead Road. Its report admitted that 'the scheme has disadvantages, not the least being the adverse effect on the attractive residences on Oval Road.'[126] The GLC, however, duly accepted the proposal.

In November, the GLC was told that the likely cost of the entire primary road programme would be £840 million.

This was crystal clear stuff. With the East Cross Route being built, the West Cross Route almost ready to go, the North Cross Route planned in detail, only the fine details of the South Cross Route were still uncertain, although the general alignment had been revealed in 1965.

You could now take a map of the capital and check whether your house was bang in the way of a motorway. One opponent of the ringways, John Adams, a geography professor at University College London, thinks that you can date serious opposition to motorway building to the time schematic plans were translated into more detailed ones where you could see where your own house stood.[127]

Actually, there was something much worse that that. If your house was in the track of a motorway, the GLC would be forced – if you were an owner occupier – to buy it from you at a fair price plus some allowance for your costs for moving as if the motorway had never been dreamed up. This wouldn't compensate you for the stress, or the heartache of losing a home you had probably lived in for years and spent money on improving, but you would at least get something.

But if you owned a house near to a planned motorway, but not actually in its track, you were – by law – stymied. You were entitled to no compensation whatsoever for the noise, polluted air, loss of view, loss of daylight and general blight on your property which you would surely be unable to sell. Only if you lived

The Brixton Barrier Block – a brutalist defence against noise from the South Cross Route

within 220 feet of the centre of the new road could you force the council to buy you out.

The GLC knew this blight would be a major issue and raised it with the housing and local government ministry in 1966. It called for a more generous compensation system to get round this difficulty, which would be included in the 75 per cent grant that Whitehall paid for approved road schemes. But the ministry did not want 'to encourage any weakening of the compensation code.' by providing better construction grants.[128] On a subsequent occasion, the ministry essentially told County Hall to get lost – saying that 'the ownership of land inherently carries with it certain risks of loss or possibilities of profits due to the activities of others on others' land,'[129] which was not how the owner-occupiers of outer south London saw their homes.

Absent a fairer compensation scheme of course, it would be in the GLC's interest to minimise land acquisition costs and skimp on environmental standards, or else see the road programme stretch out ever further into the future while its own costs spiralled and the chance of cancellation increased. Under that scenario, Acklam Roads would proliferate all across the capital.

Now that the lines of the ringways were laid down and safeguarded against development, blight spread across the proposed routes. Anyone thinking of buying your house would find the fact of the proposed motorway in the property searches their solicitor would carry out. Building societies would then refuse to lend any money, and the sale would duly fall through. Thousands of homes became effectively unsaleable on the open market and areas went downhill.

The Streatham Vale Property Owners' Association, which represented homeowners living on an estate built in 1926 and at risk both from the C Ring and the M23, records the severe blight during this period. 'Many small shops in Norbury closed and the character of the area declined. Large numbers of homes were acquired by the GLC who used them to provide temporary housing. Ownership of these houses was eventually transferred to Lambeth council, many of which have been sold to the original tenants under the right-to-buy scheme.'[130]

At the GLC elections in April 1967, Labour were hammered. They won – in an accurate reflection of national political feeling – only 18 out of 100 seats. Bill Fiske was defeated in Havering, and the new opposition leader was Sir Reg Goodwin, the only potential successor with a seat safe enough to survive the massacre.

But during the elections, road-building was a non-issue; both parties entirely agreed with the building of the ringways. The Tories came to power under Desmond Plummer, who would be the first Conservative leader of the capital since 1934. The chairman of the transport committee was now Robert Vigars, who represented South Kensington. Vigars had served on the LCC transport committee and had represented the Tory opposition on the Nugent committee. The borough elections the following year saw the Tories in control of all but a handful of London councils.

Given the close links between the Conservatives and the road lobby, they could be expected to be even more enthusiastic about building urban motorways than their Labour predecessors. They did not disappoint.

The next month the GLC announced a route for the southern part of the West Cross Route to Chelsea Basin. This would have four lanes in each direction and although it was designed to follow the railway, there would be some unfortunate side effects………. 'a slip road is unfortunately essential at this point, (near Philbeach Gardens)….the road will unfortunately encroach on the site of the college of St Mark and St John….it may affect the mooring facilities at Chelsea Basin….it will affect a number of residential properties in Elsham Road.'[131]

However the South Cross Route was proving more difficult than expected. The detailed route investigations, carried out by the GLC's own engineers rather than by outside consultants, should have been completed by summer 1966, but there had been unforeseen difficulties.[132]

One came at Wandsworth Road, where the council was building the Westbury Estate with its twin 22 storey tower blocks. Just weeks after the South Cross Route had been announced, work had to stop as it was realised that the block would be just 30 feet from the motorway. The issue was resolved by diverting the route under the estate.[133] Evelyn Dennington, the GLC housing chief, denied there had been 'any question of blame or lack of foresight.'

Another problem was the need to fit in with Lambeth Council's ambitious plans to rebuild Brixton town centre. The council had commissioned Freeman Fox to report on a possible redevelopment in August 1962. The familiar issues were in play at Brixton; the need to resolve the conflict between pedestrians and cars as well as that between through traffic and local traffic, both problems were to be solved by segregating them as much as possible. The redevelopment also aimed to provide a road system capable of supporting anticipated traffic increases.

Freeman Fox proposed widening Brixton Road and moving the entire shopping centre to a raised deck on top of this. [134] These ideas predated the plans for the South Cross Route, and so the final version of the Lambeth plan, approved just days before the first manned moon landing in 1969, incorporated a route for the motorway – and 42 huge towers.

Only one part of this vast scheme was actually built as the money simply wasn't there; a council block called Southwyck House in Coldharbour Lane. Its front was built in a threatening brutalist style, with tiny windows and unusual zig-zag design, which was designed to reflect the noise from the South Cross Route back to the road. It is universally known as the Barrier Block. The block is similar to the famous Byker Wall on Tyneside which was designed to protect

Lambeth planners' model of the rebuilt Brixton town centre, with the South Cross Route fully integrated

residents from a motorway which in the event was never built. Unlike the Barrier Block, the Byker Wall is popular with its residents, features in UNESCO's list of outstanding 20th Century buildings and won Grade II listing in 2007.

While prime minister, John Major condemned the Barrier Block as an example of 'grey, sullen concrete wastelands, set apart from the rest of the community, robbing people of ambition and self respect.' saying they were 'monuments to the failed history of socialist planning.'[135] He had forgotten that he was the chair of Lambeth's housing committee which agreed to build it in December 1970.

However Evelyn Dennington had earlier suggested that the South Cross Route could become an instrument of social engineering. She told a meeting in December 1965 concerning Loughborough Park that 'the road may be taken further to the east so as to bring about the clearance of the streets which were a problem to the borough council owing to the overcrowding of the houses by immigrants'.[136]

4 – Rage against the concrete

Protest began to coalesce – slowly – after the 1965 go-ahead for the Motorway Box. In Hampstead, residents had formed a protest group after the detailed plans for the North Cross Route were announced. Hampstead was – like Blackheath – an area whose geography made it an inevitable focus for protest. Much of the Motorway Box was planned to follow railway lines in an attempt to minimise destruction – but the three railway lines crossing the high ground of Hampstead did so in tunnel, so this option was not available here. Travers Morgan thought that a deep bore tunnel to take the North Cross Route under Hampstead would be prohibitively expensive, and so massive destruction on the surface of this wealthy area was inevitable if the road was to be built.

The Hampstead committee had been set up by a group of residents in the Eton Road area and eventually included the architectural historian Sir John Summerson, and Professor Norman Morris, a surgeon at the Royal Free Hospital. Hampstead held its first public meeting in January 1966; 300 people attended and 200 immediately joined the new Hampstead Motorway Action Group. Hampstead got in touch with activists across the river in Blackheath and the beginnings of a co-ordinated opposition began to appear.[137]

Individual groups didn't always agree with each other – Blackheath's initial impression of the Hampstead group was that 'it was mainly one of property interests. In addition they seemed disposed to launch hostile propaganda and attacks against the GLC and local authorities whereas it had been the view of the committee that the best course was to present a reasoned objection in the hope of bringing about a change of attitude.'[138] But whatever the differences, it was essential to present a united, London-wide front and prevent the GLC and MoT from playing divide and rule against different communities.

Hampstead's Labour MP, Ben Whitaker, supported his constituents, and he suggested that Labour grandee Douglas Jay call a meeting in the Commons to try to bring protest groups and residents associations together in a common front.

Jay had been a former junior treasury minister in Attlee's government, and was minister at the board of trade from 1964 until Harold Wilson fired him in 1967. He lived in Hampstead and represented Battersea North – both areas in the front line of the Motorway Box. His then wife Peggy, in turn, represented Battersea on the GLC.

Jay was a man of his times and background, educated at Winchester and Oxford; he famously once said that in matters of health 'the man from Whitehall really does know best.' His second wife said she would 'characterise Douglas as a radical in politics, but not quite a social conservative, although some of his attitudes were of their time. One has to understand that generation who came through the war, the mindset of the formation of that generation in terms of age, class, and social norms; and their astonishing commitment and belief that they could bring social justice to this country and had the personal capacity to make it happen.'[139]

Douglas Jay is almost forgotten today; a politician from a different time. But whether they know it or not, all Londoners owe him a great debt.

Jay was an early protester – the first he heard of the ringway plans was in 1964 when the leader of the Labour group on Wandsworth council told him that an acutely needed housing project was blocked because the LCC wanted to build 'some road' alongside Clapham Junction. 'On inquiring about this I discovered it to be the tip of a mysteriously much larger iceberg.' He then accompanied members of Wandsworth council to see ministers as early as May 1965.[140] Jay called the ringways 'an example of engineers' and technologists' megalomania, backed by vested interests, being given a free run almost without regard to what the ordinary public actually wanted.'[141]

On 1 March 1968, the London Motorway Action Group (LMAG) was formed. Along with Jay, two other Labour MPs, Roland Moyle (who won Lewisham in 1966) and Alistair MacDonald (Chislehurst) were present. LMAG eventually represented 13 London MPs from both parties.

The local groups at the meeting showed something surprising. Contrary to what is often assumed, the middle-class families who were starting to gentrify Georgian and Victorian property in inner London were not the core source of grassroots motorway opposition – although they did provide a hugely disproportionate number of the activists who kept a difficult campaign going. But the geographical centres of community rage were centred elsewhere, in two different types of area

- Established upper middle class areas in the path of the Motorway Box (Hampstead and Blackheath) or the C Ring (Chiswick)
- A vast swathe of lower middle class suburbia in south London threatened by the C Ring and the M23. (Streatham, Mitcham, Norbury, Beckenham, Eltham, Mottingham, Beddington, Wallington) together with areas of Redbridge threatened by the M11 and the extension of the North Circular. These areas, now considered unfashionable, were home to those who would be called 'hard-working families' in the debased political terminology of today. Many were owner-occupiers at a time when most people still rented. They felt that they had worked hard to pay mortgages on their quiet semi-detached homes in respectable areas. They felt, with good cause, that they had a great deal to lose from motorway building. Many, perhaps most, were habitual Conservative voters, and almost all the parliamentary constituencies in these areas were held by the Tories.

Opposition to the ringways in this zone was fierce – in October 1968, no less than 1,300 people crammed into Streatham Baths for a protest meeting.

The former GLC files are replete with sad letters from homeowners in the area. Mr and Mrs Pitcher from Streatham Vale wrote in late 1968 after receiving an offer to buy, saying; 'we bought this house in 1965 and spent over £500 improving and modernising it, yet Mr Cole (the GLC surveyor) made the insulting offer of £5,000, which is the same as offered to other properties in this area with gardens half the size and the house as it was in 1926.' They went on; 'the most galling part of it is that we were LCC tenants for seven years and by working and saving hard we bought this house and are now being forced by ever rising house prices to fall back on the housing list again.'[142]

J A Woodland of Mitcham wrote approving the Tory GLC plans to curb spending, adding 'there is one huge saving you can make and the same time alleviate a great deal of worry, that is dispense with the C ring road. We find it unbelievable that anyone could knock down perfectly good houses just to build a road.'[143]

The Mitcham C Road Association wrote to the GLC about the length of time 'Sold' boards were left up in homes bought by the council. The Association said

Engineers' plan of part of Ringway Two in the Falcolnwood – Eltham area of south east London

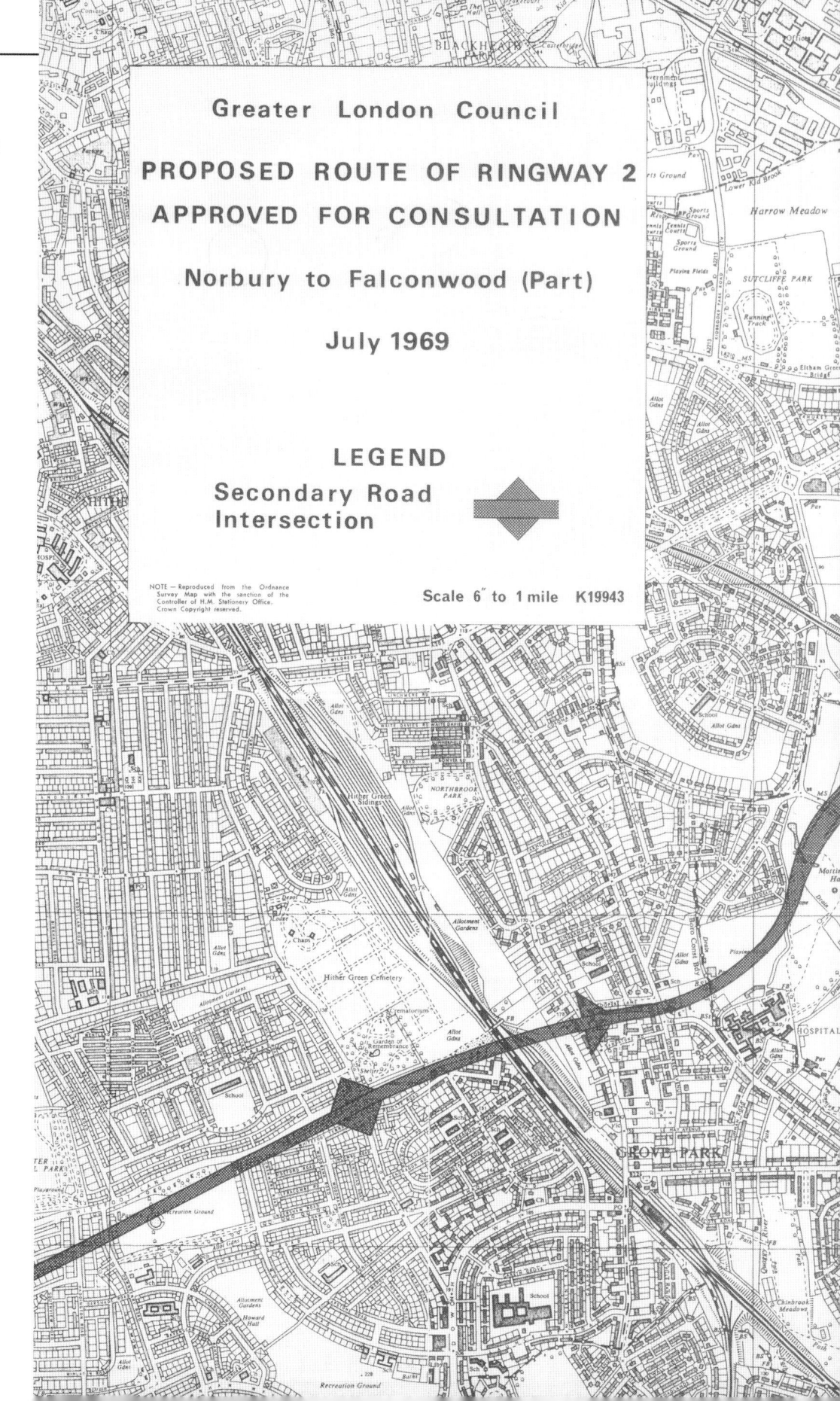

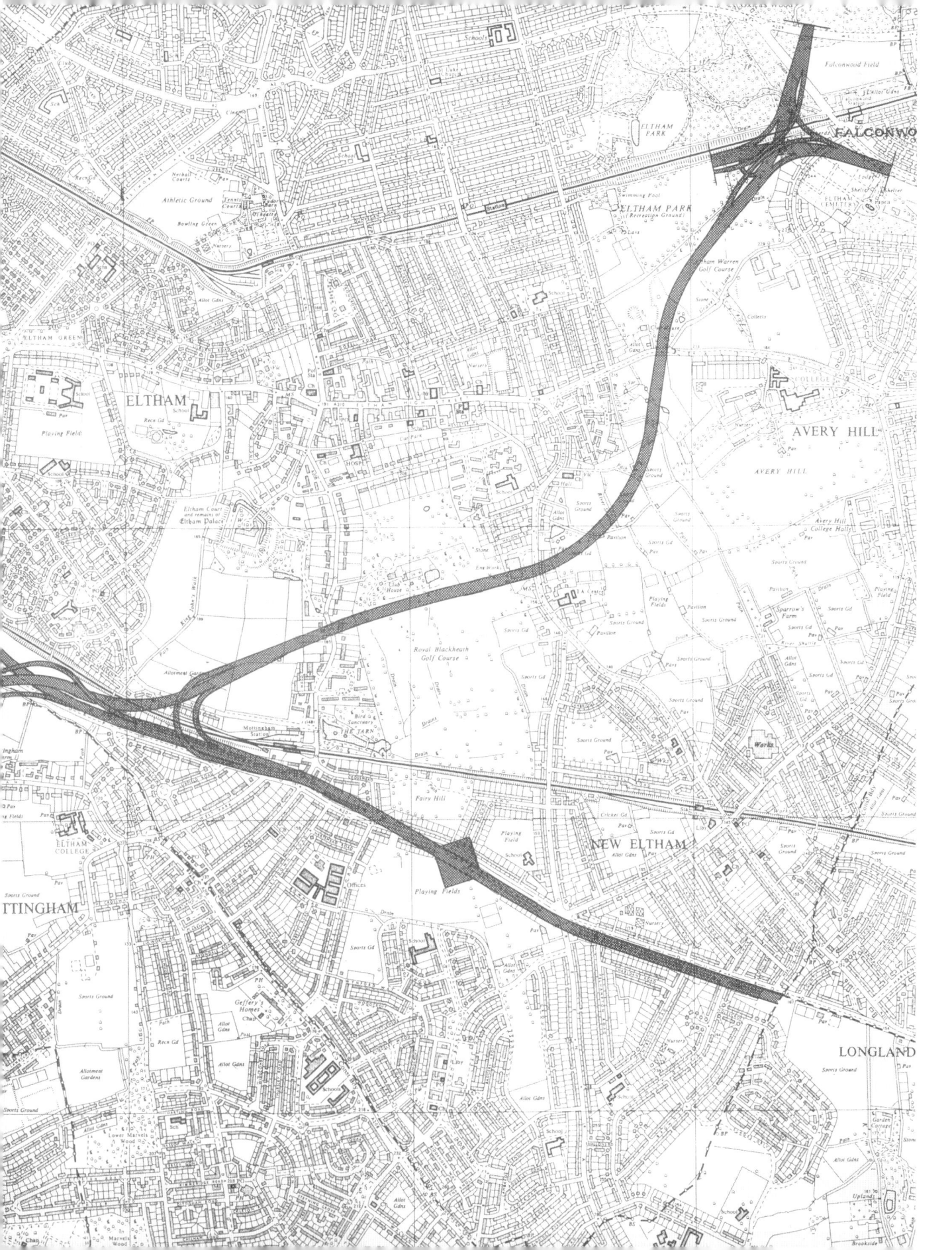

they 'invited vandalism on a large scale and can also lead to other acts of a worse nature, ie inviting people of an undesirable character taking illegal occupancy and providing means of access to other adjacent properties.'[144]

In West Beckenham, an LMAG report warned that the plight of older residents was 'acute' as replacement housing would not be available nearby; 'a move away from their friends and from an area where some have lived all their lives is a prospect which shocks and dismays them. Others, who will find themselves on the fringe, are terrified of the noise and disturbance which will ensue. Some will not be able to adjust themselves at this time of their life and have openly expressed the wish that death comes before the motorway.'[145]

With all this in mind, it was essential that LMAG be – and be seen to be – entirely non-party political and focused on this single issue. So in November 1968, Duncan Sandys, a right-wing former Tory colonial secretary and MP for Streatham, who was also chairman of the Civic Trust, agreed to become vice chairman.

The impact of motorway protest was slowly beginning to be felt in the Labour Party, now in the unusual position of being the minority party in London. Jay was always convinced that the best way of stopping the ringways was to convince the London Labour Party, which was bound to return to power eventually, to scrap the idea.

And in early 1969, the first, tentative signs of a shift appeared with the rump Labour group on the GLC moving to oppose the North and South Cross Routes. Instead, it proposed that the East and West Cross Routes be extended to meet the C Ring, which Labour still supported. Evelyn Dennington, Labour's number two on the GLC, said they had changed their minds because the government had agreed to hand over control of London Transport to the GLC, a handover which included the power to provide subsidies from the rates. Labour wanted such subsidies to be implemented, fares to be reassessed and consideration given to further tube extensions. In this situation, she thought, the North and South Cross Routes would not be needed.[146]

Jay's autobiography recalls a lunch between him and Sir Reg Goodwin in July 1969. They met at the Anchor pub in Southwark, and Goodwin assured him that it was now firm Labour policy to oppose the North and South Cross Routes and he was pretty confident that the pro-motorway faction in the Labour group, led by Ted Castle (Barbara's husband) would be defeated at the annual conference in September. At that meeting Castle tried to get the Motorway Box reinstated as Labour policy and was heavily defeated, his own speech being shouted down.[147]

Secretary of LMAG was Mary Thomas; she had been a civil servant in Jay's private office at the board of trade. She then worked worked for Tony Crosland, who succeeded Jay at the board of trade, before Jay offered her the job of running LMAG, as well as being the first secretary of the No campaign against the Common Market. In 1972 she became Mary Jay.

Another LMAG activist was Christopher Hall, who had just retired as chief information officer at the transport ministry. He had previously worked at the ministry of overseas development, and while there, led the successful campaign to stop British Rail's North London Line being closed under the Beeching Axe. The great investigative journalist Paul Foot called this campaign 'the most successful of all the campaigns to save threatened lines.'[148]

Then there was J Michael Thomson, a professor at the London School of Economics. Thomson was a leading transport economist who had carried out

The LSE Greater London Group. Michael Thomson is second from left

pioneering work on road pricing. He had served on the Smeed Committee, a pioneering study into the feasibility of road pricing and congestion charging commissioned by Marples in 1962. He also chaired the London Amenity and Transport Association (LATA), an umbrella group set up in 1967 for all the local amenity societies in the capital. By March 1969 it was obvious that a rigorous and independent analysis of the motorways was essential for the public inquiry into the GLDP. One key reason for the progress the ringway schemes had already made was that the intellectual case for them was put together by the road lobby in such a way as to chime with the commonsense experience of the ordinary motorist.

LMAG and LATA agreed to set up a working party to really assess the implications of the plan. Chris Hall and David Hunter, a lawyer from Camden Town, represented LMAG and the group included a number of high profile experts, including Lord Esher, a former chairman of the Royal Institute of British Architects, Peter Hills, a traffic engineer who had served on Buchanan's *Traffic in Towns* inquiry, and Dennis Gilbert, a traffic engineer who had also worked for Buchanan.

Secretary of LATA was Tim Pharaoh, who had just arrived from Edinburgh to accept a job working for Thomson at the LSE. The first assignment Thomson gave him was to work for LATA. Thomson was then working on an LSE project on London governance, and this needed to have the active support and co-operation of the GLC. However County Hall soon got wind of Pharaoh working for LATA and demanded he stop. Pharaoh's over-professor told him that he had to stop his LATA activities. Pharaoh was highly reluctant and so this gentleman suggested that to continue he should use a pseudonym, and hence some LATA documents appear under the name of Tim Martin.[149]

Two central tasks for protesters were to
- Make people aware of what was being planned and what it meant for them
- Get them to understand that this was not inevitable and could be fought off

Motorways in Suburbia, the M23, Ringways 2 and 3, and Parkway E

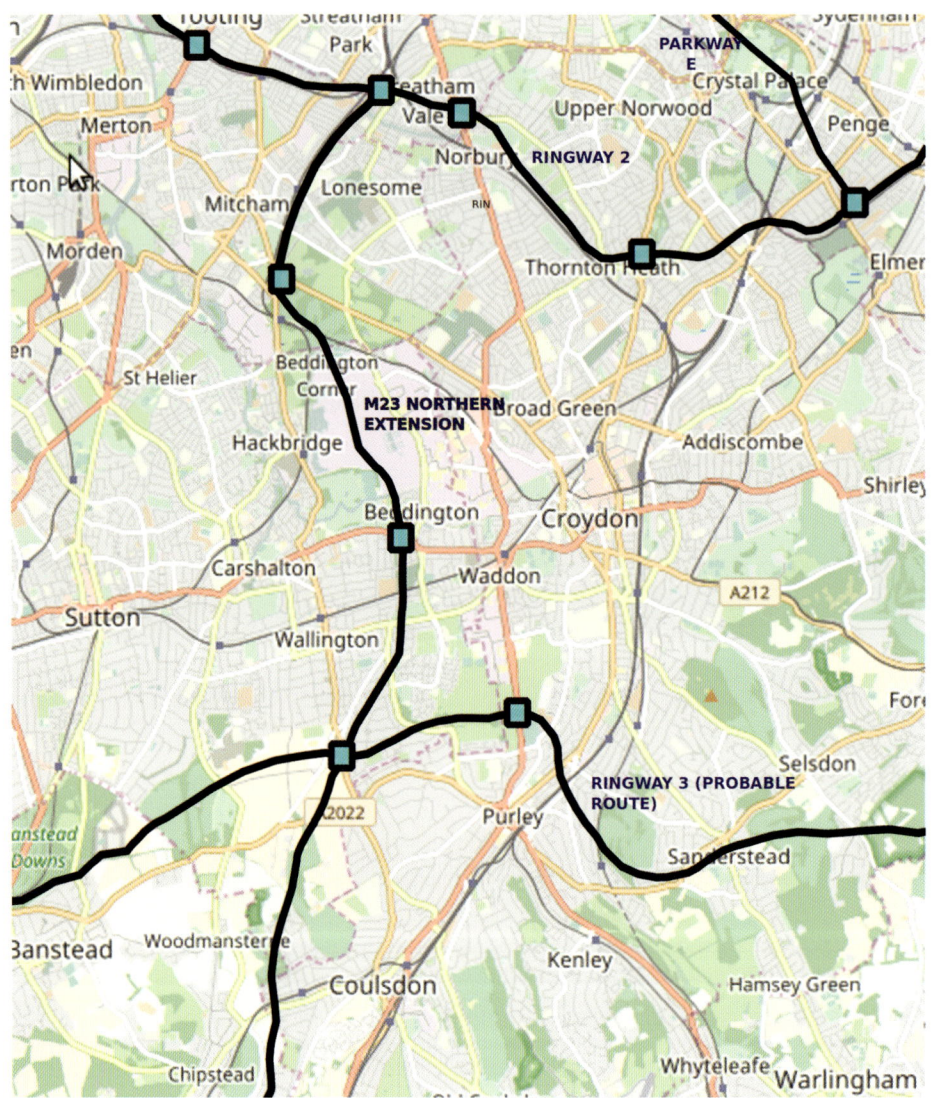

Planning professionals were often surprised at the apparent lack of public interest; reporting on the controversies in Blackheath, the *Architects' Journal* noted that 'the LCC's road programme seems surprisingly little known'.[150] One Blackheath resident, Elizabeth Bennett, wrote to Roland Moyle in October 1968 saying, 'my feeling is that people in Blackheath are surprisingly apathetic to the proposal'.[151]

This was also the experience of Sara Neill, then a librarian in her late 20s. She was an active member of Chelsea Labour Party and was a committee member of the Kensington and Chelsea Residents' Association as well as being an LMAG activist. Today, she recalls the difficulty of getting people to do something 'You knew about the schemes if your house was in the way, but otherwise people thought you were somehow prehistoric, like you were fighting progress.'[152]

Tony Belton, then a young councillor in Wandsworth, recalls a meeting he organised for Jay at Latchmere Baths in Battersea 'and there really was just one man and his dog present. To say I was disappointed was an understatement.'[153]

A reporter who visited Eltham talked to two young mothers outside their house which would be demolished, yet who still believed that 'the road would burrow underneath like the Victoria Line, leaving them unscathed.' An older woman 'was merely happy that her house was not to be taken 'I don't want to move, I don't want to live anywhere else,' she said, 'not realising that the scene would change with the new road a mere three houses away.'[154]

One explanation for this perplexing apathy is that planning strikes most people as a business tedious in the extreme. They know that most plans never materialise as they take years to mature and are frequently cancelled along the way with life continuing as before. Planning is also an area where the bureaucrats consider that they know best and do not actively invite public participation. Much discussion goes on behind closed doors and a scheme can proceed a considerable distance before people wake up and start to protest – and by then it may be perilously late.

Still, the first LMAG newsletter in March 1969 had recorded progress, saying that 'we have moved from the stage in which uninvolved observers tended to say 'well you can't stop progress' to the point whether they question whether urban motorways are progress at all.'[155]

Money was also a constant problem. Fighting the GLC and the transport ministry was not a cheap activity and both could spend taxpayers money pretty much with no limit. According to Mary Jay, the largest chunk of funding for the campaign came eventually from the trades unions, especially the TGWU, which, under the leadership of Jack Jones, had become a more leftish organisation which took a wider view of its responsibilities, which it thought did not end at disputes over wages and conditions.[156]

Jay also worked hard to get the London boroughs affected by the ringways to oppose them; several did so, including Camden, Hackney, Southwark, Ealing, Hackney, Lambeth and Croydon. When the Tories lost control of Lewisham council in spring 1970, it too joined the opposition. Two councils – Lambeth and Camden – supported LMAG financially with donations of £1,000 apiece, which was also important. This kind of support, however much in the interest of residents it was, would probably be illegal today.

In addition, he worked to build a coalition of all the MPs whose constituencies were affected. There was only one holdout – Marcus Worsley, the Tory MP for Chelsea. Although the World's End area of his constituency was at risk from the West Cross Route, he was a consistent supporter of the ringways, and reflected a certain view in Chelsea that the unwanted traffic was better directed over the river to the 'obsolete housing' of Battersea.

In the end LMAG raised £20,000 during its five year life, which was enough to pay its legal costs and leave some over as a modest fee for the transport economists who worked on its objection. By contrast, the BRF, which was for ever complaining about its lack of resources, had an income of £116,000 in the year 1970 alone, with the oil companies being the largest contributors.[157]

While Thomson's group worked to undermine the intellectual and transport case for the ringways, campaigners had to confront another major issue. With the West and East Cross routes already being built, they were afraid that the momentum to link them up and complete the box would become irresistible.

Jay's top-level political experience was central here – he knew ministers personally and as political colleagues. As such he was a consistent and effective high-level lobbyist against the ringway project.

Aerial views of what the two options for
the Dalston interchange on Ringway 1
would have looked like

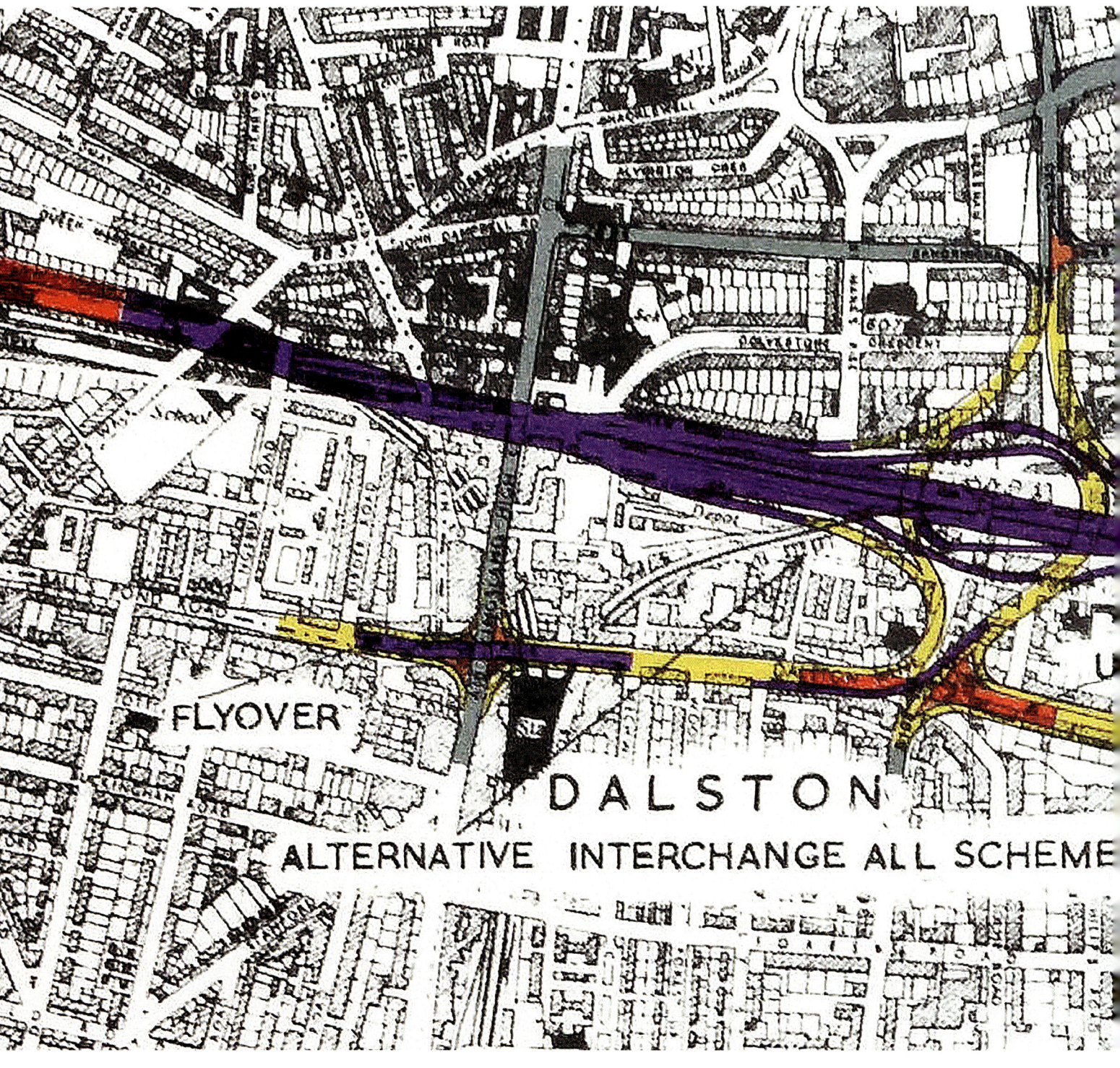

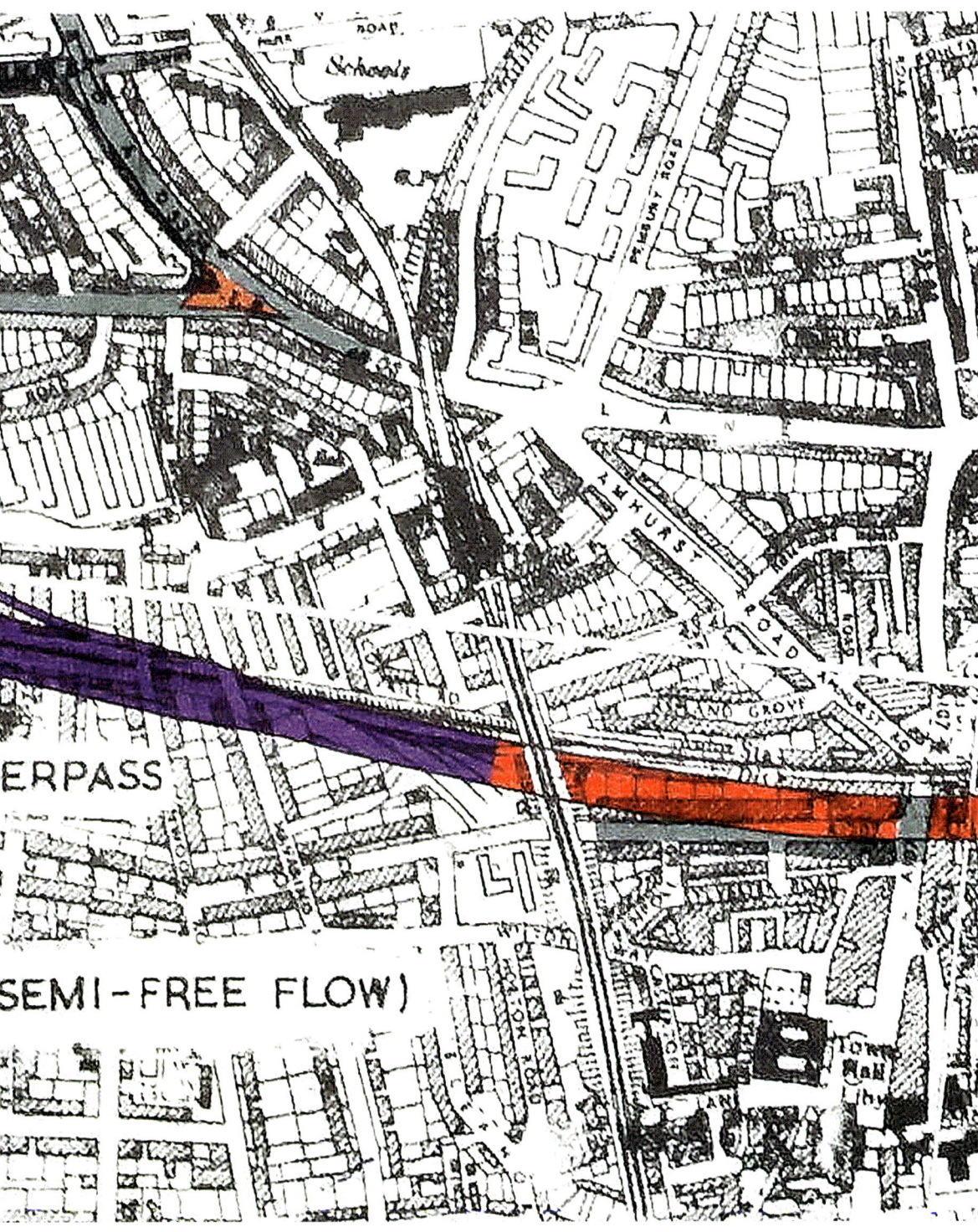

This spread and next: GLC engineers' drawings showing options for the North Cross Route interchange at Dalston. Lines in red indicate where the road would be depressed below the surface, grey where existing roads were to be widened and improved, yellow where a road would be built at surface level, and purple where the road would be elevated

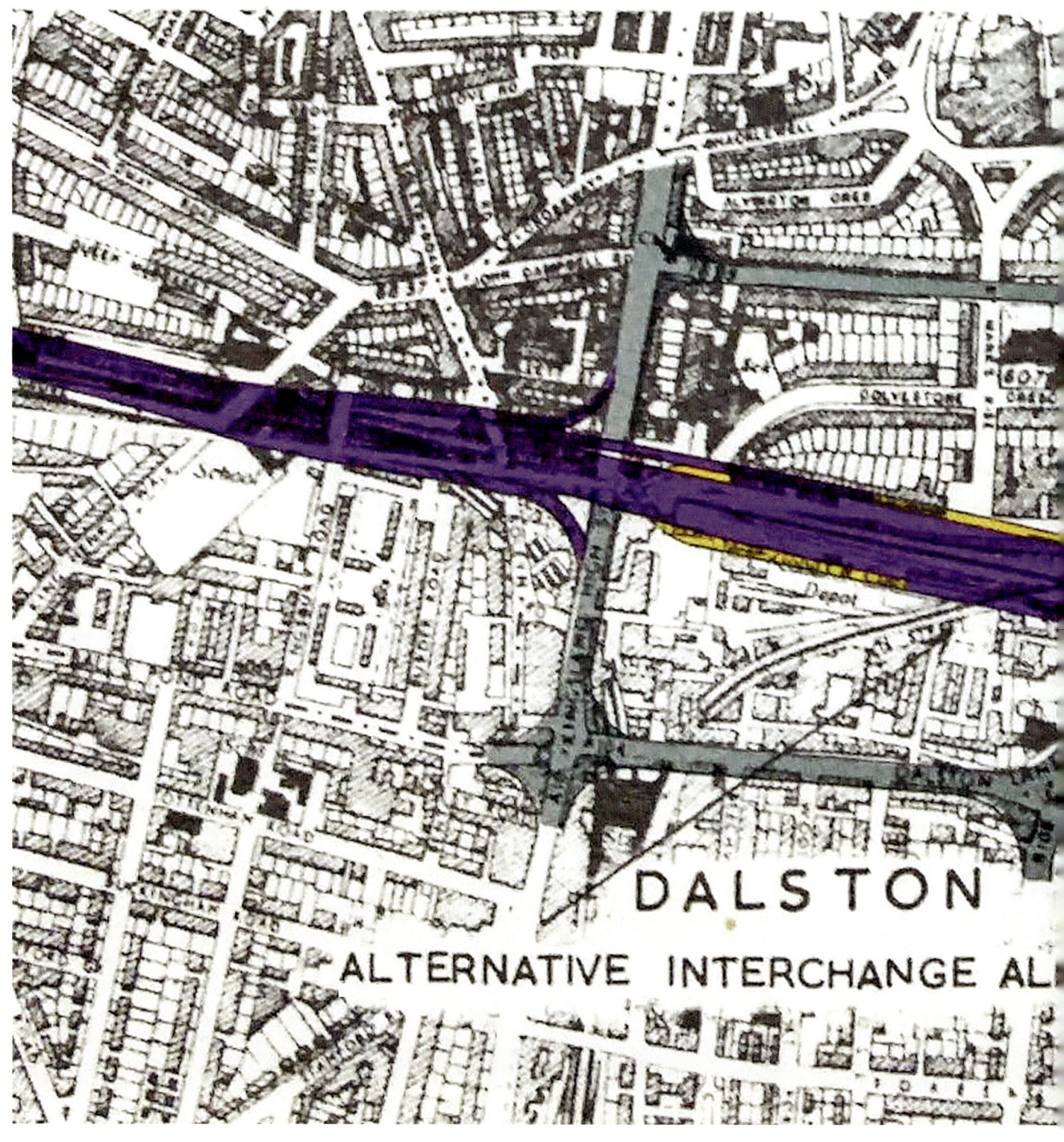

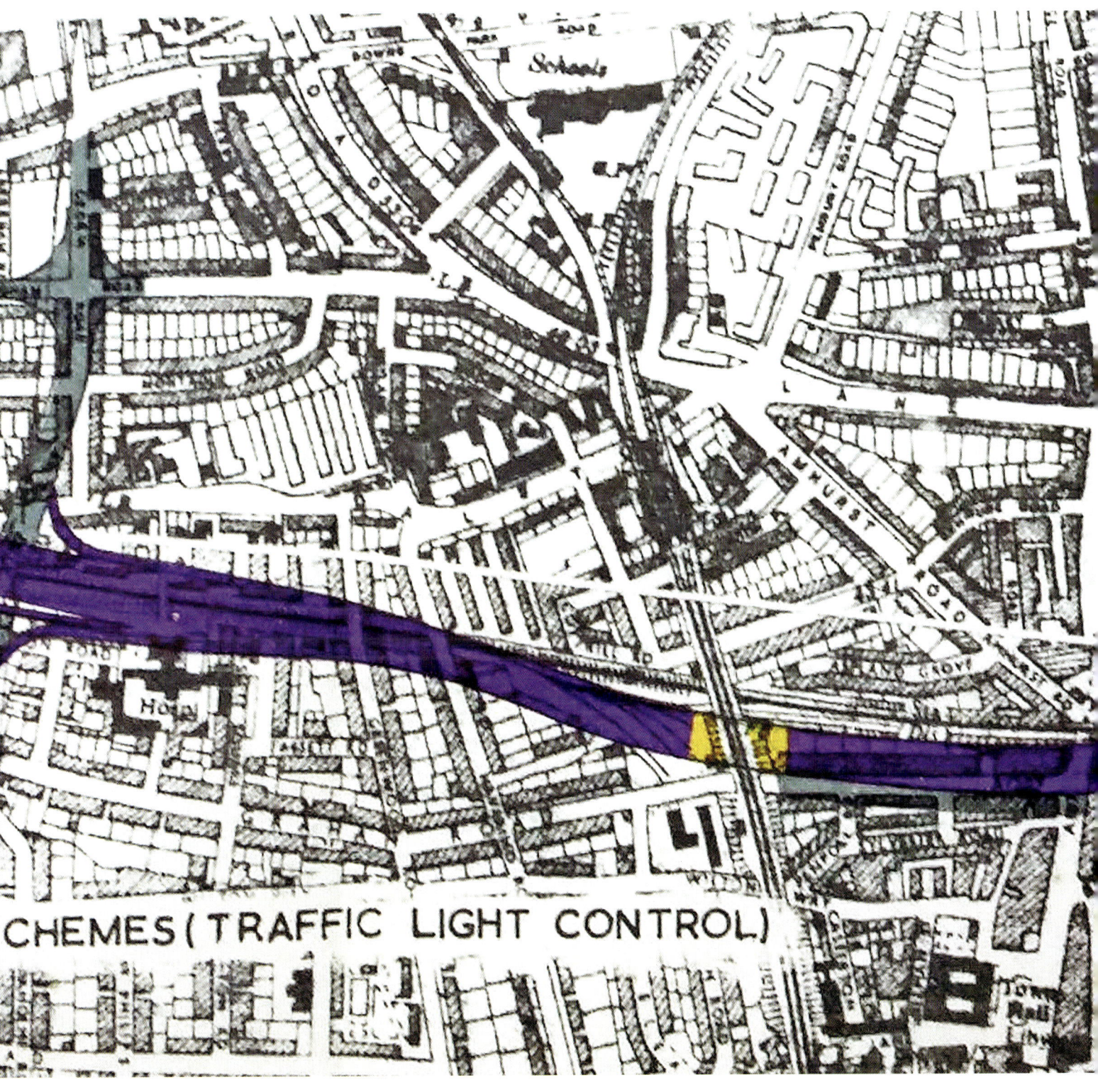

When 40 year old Richard Marsh took over as transport minister in April 1968, Jay successfully won assurances from him that future motorway projects would only be approved if they could be justified 'on their merits.'[158] Any other outcome would have totally prejudiced the eventual inquiry into the GLDP. Marsh had also confirmed to Jay that the government was not committed to the building of the Motorway Box.

However Marsh's own personal attitude to the ringways was guarded. He had publicly accepted the need for a network of primary roads although he carefully said that they would have to be considered as part of the GLDP.

In May 1968 he approved 27 London road schemes 'on their merits' to join the Preparation List for schemes where a high-level knowledge of cost, benefit and environmental impact existed. It helped ensure there was always a pipeline of schemes ready to be built when resources became available, and a road which made it onto the list automatically qualified for 75 per cent government grant.

The 27 included the West Cross Route south to the Thames, the C Ring from the A13 in east London, via a Thames crossing to the A2 at Falconwood, and the Sidcup road link from the A20 to the East Cross Route.

LMAG feared that Marsh was privately sympathetic to the GLC plans on advice from his officials, who it was beginning to be realised, had a deeply ingrained pro-road bias.[159] When Marsh met members of LMAG in May 1968, he told them that 'something should be done about London's traffic problem, but he did not think that public transport or parking policies were realistic alternatives.'[160]

When Marsh succeeded Barbara Castle as transport minister, he asked of his officials what the attitude towards the ringways should be, and in particular, had the GLC had properly thought the whole plan through? The answer from the DoT civil servants was 'a qualified Yes.' They continued; 'No informed opinion within the ministry believes that London can come to terms with the internal combustion engine without the Box or something very like it.' A top transport civil servant, John Garlick, said that London needed some sort of high capacity road system not far from inner London, complaining that 'people accept readily the need for investment in public transport, the total demand for which is falling, while objecting to investment in roads, the demand for which will increase for decades.'[161] Garlick had previously been principal private secretary to Ernest Marples, he was a passionate driver and rallyer and was so in love with the car, that even as a senior civil servant, he took a 1st class City and Guilds certificate in motor mechanics.[162]

The ministry had in fact been a consistent behind-the-scenes backer of the London ringways and worked closely with the LCC to plan them. Three years previously, when Jay took Wandsworth councillors to see Barbara Castle, the civil servants' briefed her that while they were not committed in detail to all the GLC's plans 'the ministry accepts in general the GLC's analysis,' and that 'a Motorway Box is at best an essential minimum provision.'[163]

In later years, environmentalists would complain bitterly about the grip the roads lobby had on the transport department.

In summer 1972, Garlick was promoted from under secretary at the DoE to deputy secretary. The road lobby obviously regarded him as one of its key supporters in Whitehall as the secret minutes of the BRF public affairs committee described his promotion as being 'in some ways regrettable from the Federation's point of view.'[164]

When Garlick retired, by this time as permanent secretary, he turned up on the public affairs committee of the RAC. Another top transport civil servant to go the same way was William Glanville of the Road Research Laboratory (the man who thought it a good idea to bring the M1 to Marble Arch). Both Garlick and Glanville sported knighthoods by this time.

Part of the problem is that once a particular culture takes root within a ministry it is very hard to change it – civil servants can spend decades in the same ministry – few transport ministers have a tenure of more than a few years, and even ones who are not particularly sympathetic to the roads lobby can find their initiatives blocked or slowed down while the civil servants wait patiently until he or she is moved around in the next reshuffle.

Jay was soon complaining that the assurances he received from Marsh were not being honoured. Protesters were being told, complained Jay in a letter to Marsh's successor as transport minister, Fred Mulley, 'that since certain stretches of motorway had already been built, the rest must be completed.'

Meanwhile, the ministry was resisting GLC attempts to limit the environmental damage from their motorways. As the transport ministry would be paying for most of them, the civil servants wanted them to be built as cheaply as possible.

At a meeting in July 1967 called to discuss the Eastern Avenue extension, G W Haslam of the MoT's London highways division told the GLC he was 'concerned' that the GLC preferred route, which ran close to Hackney Road, was £8 million dearer due to rehousing costs than a route using a drained Regent's Canal. This diversion, complained Haslam, 'appeared to have no traffic advantages.' A document from Haslam moaned that 'the line adopted by the council to safeguard is the most expensive of the lot, and the cheapest route through London Fields is not recommended by the consulting engineers.'[165]

The MHLG later approved the GLC's route because it wanted to keep options open for developing the canal as a public amenity.

This was the second time that GLC attempts to build in east London with some concern for local amenity and environment fell foul of the men from the ministry. The GLC's in-house engineers wanted to minimise the noise and pollution where the North Cross Route passed through the densely-populated eastern part of Hackney. So they proposed running the motorway in cutting and alongside the North London Line rather than building it on viaduct as originally intended.

But G E Rowland, head of the MoT's London highways division, complained that this route would add £3.6 million to the cost, arguing that as the route would in any case be alongside the railway viaduct there seemed no reason why it should be in cutting. Rowland demanded that any further cases like these should be referred first to the ministry before being considered further.[166]

In south London, the planned M23 to Crawley and Brighton was a route closely associated with the ringways. This was a government project and its London end would terminate, according to the 1964 outline plan, at Tooting Bec Road in Streatham.

However the exact location of the northern terminus was a headache. Everyone involved in the project (a list which did not, of course, include local residents), agreed that the original plan would throw far too much traffic onto local roads which would not be able to cope. Enter the GLC's decision to resurrect the C Ring, if only the M23 could be made to terminate at a C Ring built to motorway standards, then the traffic could be evenly distributed throughout south London.

Like the C Ring, the M23 would have been another devastating project for outer south London. It would have started at Hooley in Surrey and run to the west of the existing A23 through a mixture of Green Belt land, and public open space. The rising country on the edge of the North Downs demanded a 100 feet viaduct across the Chipstead Valley. The M23 would then continue north, eventually following the Victoria – Portsmouth railway to Tooting Bec Road, (See map page 64).

Even the GLC quailed at the environmental damage this route would cause – it would gobble up 36 acres of open space between Tooting and Beddington, while the character of Beddington Park and surrounding buildings would be 'seriously affected visually and by noise as the road will be on embankments 30 feet above ground.'[167]

A civil service ministerial brief, submitted by L E Dale in December 1964, indulged in a piece of self-reflection rare for the period. If actual doubt about motorway building never entered the bureaucratic mind, there was at least an occasional gulp at what it really meant – and the opposition it would surely generate. Dale warned that the M23 'can only be built by making demands on property and amenity.....cost and other factors drive us to impose certain effects which are bound to be unpopular.' He went on, 'Mitcham Common is not one of London's best by any means, but the fact that we have chosen a route through it instead of through property will not prevent an outcry from those who see London's open spaces as sacrosanct. We have, on the other hand, selected a route through houses in the Beddington – Wallington area instead of across the nearby vacant Croydon Airport. The airport is already planned for development and it seemed that it was better to avoid the new development and disturb the old.'[168]

Outline plans for the M23 were published in December 1966 and the viaduct at Chipstead Valley proved especially controversial as it would have passed directly above two schools. A protest meeting at Chipstead Valley School in early 1967 attracted over 500 people 'What safety precautions will be taken?' asked a protester at the meeting, but the local newspaper reported that 'any answer there may have been was lost in a barrage of cries of Aberfan.'[169]

The bandwagon rolled on regardless, a public inquiry at Wallington in October only recommended shifting the viaduct slightly to avoid the schools, and the M23 was approved by Marsh in May 1968.

But by March 1967, the MoT knew it had a major problem. The M23 depended partly on the C Ring, but the GLC made it clear that it would not be able to pay for this for a while, leaving the MoT with the awkward choice of either;
- Delaying completion of the M23 by three or more years, at a cost of £4 million a year, or
- The MoT building and paying for the C Ring between the A24 at Colliers Wood and the A23 at Norbury station, and then handing it over to the GLC. The M23 could then terminate on this link at Streatham Vale

The GLC also had a scheme – never formally approved, although included in the GLDP, to build a link road from the end of the M23 to Parkway E at Loughborough Junction. This dual two lane road would have affected 950 homes.[170]

The M23 terminus dependency on the C Ring was of course a flagrant breach of the assurances given to Jay and the LMAG. 'It seems,' said their objection, 'perfectly plain that these link roads are 'not viable in their own right' and have not been chosen on their merits without prejudice as to whether the C Ring is or is not to be constructed.' After all, if the C Ring were not built, then an eastward link to the M23 at Norbury would certainly not be 'justifiable on its own merits' – it would mean northbound traffic from the M23 turning east and then southeast for 1.5 miles before hitting the A23, and then turning north again.

It was the same story with the controversial southern section of the West Cross Route where the GLC wanted to go ahead without waiting for the GLDP inquiry. The GLC presented a motorway as a relief road to crowded north/south routes in Earl's Court and Fulham and insisted that it stood entirely on its own merits. Vigars also carefully insisted that the West Cross Route link to the Embankment was; 'justifiable in its own right independent of the primary network as a whole or of Ringway 1 of which it will form part'.[171]

This was bureaucratic subterfuge; LMAG had carefully checked and found that the GLC had no plans to protect the relief that would be initially enjoyed in Earl's Court Road, Warwick Road and neighbouring streets. The GLC could have scrapped the one-way system to slow traffic down, used traffic management measures to discourage through traffic, or even pedestrianised the shopping areas on Earl's Court Road. But of all that there was nothing.

The interchanges at Cromwell Road and Chelsea Basin had no validity if the West Cross was just to be a relief road, and the more of it was built, the greater would be the pressure for it to be extended over the river to Battersea. In that case, it should be considered at the GLDP hearing and not before.

In 1970, Peter Walker, the environment secretary, gave the ringways a boost and at the same time helpfully undermined the upcoming inquiry into the GLDP. He agreed with the GLC that the objections to the West Cross Route could be handled at a separate inquiry. The civil servants approved the GLC's request in just 10 days, prompting *The Guardian*'s planning correspondent to observe that 'the Whitehall machine has moved very briskly indeed.'[172] The local inquiry took place at Fulham Town Hall in spring 1972, in parallel with the GLDP hearing. The inspectors submitted their report in November 1972, but the government decided to sit on it for a while.

The ringway bandwagon was beginning to be watched in the treasury however, which would be picking up 75 per cent of a very large bill.

Roy Jenkins, a hugely-successful home secretary, had taken over as chancellor in 1967 after the sterling devaluation. He had no choice but to run a tight financial ship, with the 1968 budget upping taxes by a record £923 million.

Jenkins had heard of the GLC's schemes and on 20 January 1969 he asked his team for a summary of what was going on. The treasury civil servants were cautious. G S Downey provided a report advising that killing the project at this stage would 'be very difficult indeed. The opportunity to do so will arise in the context of discussion on the development plan when the full weight of objections can be assessed.' D McKean said that 'the plan as a whole is the GLC's and they cannot be stopped from putting it forward.'

Next month, Jenkins had a private discussion with Jay about the ringways, and replying to his civil servants, he stood firm. He noted that the GLC could not be stopped from putting the plan forward 'but assumes that they can be stopped from doing it.'

His stand was on political principle, not merely about the parsimony to be expected from a cash-strapped chancellor. A minute records that Jenkins thought it 'important that the government should range itself alongside those who are outraged by the GLC's proposals and that an early statement should be made committing the present administration to frustrating the present scheme to the maximum of their power.' Jenkins took the issue up with Richard Marsh who, despite his ambivalent public comments on the ringways, confirmed that he 'did not approve' of the scheme.[173]

The entire project now hung in the balance. Jenkins was fighting desperately to restore economic stability – his 1969 budget included another £340 million rise in taxes to further limit consumption. And the cost of the ringways was going to be unacceptable. If the treasury could have killed the scheme on cost grounds then that would have been the end of it.

Yet Jenkins' strong disapproval remained secret. The reason was that Harold Wilson, and the government's legal advisers, had gagged ministers from speaking out publicly.

In April that year, Number 10 warned that that ministers 'should adopt a neutral attitude in public towards the GLDP and the Motorway Box.' This gag was on the grounds that the GLDP would be handled at an inquiry or hearing and 'any ministerial comment may well prove embarrassing to the minister of housing who will have a statutory duty to determine the future of the GLDP.'[174]

In public the line held. Ministers kept quiet – and a golden chance to kill the motorways off once and for all was lost. In private there were mutterings of dissent – Reg Freeson, a junior housing minister – told his boss that the ruling meant 'we must abdicate political responsibility for about 18 months' on a central issue 'at the very time when the Tories are mounting a major assault on Labour government social policy.'

While the treasury was uneasy, but unwilling to actually do anything, the transport ministry officials were busy helping things along, despite their boss – Richard Marsh – telling Jenkins that he did not approve of the ringways. The apparent divergence sheds some light on who was really controlling transport policy in Britain.

In April 1968, John Garlick at the MoT had written to Peter Stott confirming that 'The ministry accepts the need for a system of primary roads designed in particular to improve the efficiency of orbital movement......we have come mutually to the conclusion that a network of orbital roads connected by radials will be required.'[175]

Meanwhile, at County Hall, the unexpected upsurge in protest had put the Tory leadership on the back foot. The leader's meeting minutes[176] for 28 November 1968 discussed a GLC publicity campaign for the Box designed specifically to counter LMAG. 'Visual aids should show how London might be jammed with traffic without it.' Another proposal was to reopen the stalled campaign for better compensation. The GLC reckoned that a fairer compensation scheme would add 10 per cent to construction costs – so delaying completion – unless Whitehall would cover this through grant.

It is hard to understand why they were so surprised at the growing protest. While few people opposed road building in the 1950s, nothing on the scale of the London ringways had ever been proposed with such seriousness and such commitment in a densely-populated area. There was one – Conservative – voice who had warned with great prescience what would happen if such plans were announced. He was Richard Nugent who had chaired the 1957 committee. He warned in 1959 that 'although many people welcome the idea of such a motorway, when they realise what is involved, they decide it is something which they would not be keen to have near their homes. There is no getting away from the fact that the cost, in terms of amenity and in sociological terms, of splitting up whole communities is very heavy.'[177] Nobody remembered his warnings.

The Conservative-supporting newspapers were notably lukewarm about the ringways, and the GLC was soon looking around for allies. Minutes survive of an extraordinary meeting between the council and the BRF in January 1969. The initiative seems to have come from the GLC press office which established contact with the BRF, eventually meeting with the BRF's chief lobbyist, Robert Phillipson.

At that meeting were present, among others Plummer, Vigars, the GLC's director of public information and the chief press officer. The minutes[178] record how Plummer 'welcomed the Federation's offer of cooperation and support.' In order to help, the BRF asked for huge amounts of detailed information which certainly would not have been given to objectors. In fact, objectors were routinely denied copies of detailed plans, being told instead to visit the display at County Hall, which, of course, was only open during working hours.

This meeting then discussed various publicity tricks which might also be used. They included
- Letters to the press supporting the ringways coming ostensibly from members of the public but which in fact would be inspired by the Federation
- An opinion poll whose wording would be designed to drum up further support
- The BRF putting itself forward as an objector on the grounds that the ringway plans were actually inadequate, 'thus demonstrating that the GLDP was not over-favourable to motorists'

Plummer said he would think about this last idea.

The meeting was clear about the implications of giving inside information to the BRF; 'this could mean the provision of information in advance of it becoming generally available' while it was still in the council's coordination and consultation machinery. The GLC's only qualm was the 'danger of repercussions if information on housing aspects were too localised.'

The BRF itself was becoming worried about the success of anti-motorway activism – in spring 1969 it set up a special London roads working party and the minutes of the first meeting noted that; 'unfortunately the action groups opposing the primary roads network had been most successful with their publicity.'[179]

In 1969, work went on at County Hall to finalise the draft GLDP, and it was announced that the Motorway Box and the C and D rings would be renamed Ringways 1, 2, and 3 respectively, terms which will be used from now on.

GLC leaders conducted a series of roadshows under the London's Future banner and Vigars in particular fought his corner bravely, being quite prepared to argue his case at what he knew full well would be stormy meetings with him in the firing line. At one in Battersea he insisted that motorways are NOT monsters ploughing willy-nilly through residential areas.' In Camden he promised – against all the evidence – that 'the GLC has no intention of arbitrarily bulldozing its way through established communities.'[180] In May 1969 he cheerfully spoke at a meeting organised by the Chiswick Motorway Liaison Committee.

On 13 March Vigars announced more enhancements to the West Cross Route and revealed what would happen – absent the new bridge over the Thames – to the southbound traffic. The plan was for the route to cross over Fulham and King's Roads before splitting near to Lots Road power station. One branch would

1969 – The first sceptical examination of road building

link onto Chelsea Embankment which would eventually funnel traffic onto Battersea Bridge, with the other would funnel traffic to Wandsworth Bridge. Some 800 families would have to move home as a result.[181]

The GLDP was launched on 20 March – with the objective, taken straight from the LTS – to double the amount of road miles by 1991. From the 23 million vehicle miles in 1962, there was expected to be 50-60 million vehicle miles by 1991. In August, the GLC delivered the final version of the GLDP to Whitehall.

Vigars was in an uncompromising mood when challenged about the ringways, saying; 'Of course there is a need for further improvement of our public transport but London's fundamental mistake has been to neglect the roads. The ringways are intended to deal with different problems – the need to provide for movement outside central London and the need to take heavy traffic out of the residential and shopping streets.' He claimed that Ringway 1 would take 20 per cent of the present traffic away from central London; 'life with the ringways will be safer, quieter, and healthier for the great majority of Londoners.'[182]

Vigars remained in this same uncompromising mood all that summer – speaking again in south London in July he said it was 'high time we stopped considering the need for a ring road system and got on with the job.' He insisted that he had been pressing Whitehall to pay for soundproofing of homes close to new roads and to buy up and demolish homes too old to protect in this way. But a GLC press release headed 'owners of blighted properties may get new deal'[183] was still very far from the truth. It turned out that environmental measures on the West Cross Route alone would cost £2.2 million; a six per cent budget increase which would not, as it stood, qualify for a government grant.

The GLDP did not quite ignore public transport. It suggested schemes dating back to Abercrombie and the BTC's 1948 proposals,. These included electrifying most main line suburban routes, as well as building the Fleet Line, which would take over the Stanmore branch of the Bakerloo, and then run via Bond Street and Charing Cross before following Fleet Street to the City.

But there was nothing as to how this would be paid for, or by whom, and when. The reality is that these ideas were sops to public transport – In 1967 the council had said clearly there were 'only a few areas where substantial increases in rail capacity are needed.'[184] The real, practical focus of the GLC's work remained on building motorways ready for a predicted explosion in orbital, cross-London traffic.

Indeed Vigars' proclaimed public commitment to improving public transport was undermined by how the GLC achieved control of London Transport. This was a good idea – and it meant that the GLC really could function as a strategic transport authority. The GLC took over London Transport from central government on 1 January 1970. But Plummer's condition had been that it must be in a financially viable state, defined as the ability for the new London Transport Executive to put £2 million into reserves in its first year of operation, and to be able to keep reserves at least this level.

So Whitehall wrote off 100 per cent of its capital debt, and commuters were hit with a huge fare increase designed to raise £8 million a year. The transfer meant that the GLC had financial responsibility for the level and pattern of services it wanted, but Plummer insisted that under no circumstances would ratepayers' money be used to subsidise London Transport, so the shift of control to County Hall meant that few benefits were delivered to the travelling public.

The housing issue was central to the campaign against the ringways. The GLC accepted that significant rehousing would be needed, but this awkward fact was made light of on the grounds that the properties affected were mainly 'obsolete' and would probably be demolished in any case under slum clearance schemes. The GLC said that because Ringway 1 would go through 'housing problem areas' the latter 'present a unique opportunity....for building the road and redeveloping the lateral lands in a way that will permit this major highway to be satisfactorily assimilated into a relatively densely developed area.'[185]

This sort of argument was recycled by the civil servants in the transport ministry and briefed out to ministers – when Jay met Richard Marsh in March 1968, Marsh told him that 'parts of the proposed line of the route of the box would pass through areas where amenities were not great.'[186]

Just how many houses actually would be lost to the motorways was a matter of great controversy. The GLC's final estimate was that 20,000 homes would be directly lost.[187] LMAG argued that this would represent a greater number of households, possibly as many as 60,000.

The GLC had retained Colin Buchanan to advise on the plan. They asked him to look at the north-east London area as a sample, and he reported back that in that area alone, building the primary roads could cost 5,007 homes directly and 7,245 indirectly.[188] If this ratio of direct to indirect was accurate, then the GLC's London-wide figure looked like a big understatement. LMAG thought that in reality, a minimum of 60,000 people would be displaced, with 100,000 a more realistic amount.

As as we have seen, in early 1970, there were 192,000 applicants on the housing waiting list. People in serious housing conditions already waited years to be rehoused, and demolishing the homes of another 100,000 people would dramatically worsen their position.

Where would they all go? To another expensive New Town with all the disruption and dislocation that implied? There just wasn't the land available to rehouse everyone displaced by the Motorway Box in inner London, after all, building the primary road network would demand an astonishing 6,200 acres, or 9.7 square miles of scarce land.

It is impossible to plan in detail for what you can't see, but we now know that this 'obsolete' Victorian housing which had been the target of intensive slum clearance programmes, could easily become desirable, once restored and repaired on such a scale as to change the look and feel of an entire community. A walk around Battersea, Islington or Hackney today illustrates the point.

Soon after the GLDP's launch, Plummer went on a seven day working visit to the US to study the effects of motorways on the environment. He returned full of enthusiasm, saying 'their roads convince me that our plans for ringways are absolutely essential if London is to remain a major world city.'[189]

However several local councils were becoming unhappy about how the GLC was planning the ringways. Essentially, County Hall devised them in conjunction with the ministry and the consulting engineers, and local councils were kept in the dark until core decisions had been made. Tory-controlled Bromley complained in 1969 that it was 'being kept in ignorance of the plans now under consideration and will have no opportunity of commenting on relative merits before a decision is reached by the GLC to select one as the preferred route.'[190]

Meanwhile, in the same year, the transport minister, Fred Mulley, set up an Urban Motorways Committee to report on the problems that urban roads were causing, and to come up with solutions. The solutions required were ones which would make such roads more acceptable to the citizens, the committee was not to question whether they needed to be built in the first place. Its members included familiar faces from road mania; Peter Stott from the GLC, John Garlick from the MoT, Hubert Bennett, the former GLC architect, and Alfred Goldstein, a partner at Travers Morgan.

Michael Thomson's report appeared in October 1969, simply tilted *Motorways in London*. Its 194 pages did not make easy reading. Thomson was a top transport economist and he built up his case slowly and methodically, going back to first principles to define the transport problem from an economist's point of view, before looking at the GLC's proposals and their history.

But the patient reader learned a lot, because here was a comprehensive and rigorous demolition of the transport case for the motorways.

Thomson took apart the flawed thinking which underlay the assumptions in the LTS and transferred to the GLDP, that cross-London traffic would be the future priority, rather than commuter traffic to the centre.

The LTS thought that the traffic in London could double between 1962 and 1981. But this forecast – the central case for building the ringways – contained all sorts of questionable assumptions – it could happen *if* the roads network were expanded by an equivalent amount to handle more traffic, *if* parking places were provided, *if* there were no traffic management such as bus lanes or parking meters, and *if* there were no improvements made to public transport. Ignoring these assumptions meant that 'the forecast had thus been held to provide the need to bring about the assumptions.' This, he went on, 'is an example of trend-planning of the worst kind – making a forecast and then planning to bring it about.'

Surprisingly, *The Economist* agreed. This was then a pro-road/anti-rail journal which once described the motorway box as being 'cheap at the price,'[191] a comment gratifyingly received at the transport ministry. But it saw through the LTS – 'beneath its complexity and all the usual brouhaha about it being done on computers, this is a simple exercise in extrapolating trends.'[192]

Motorways in London carefully explained the counter-intuitive fact, not understood at the time, that building more roads could never solve traffic congestion because they generated more traffic to use them. Thomson was not the first to observe this phenomenon – Bressey referred to it back in 1938 and several American studies observed it in the mid 1960s, when traffic jams in motorway-dominated Los Angeles became notorious, but Thomson explained to a UK audience just how this entirely counter-intuitive state of affairs came about, which was a big step forward.

This in turn meant that the Predict and Provide philosophies which 'predicted' the likely future demand for roads and then proceeded to 'provide' them, were not merely bound to fail, they would actually make the traffic situation worse. Although Predict and Provide had dominated road planning for decades, the motorways would be, quite irrespective of their effects on housing or on public transport, failures in their own terms.

Another transport consultant, Stephen Plowden, who worked with Thomson in preparing the LMAG evidence for the inquiry, pointed out that 'the amount of traffic is governed by what is regarded as a tolerable level of congestion.'[193] That is, build more roads, or widen old ones and traffic increases until its reaches the same level of congestion as before, at which point people take to public transport or walk or don't make the journey at all.

> **How building roads generates more traffic**
>
> In the short term…
> - New roads relieve those close to them – so on the opening day the traffic switches
> - Other drivers find that the new roads make alternative destinations available to them and they too will divert to the new road to take advantage
> - New fast roads allow drivers to make longer journeys, either through longer but quicker routes or changes of destination. Longer journeys inevitably mean more traffic for the same number of trips
> - Improved journey times start to affect public transport. Some rail passengers begin to drive instead and bus passengers also start to use a car.
>
> In the medium term
> - Drivers find that some destinations have become easier to reach, and that trips they never previously considered have now become possible. So they make them
> - The enhanced advantages of having a car encourage more people to buy one, so more journeys shift away from public transport
> - This increased car ownership itself stimulates more journeys on the old roads as well as the new
>
> By this point the new roads may be as congested as the old ones and congestion on the old ones is only marginally better than before.
>
> It is easy at this point to assume that 1) the rapid traffic growth is the result of greater affluence leading to greater car ownership, 2) that the new roads were built just in time to avoid total chaos, and that, by extension, 3) yet more roads are needed to meet future growth
>
> But in the longer term
> - Improved roads lead to greater dispersal of work, involving longer journeys and hence more traffic for the same amount of activity. Simply put, new roads encourage longer commutes
> - This dispersal tends to take jobs to outer areas less easily served by public transport, and it boosts the shift away from public transport towards car ownership
> - The erosion of demand for public transport leads to higher fares and worsened services in a vain attempt to balance the books. This causes more journeys to shift from public to private transport, adding to congestion and starting a vicious circle in public transport finance
> - Increasing road congestion and worse public transport traps people in locations they would not have chosen if they had foreseen what would happen. This leads to demands for yet more roads, as well as demands to restore the quality of public transport
>
> From J Michael Thomson – *Motorways in London*

Thomson also criticised the GLDP for its obsession with road transport to the exclusion of public transport, which carried 38 per cent of all journeys and 50 per cent in the peak.

Amazingly, the GLC never really addressed the issue of generated traffic. Yet the GLC had inherited from LCC days its own evidence that generated traffic was no myth. In July 1964 Peter Stott briefed councillors on the effect of the Dartford Tunnel – opened in November 1963 – on the Blackwall Tunnel. It turned out that, initially, traffic through the Blackwall Tunnel fell by 12 per cent. But afterwards, traffic increased again and by April 1964 it was only 4 per cent below the pre-opening level.' Stott argued that these patterns reflected traffic diverting as far west as Waterloo Bridge due to congestion at Blackwall.[194] But once again it seems that awkward evidence which conflicted with the official view was simply ignored.

As an economist, Thomson looked hardest at the economic case for the ringways. To understand this we need how to assess the financial benefit of road building.

In order to win financial approval, something better than the facile 'it reduces traffic congestion' is required. Evidently in a world where resources are limited, priority calls have to be made and to do this the supposed benefits have to be quantified so that comparisons can be made. The quantification has to be in the one currency everyone understands – money.

Consider a lorry driver who spends three hours (that is 180 minutes) taking a load of widgets from a Midlands factory to an East Coast port. If we suppose that he spends 30 minutes of this time in traffic jams, we can say that a road project to end this jam would make him 16 per cent more productive. (30 /180 x 100 = 16.666). Pre-road, 16 per cent of his wages are being wasted, as is 16 per cent of the petrol used to keep the engine running. And we can try to quantify too, any cost of delayed delivery of exports.

We can scale up this trivial example to devise some kind of figure for the total cost of road congestion, and, based on the cost of the roads needed to fix it, we can come to a view whether it is worth spending the money or not, or whether, for example, other projects would deliver a better return.

And this is indeed what happens. Attempts to put a monetary value on traffic congestion appear in Abercrombie's report, which quoted Frank Pick of London General Omnibus to the effect that it cost his company £1 million a year. Abercrombie quoted other research which put the cost of jams in New York at £70 million per year, adding that the figure for London could hardly be much different.

UK road building economics were justified by one-dimensional models such as this, with no accounting for environmental damage, and a set of questionable and hidden assumptions which made road building – in strict monetary terms – look a much better bet than it actually was even in its own terms. We shall see later (page 141) how this model – called COBA – finally unravelled.

For the ringways, the LTS calculated that the return on investment would be 8.8 per cent. This was based on building Ringways 1 and 2, (with Ringway 3 assumed to be already built by the ministry) plus the radial connections between them at a cost of between £800 million and £1,300 million, plus parking and interest costs of £150-200 million and improvements to secondary roads costing £200-300 million.

The government normally demanded a 10 per cent return on road projects, and Thomson argued that this figure should really have been higher in urban areas where the unquantifiable costs in noise, pollution and damage to amenity should be factored in too. So in strict economic terms, the motorway programme wasn't worth the money it would cost.

In fact, the situation was still worse because of the astonishing assumptions made to generate the 8.8 per cent return. How valid were they? Thomson looked at these assumptions and found seven different holes

- No allowance was made for the cost of improving secondary roads
- A substantial – but entirely uncosted – set of public transport improvements was assumed to have been put in place, with no fare rises, to ensure that total loading on public transport would be the same as in 1962
- No allowance was made for disruption cost during building, nor for interest on construction work in progress, estimated at £90-10 million.
- An astonishing one third of the benefits of building the ringways were to come in the form of 'tax benefits,' the notion that extra spending on cars, petrol, maintenance, labour etc would generate higher tax revenue than the spending from which it was diverted. Thomson thought any diversion to motoring-related taxes would actually come from luxury goods and services rather than other things, and in any case these were then taxed more heavily. The lack of evidence meant he refused to consider these supposed benefits.
- Another 15-20 per cent of benefits came in time savings, which, it was argued, should be 50 per cent higher in 1981 than in 1961. But how reasonable was this? in a wealthier and more productive society the value of a man's labour hour could well fall rather than rise.
- It assumed that existing roads would carry much larger volumes of traffic than in 1962 without any fall in traffic speeds.
- Predictions of growing traffic were based on a growing population along with increased car ownership and income. Yet London's population had been falling for years and did not start to rise again until 1983.

To test all this, Thomson devised a complicated model with nine variables to represent the traffic benefits of building the system. This yielded the following results:

Table four – The real costs and benefits of the ringways

Section	Miles	Plausible range of traffic benefits (£m pa)	Preferred estimate of traffic benefits (£m pa)	Estimated capital cost (£m)	Annual rate of return %
Ringway 1	30	12-40	23.7	450	5.3
Inner radials	44	9-35	18.1	350	5.2
Ringway 2	49	11-40	21.0	310	6.8
Outer radials	114	18-70	35.9	410	8.8
Ringway 3	100	15-60	29.8	200	14.9
TOTAL			128.5	1720	7.5

In line with his view on the implausibility of the supposed tax benefits, Thomson excluded them from his calculations.

But it was clear enough that although the outer ringways would attract less traffic, the return on capital was much better because they were much cheaper to built, whereas Ringway 1 and the inner radials (the roads bringing the motorways nearer the centre to join Ringway 1) showed a poor return. Thomson's calculation also showed that it wasn't necessary to view the network as an indivisible whole, different sections yielded different results.

Thomson delivered a massive shock to the road lobby, which had very successfully set a bandwagon rolling to the point where urban motorways had been accepted as an inevitability representing a progress which was irresistible. Until now, they had been the technical experts, and sources of expert opinion, on all matters connected with roads and were regarded as such by the transport ministry.

THE THREAT TO CAMDEN

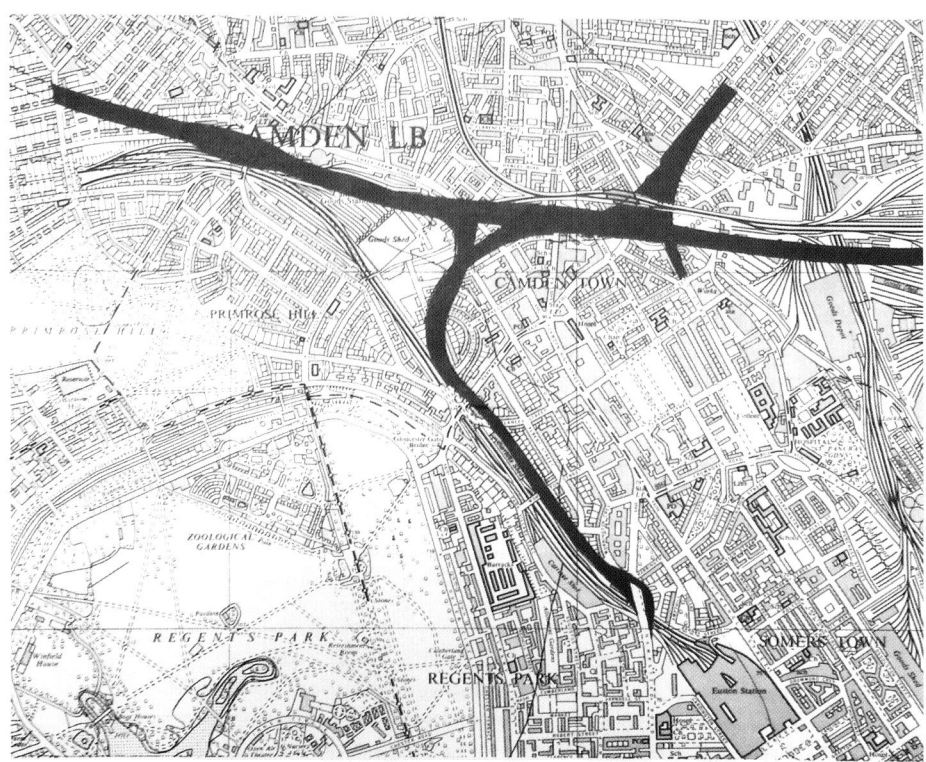

CAMDEN TOWN MOTORWAY ACTION GROUP

This map shows, better than any words, just what kind of a mess the proposed Ringway One and the Camden by-pass will make of the heart of Camden Town. It is to stop this threat that the Camden Town Motorway Action Group (as part of the London Motorway Action Group) appeals for your urgent support in fighting our case at the forthcoming Public Inquiry.

But here for the first time was a comprehensive demolition of their case and the ideas underlying it. Mary Jay recalls its impact; 'you could forget the effect of the environment, forget the housing, Thomson had demonstrated that even on its own terms the whole thing would not have worked.'[195]

The BRF replied quickly to Thomson, calling his work 'an appeal to the puritanism of Cromwell,' complaining that the ringways were 'subject to the most vigorous attacks by a small number of highly vocal objectors. These attacks are made in ignorance and in defiance of the wishes of the silent majority. The only alternative to the construction of the motorways is a greater restriction on personal movement than would otherwise be necessary.' [196]

The detailed arguments against Thomson, it turned out, were provided by the GLC itself following their meeting in 1969; Phillipson phoned John Fitzpatrick – assistant director in the GLC planning and transportation department – who helpfully provided 10 pages of critical – and confidential – comment. Fitzpatrick admitted, however, that where Thomson differed from previous anti-motorway material 'is in the quality of argument, its comprehensiveness and in its attempt to dispute the economic evaluation carried on in the LTS.'[197]

The *Architects' Journal* said Thomson's work was 'not desirable reading but essential reading.' The reviewer admitted that his review was more heated that Thomson's austere and ice-cool analysis; he said Thomson 'confirms one's worst fears of traffic engineers as 'trend planners' of the most superficial kind. It is surely obvious to everyone except them that the provision of more and more road capacity to meet the pressure of unrestricted demand and without regard to the true economic and social costs of such roads is not likely to do anything more than reproduce the same problem on a larger scale.'[198]

Motorways in London provided a great soundbite for the media; an easy-to-understand estimate of the costs of the ringways.

Thomson thought that when everything was taken into account, it would hit £2 billion (£28 billion in today's money). That would be more than London's third airport, Concorde and the UK's share of the Channel Tunnel put together. In fact, it would easily be the largest public works project in the UK since the war.

The GLC's own cost estimate was £680 million, but it turned out that this excluded
- Interest on work in progress
- Work already planned
- The cost of upgrading secondary roads which would feed traffic to the ringways

In December that year, LMAG filed its formal objection for the public inquiry, based on Thomson's work. Fighting at an inquiry of this kind was a daunting undertaking for a small group, even one with experienced political leaders. David Hunter, a barrister, and LMAG member, thought presenting a case would cost a minimum of £10,000 (£143,000 in today's money) but for maximum effect it really needed twice that. LMAG funds at the time were £4,000.

LMAG minutes record constant appeals for money, along with records of jumble sales and collections needed to keep the campaign going. Eventually, the money was raised and top City law firm Clifford Turner was appointed for the group. Viscount Colville, who had appeared for Oxford council at an inquiry into the city's Green Belt, was appointed to actually present the case. The LMAG minutes gratefully noted that Clifford Turner was 'sympathetically conscious of the group's lack of funds.'[199]

In January 1970 the GLC revealed that the total cost had increased to £1,695 million. Since Thomson's estimate had also included Ringway 3 where Whitehall picked up the bill, his estimate was clearly not far off. The GLC presumably realised that they would be under attack at the GLDP inquiry over costs and so it made good political sense to get the bad news out of the way now and let the hubbub quiet down a little.[200]

Table Five – 1970: costs going up....

	1967	1970
Primary network (ie the ringways)	625	850
Secondary network	210	240
Extra environmental improvements		40
TOTAL	835	1130
MoT costs for primary network	271	255

As the 1970 GLC elections approached, with both Labour and Conservatives united in support of the ringways, another protest group prepared to stand candidates on a Homes Before Roads platform. The coalition was the brainchild of Derrick Beecham of Chiswick, an old Etonian who was a scion of the Beecham's pharmaceutical family, and who had Sir Thomas Beecham as an uncle.

Its press officer was Terence Bendixson of Chelsea, a planning and environment writer who was then a journalist on *The Observer*. Bendixson, who stood against Vigars in Kensington, recalls; 'in the end we stood 92 candidates, and that meant we got TV time for a political broadcast. This was really important. It got us ahead and above the normal chatter and noise in politics.'[201] Stephen Plowden says it was important that for the first time, the actual name of the party was on the ballot form, previously, only the candidate's name appeared.

The candidates were a varied bunch – a surprising number were planners, lawyers and architects; Gerry Foley of the Chiswick Motorway Liaison Committee stood in Ealing and Stephen Plowden in Islington, but Fred Davis in Lewisham was a pub landlord, Heather Stubbs in Hammersmith a housewife. Bendixson again 'we found candidates by ringing someone up on the lines of 'do you know anyone who could.......that sort of thing. We said to them don't worry, you won't get elected, you just need to stand.'[202]

HBR operated separately from Jay's group. LMAG – ran by party political figures of some seniority and who obviously could not break party discipline – did not formally support HBR. Roland Moyle in particular thought standing candidates was dangerous, since the minority of voters who actually did vote would stand by established loyalties in a first-past-the-post system. The inevitable failure of HBR to win any seats might then be used by the motorway supporters at County Hall to undermine the entire campaign.[203]

HBR was a loosely run, very ad-hoc coalition; 'I had no idea what was happening in Camden or Hackney,' says Bendixson, 'we saw ourselves as guerrillas really, fighting the established powers. We did a few public meetings but nothing really big at Central Hall, nothing like that.'

London voted on 9 April. The Tories kept power on a low (35 per cent) turnout and they won a small majority (51 per cent) of all votes cast. Labour's improved

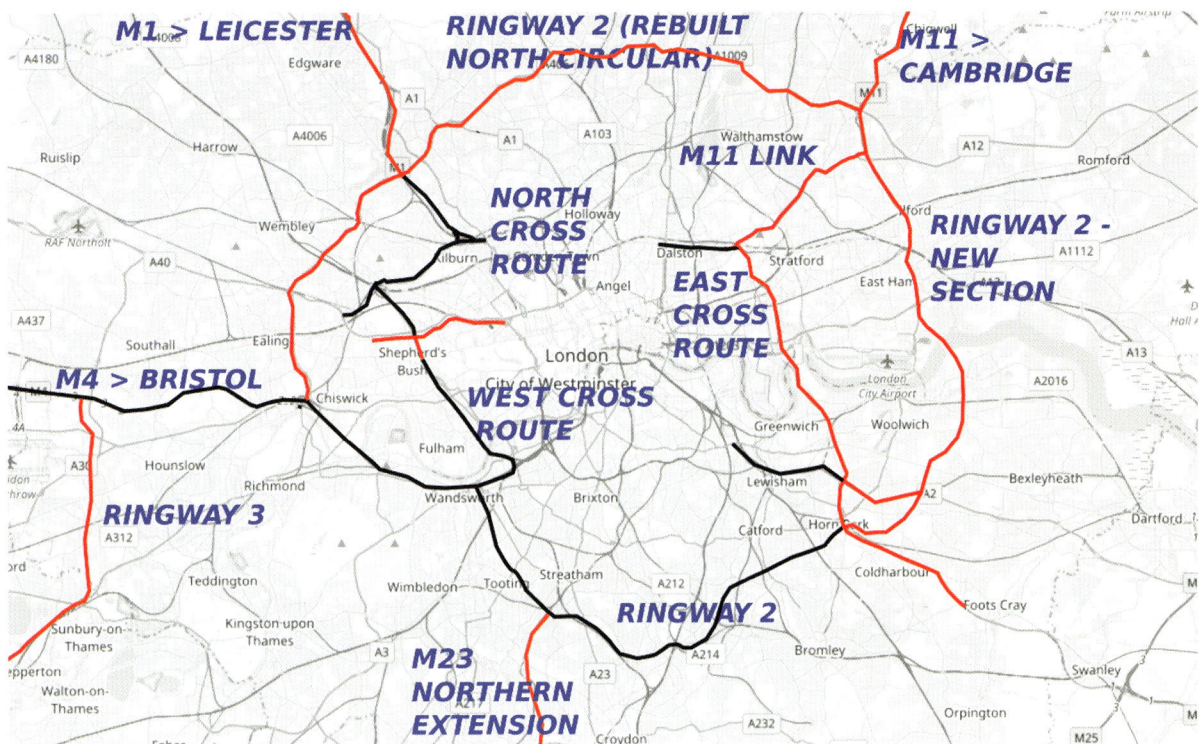

The ringways 1970 – phased construction plans. Phase one routes in red, phase two in black

vote was considered promising enough for Harold Wilson to call a general election two months later – which – against all expectations, he lost to Ted Heath.

HBR won 81,215 votes – and with each elector having multiple votes this meant that around 27,000 people voted for the coalition. All but four boroughs in outer east London were contested.

No one was elected, just as Moyle had feared. In fact, results were universally poor, hovering around the 1.5 – 2 per cent mark. There seemed to be no stand-out areas of local strength either; best result came in Newham (2.9 per cent), followed by Ealing (2.3 per cent) and Camden and Croydon (both 2.2 per cent).

Areas where there was large scale opposition to Ringway 2 in south London (Lambeth, Croydon, Lewisham) did not reflect this at the ballot box. As Roland Moyle had feared, party loyalty prevailed in a first-past-the-post system.

However Beecham called the result 'slightly better than expected...my campaign certainly had a far reaching effect on the Labour Party and helped them win the Inner London Education Authority. Our campaign was a massive public relations exercise yet the whole thing was achieved in three weeks and cost £900.'[204]

The exercise seems to have taken it out of Beecham, who had earlier promised to stand in the Brentford and Chiswick seat at the next general election. He described himself as 'physically exhausted' after getting fours hours of sleep a night for the previous three weeks.

In the summer of 1970, the GLC announced the phases in which it planned to build the network. It was becoming clear that the entire plan was all too much to digest at one sitting. Leaving aside the unpromising economic situation, and delays caused by the pending inquiry into the scheme, there remained a serious shortage of construction workers and project staff.[205]

So the GLC split the plan into three phases. Phase One (see map on page 87) was estimated to be complete by 1981. Phase Two, which included most of Ringway 2, would then be complete by 1991. That left almost all of the difficult sections of the North and South Cross Routes to be completed in a Phase Three. That meant 20 years or more of blight and uncertainty in the affected areas.

The Eastern Avenue extension between Hackney Wick and Islington was now not expected until at least 1985. It was now regarded as a secondary rather than a primary route and as such had been quietly deprioritised in favour of the North Cross Route.

Amid the controversy, palpable progress had been made with the Phase One schemes. Plummer had opened the second Blackwall Tunnel on 2 August 1967 and a plaque marking the event is still in place. The new cast-iron tunnel featured fluorescent strip lighting and emergency telephones and unlike the old tunnel, there were no sharp bends. It was designed by Mott, Hay & Anderson, and built by Balfour, Beatty. The tunnel needed special precautions to protect it from the contaminated subsoil near the East Greenwich gasworks, which was one of London's most poisoned and polluted sites. The older tunnel – now used for northbound traffic – was then closed for repairs and renewal, reopening in April 1969.

On 25 April 1969, the new Blackwall Tunnel southern approach – the first stretch of road built by GLC to motorway standards – was opened by Richard Marsh, who said 'the nation has paid a high price for its inadequate road system.' But he continued to hedge his bets on the ringways, saying; 'we shall have to decide whether the plans are likely to meet the claims made for them and whether the cost is commensurate with the resource they will require.'[206]

The building contractor was Fitzpatrick. The cost of the actual building work was £4.2 million, but taken together with the cost of buying land, and all the preliminary works, the total cost came in at £9.7 million.

But the warm glow of engineering achievement didn't last.

A year later, in July 1970, Westway finally opened. It had cost £36.5 million, including the cost of land acquisition. The actual building cost was £15.3 million. Laing was the sole contractor on the project. The chief engineer was John Baxter of G Maunsells, the engineering consultancy, Baxter's glittering career saw him become president of the Institution of Civil Engineers in 1977 as well as winning a CBE. But at his death in 2003, *The Guardian* called him 'the man who masterminded London's most hated road'.[207]

In fact, the Westway was similar to some other schemes – the 1965 Chiswick Roundabout to Langley section of the M4 for example with its long elevated section, or the Five Ways interchange on the M1 at Hendon, in terms of engineering and impact. It was the political and environmental climate which had changed.

The project also included the 1Km length of the West Cross Route, which joined Westway at an elevated roundabout. Spurs off the north side, built for the link to the North Cross Route, can still be seen today.

The engineers were naturally proud of their achievement. At its opening, the road was the largest continuous concrete structure in Britain and unlike the concrete, system-built tower blocks going up all over Britain, the Westway was built to last.

Westway was made mainly of pre-stressed and post-tensioned concrete construction, With this approach, the concrete sections are cast offsite and moved on heavy lorries to where they are needed. They are then assembled, heavy

Sheer, brutal, scale; the Westway at Paddington

cables are strung through all the sections and jacked tight; this produces a set of rigid spans capable of carrying heavy traffic.

It was built with a whole set of innovations; the number of expensive joins between the sections was kept down to provide a smoother journey; electrically operated metal mats were embedded in the tarmac to protect against winter ice.

The ¾ mile section from Acklam Road to near Torquay Street in Paddington features a continuous curve over the main line from Paddington. At the eastern end, the project needed a major realignment of Harrow Road into a dual carriageway complex.

Love it or loath it, the Westway remains an iconic structure which is a recognised part of London's cityscape. But the residents of Acklam Road whose homes faced directly onto an urban motorway didn't share the pride in the engineering achievement. At the opening, residents unfurled banners saying 'Get Us Out Of Hell' and barracked junior transport minister Michael Heseltine, who admitted, 'you cannot help but have sympathy for these people.' *The Guardian* suggested that Heseltine had rewritten his speech at the last minute, swapping praise for the engineers and planners in favour of a pledge to help those living in the Westway's shadow.[208]

At that time, North Kensington was just beginning to recover from the 1958 race riots and had become a key locus of London community activism and radical politics. Portobello market became the hangout-of-choice for top musicians; The alternative paper *Oz* was based here and in 1968 the Mangrove Café was opened on All Saints Road as a focus for the embattled black community – the police raided it no less than 12 times between January 1969 and July 1970.

A plethora of community groups fighting on housing issues had sprung up; lack of open space was another issue, GLC standards laid down that there should be at least 173 acres for North Kensington's population of 77,000. Instead there were less than 20. So most children had no play options but the street, and on average, one child was injured in a traffic accident every five days.

Into this high-stress environment an urban motorway was a disaster. George Clark, a local community worker and former CND Aldermaston marcher was chair of Golborne Social Rights Committee which fought for those whose lives were being devastated by Westway. He told *The Times,* whose report of the opening was headed 'sleepless night for Westway residents.' that 'it was like being in the middle of a factory. It is essential that people in this street should be moved as fast as possible.'[209]

Westway had been built very close to first floor windows of homes in Acklam Road, a fact the LCC architect had warned about in 1963; residents threatened to blockade the road unless the GLC took action. One man, 57 year old George Burton, who lived in a second floor flat, said he and his wife and daughter did not get to sleep until 2.30.

There was no duty, or even power, to compensate and the ministry refused financial help. The GLC hurriedly found legal grounds for action and took a declared one-off step to buy or soundproof the affected homes at the council's cost. Subsequently it decided that no future major improvements would be built until fairer compensation was available. Vigars wrote to the new Tory transport minister, warning of the risk of 'the council's ringway proposals falling into disrepute if parsimony outweighs humanity in this extreme situation.'[210] The Tory leader of Kensington council said that he had asked the GLC to delay opening until people had been rehoused.[211]

Below the Westway there was now a huge corridor of wasteland. Other areas near the road remained semi-derelict and became home to a mixture of hippie squatters, drug addicts and homeless people. By the side of the West Cross Route at Freston Road, over 100 squatters moved into empty houses after construction had been completed and declared their independence as the Free and Independent Republic of Frestonia.

Apart from an area designed as open space at the western end, the GLC had no plans for anything except a car park. The North Kensington Playspace Group had been founded in 1966 by Adam Ritchie, a photographer who had seen neighbourhood action at work in New York's Lower East Side. 'A more inappropriate and negative use for the space could not be imagined,' said Ritchie at the time. The Playspace Group then discovered the GLC had no legal authority to build a car park anyway – it had forgotten to put in a planning application to Kensington Council.

Agitation in the overcrowded and devastated area continued with the support of architect Sir Hugh Casson and Peggy Jay. The first gain was an adventure playground carved out of the motorway site at St Mark's Road by the contractors John Laing, who also footed the bill.

The Playspace Group became the Motorway Development Trust in 1968. It had a hard time to maintain its independence in the face of a local council which was the habitual target of community activists in North Kensington. It started with a £25,000 council grant and eventuality made the transition from being a protest group to a charity with an annual turnover above £6 million and assets of over £20 million.

Up and down the Westway

The Westway has become a cultural icon, easily the nearest thing Britain has to a Route 66.

It helped that it crossed the counter-cultural powerhouse of Notting Hill; the M1 or M6 were never going to feature in music lyrics. Yet there is something about the presence of the Westway that forced itself into song.

Punk band The Clash featured the Westway in their 1978 hit London's Burning, *'I'm up and down the Westway, in and out the lights. What a great traffic system, it's so bright. I can't think of a better way to spend the night, than speeding around underneath the yellow lights.'* A 2000 documentary film about the legendary band was even called *The Clash: Westway to the World*. When The Jam cut *This Is The Modern World* in 1977, the cover image was taken under the Westway.

In the Blur song *For Tomorrow*, a couple have lost their way – the full line is: 'London's so nice back in your seamless rhymes, But we're lost on the Westway'. The Westway is also mentioned in two other Blur songs *Fool's Day*, and *Under the Westway*. The Dirty Pretty Things refer to it in the song *Truth Begins* quoting 'The Westway walls so tall and bleak, Reflect the words we dare not speak.'

Driving the Westway is still a thrilling experience at night. You start at Holland Park roundabout, curve left onto the West Cross Route and drive past the vast bulk of Westfield's mall on your left. Pass other office blocks on your right, one looks like a multi storey car park by day but is bright yellow coloured at night. The whole carriageway is brilliantly lit from the centre. In no time you see the flyover carrying the Westway overhead and you're at the roundabout. Road signs are green not blue; this isn't a motorway any more. Right hand lane for City and West End, onto the roundabout and under the flyover. Keep turning right, the roundabout is bigger than it looks in the absence of the North Cross link road. At night you can't tell that it is elevated.

Then up onto the Westway, two tower blocks on your right and suddenly you need full headlights. The absence of lighting means it is strangely dark as you pass over North Kensington with treetops on both sides, The sky is navy blue not black, brake lights ahead reflect red off the wet surface. To your left you see the Trellick Tower block, its stairwells picked out in lines of brilliant white and individual flats lit in varying other colours. Once a dumping round for Kensington's homeless and drug addicts but now a desirable residence.

Keep curving gently to the right – five more tower blocks are now visible ahead – it's an illusion; you pass them to your left in a while as Westway continues to curve right. London's tower blocks look stunning at night after rain has washed the dust from the air. You can't see landmarks like the Shard or the BT tower from here – but the sense of excitement would tell a complete stranger he was approaching the centre of Europe's largest city.

Soon you thread the Harrow Road junction....make sure you're in the middle or right hand lane and follow the signs 'The City, King's Cross, Euston (Ring Road East),' Suddenly you face the vast, brightly-lit wall of the redeveloped Paddington Basin area. Over the Marylebone flyover, cut speed, and hope you'll be lucky with the phasing of the lights – if so you'll enjoy one of the sights of London – green all the way down the Marylebone Road. How stunning and luminous a set of successive green traffic lights really looks on a damp London night.....

Underneath the Westway junction with the West Cross Route. Scenes like this would have been repeated in many parts of inner and outer suburban London.

The view from back gardens

We now know that the Westway was built – like other urban roads at the time – on the cheap and with minimal attention to the environmental impact.

As the row over the Westway died down, the BRF released – in October 1970 – the results of its poll on the ringways. It was based on 1.900 people and showed, apparently, that 46 per cent were in favour to some extent or another with only nine per cent against. The rest said they did not have enough information to say. 80 per cent said that the ringways were essential if London was to maintain its position as a great city. [212]

The real point of the poll, according to internal BRF documents, was to convince election candidates that there was no advantage in taking an anti-motorway position. It noted, astutely, that most candidates, and indeed most voters, were in areas unaffected by the plans and might be presumed not to care too much. Westways would be the exception – not the rule.

But the fight against the ringways brought the activities of the road lobby into the daylight. Like all lobby groups it preferred to operate behind the scenes, influencing ministers and civil servants with the minimum of publicity. But now the concerned citizen had become aware that motorways in cities didn't just happen – public opinion had been expertly manipulated and the case for them, both intellectually and financially, was being pushed by a self-interested lobby group, which had its supporters entrenched deep within Whitehall.

The road lobby's Whitehall friends were quite happy to advise it on political tactics too; one BRF minute noted that ministry officials 'felt that if the Federation's aim was to secure the adoption of the basic network as a strategic target then it might be better to press for that as a single entity and have one enormous public row rather than get it in bits and have a cumulative series of only slightly less hostile rows which, in the medium term, might well weaken any politician's resolve to continue the decision pattern until the network was established.'[213]

And as Derrick Beecham had observed, the anti-motorways campaign had affected the Labour Party, and there were signs that the all-party consensus for motorway building was finally beginning to break down. Still, as late as February 1970, the BRF public affairs committee could note that the Labour GLC manifesto was 'not unfavourable.' With the Motorway Box essentially kicked into the long grass pending the GLDP inquiry, the BRF noted that 'this policy meant that there would not be a major clash between the Tories and Labour on the roads issue.'[214]

But a year later, things had changed and the BRF viewed the new climate with alarm. In the autumn of 1971, its public affairs committee heard a candid analysis of the political situation as a result of anti-motorway activism.[215] It noted that;

- Senior civil servants now had real concern about public opposition to urban motorways and the effect this could ultimately have on political decisions
- Political stances between the major parties had become more rigid with clear polarisation for and against from Conservative and Labour
- The weight of opposition to roads in London could affect political decisions in other cities simply because of the 'local' impact it was having on government ministers and MPs
- In London, fringe groups had encouraged very strong opposition, broadly from two standpoints; first from those adversely affected by loss of housing or amenity, and second from those more articulate groups who are opposed on a more general level of principle. This strand of opposition was marked by an increasing antagonism towards the motor car and towards the whole concept of economic growth.

It wasn't all bad news. The BRF noted that the government's plans for national trunk roads were 'remarkably close' to the target urged by the BRF, while in most provincial cities there had been 'no strong local reaction' against road schemes, with citizens accepting 'planners' explanations about the need for primary networks without marked enthusiasm but equally without noticeable antipathy.' Urban roads too, it turned out, generated much more opposition than inter-city motorways built through open country.

5 – Defeat into victory

In March 1970, local government minister Crosland announced that the public inquiry into the GLDP would be handled by Frank Layfield QC. He had only taken silk in 1967, but was already regarded as one of Britain's top planning law experts. After the war he had been at the ministry of town and country planning – where he was worked on the setting up of new towns – and then with a firm of planning consultants, before qualifying as a barrister in 1954. Supporting Layfield were four inspectors and five assessors.

Layfield himself went on to run the the 340 day inquiry into the planned nuclear power station at Sizewell in Suffolk.

The inquiry would be in three parts; Stage One for objections to the actual strategy of the plan, Stage Two for the local implications, and Stage Three as a final wash-up session, including objections to new evidence presented by GLC as well as providing a chance for the panel to raise further questions. Some hearings would be in the evening to suit objectors working during the day, and they would take place in different areas too.

The ministry planned to handle 10,000 objections – in fact they got 28,000. The vast majority concerned the ringways and a list of the residents' associations objecting reads like a gazetteer of London.

The GLC's written statement[216] – the legal core of the GLDP – argued that without the ringways there would be 'a continuation of the present conflict between roads and environment but over a wider area and of a more intense character.' To avoid this, huge new capacity was required to provide for the anticipated increase in orbital journeys, Traffic restraint was, it claimed, not an option outside the central area – it would be technically unfeasible and socially undesirable.

Layfield carefully ducked the question of whether individual inquiries such as that on the West Cross Route were in fact prejudicial to his report. He said that this decision rested with Peter Walker, the trade and industry secretary. Jay had written – unsuccessfully – to Walker asking him to postpone this inquiry.

LMAG and LATA issued a comprehensive rebuttal of the ringways; a sequel to *Motorways in London*. A huge amount of extra documentation had become available, and LMAG had done more work too. The result was a much more hostile, 300 page document, written by Thomson with help from Stephen Plowden. It featured an introduction by Jay as well as (literally), appendices labelled A to Z.[217]

In Hampstead, Professor Morris wrote a detailed document for the inquiry which looked at the levels of respiratory and stress-related illness which came from living near urban motorways; no minor issue given that it was claimed that one million people would live with 200 yards of one of the ringways.[218]

As suggested at its private meeting with the GLC leadership, the BRF decided to object, which meant it would only be cross-examined by the panel itself, not by objectors. The BRF fought hard for Ringway 1, insisting that it should be the first to be built, not the last as the GLC now planned, and the Federation's counsel – Anthony Cripps QC – said that a motorway network without Ringway 1 would leave London with only a rump of a network.

The BRF's chief lobbyist, Robert Phillipson, told the panel that of all the freight moved in 1969, 88 per cent went by road. He said that construction costs should be financed from new borrowing, not from current revenue, as this would be 'unreasonable' on local councils who would not be able to pay their share.

The BRF had a bright idea when it came to reducing the building costs of the North Cross Route. They looked enviously at British Rail's North London Line, which then ran a passenger service from Richmond to a City terminus at Broad Street, and had a freight-only section from Dalston, via Hackney to Stratford.[219]

If only this awkward railway could be wished away, the motorway could occupy its trackbed. At the enquiry, a BRF witness, Professor Alan Day of the LSE, said 'what apparently has not been done is a costing of using the actual rail bed as the route for the motorway. The social cost would be the loss of the rail facilities. As far as the passenger transport is concerned they appear to be very lightly used. As far as freight is concerned it appears that parallel routes are available across north London and it may be that the decline of the upriver docks will in any case reduce the freight demand.'[220]

The North London Line had been marked down for closure under the Beeching plan, but had been saved after a vigorous local campaign. But even had the passenger service been axed, BR would still have needed the line as this was one of London's strategic freight routes, taking traffic from the docks to the north and midlands. The Layfield panel asked BR how they felt about Day's proposal. BR replied firmly that the line's 'strategic importance cannot be overstated.' It was, they explained, impossible to surrender the line for Ringway 1 without an alternative cross-London rail route being built. This would cost some £65-100 million, while the cost of additional land could easily add a further £35-45 million.[221]

This proposal exposed some surprisingly sloppy thinking from the roads lobby. Roads actually need more space than railways and the cutting carrying the four tracks of the North London Line through Islington could only have carried two lanes of road traffic – not four, a fact that road engineers ought to have appreciated. The rail into roads conversion cult[222] was dealt a death blow in 1984 when BR chairman Sir Peter Parker called its bluff. BR commissioned consultants from Coopers and Lybrand to investigate the feasibility of converting some routes to road. The consultants identified exactly this objection, just as, it seems, Parker realised they would.[223]

The BRF's other key witness was Tom Williams, professor of engineering at Southampton University. He claimed that if the North Cross Route were not built 'it would be necessary to double the capacity of six ordinary four lane general purpose streets with all the destruction of frontage development, severance of activities and damage to local amenities that this would entail.'[224]

There was substantial opposition to the ringways from the Victorian Society and poet laureate John Betjeman, as concern for the built heritage rose steadily in the late 1960s. Betjeman, the saviour of St Pancras station, had called the GLC's route 'a line of death,'[225] and he was an important voice against more motorways. Ironically, the group around Michael Thomson had slightly mixed feelings; Tim Pharoah recalls 'they rather got in the way – it wasn't a question of being sentimental about old buildings – we needed to win a clear argument on the transport case that these motorways would not work.'[226]

The inquiry heard some interesting evidence from Camden Council which had looked at the impact of the interchanges proposed. These interchanges would have been one of the worst effects of the ringways as they would have demanded huge amounts of land, and sterilised the immediate neighbourhood making it

The junction between the Westway and the West Cross Route, taken just before opening. The links to the planned extension to the North Cross Route are clear to the right of the roundabout

harsh and unforgiving for both pedestrians and cyclists. Even the GLC admitted that they would 'probably be fairly large and have a considerable effect on the environment in which they are built.'[227]

Ivor Walker, of Camden's planning committee, told the inquiry that 12 acres of Camden Town would be covered with motorways – the borough would lose one tenth of its built-up area if the ringways were built to the latest recommended standards.[228] It would also, he said, be difficult to rehouse those displaced within the borough.

The effect of these vast spaghetti junctions had actually been mentioned in *Traffic in Towns*, which said that they were 'particularly voracious consumers of space, needing up to 40 acres or even more.' By comparison, the land between Piccadilly, Lower Regent Street, St James Street and Pall Mall, only occupies 35 acres.

The problem of the interchanges dovetailed neatly with the fact if the ringways were built, traffic would then increase massively on the secondary roads (which included most A roads), because most journeys in the capital naturally began and ended there.

It turns out that an ordinary two lane road can handle 20,000 movements a day, a four lane road 40,000. But Thomson thought that there could be 1 million trips per day on Ringway 1, which meant 2 million entries and exits, either to other motorways or to the A roads. He warned that if more than a small proportion used the A roads, these roads would rapidly clog up, and 'traffic delays on the feeder roads could rapidly whittle away time savings achieved on the motorways themselves.'[229]

Solving those issues would mean knock-on upgrading works on these roads to handle more traffic. This wouldn't be cheap – the GLC engineers thought this upgrading would cost 50 per cent of the entire price of the ringways. The GLC never revealed which A roads would need the Finchley Road treatment however.

Conditions, as a result of widening and more traffic, would worsen rapidly on these roads, They would indeed, thought LMAG, probably be worse than on the ringways themselves, with the noise, dirt stress and ugliness making some areas really unfit for human habitation. The GLC's secondary roads policy said specifically that only in rare cases would special provision for pedestrians be provided.[230]

A confidential report from Colin Buchanan agreed; it warned the GLC that its planning needed a 'considerable switch of priorities from the primary to the secondary network.' Buchanan thought that the environmental battle would probably be joined there and added that the GLDP was 'in danger of misleading the public on the state of affairs that will develop on the secondary network.'[231]

In June 1972 the dam broke – and Labour finally switched sides. A decade after its leadership first started working to build motorways, the party announced that it would kill the ringways if it regained control at County Hall. Sir Reg Goodwin, a traditional moderate, said that 'Labour pledges itself to abandon the disastrous plans to build two motorways which threaten the environment of central London.' He called on the GLC not to sign any contracts which would allow works to be started before the next GLC elections 'so that London's choices would not be pre-empted.'[232]

London Labour in fact had rethought its views on transport, and a pre-election discussion paper considered a whole number of revolutionary ideas, including scrapping fares altogether, or at least introducing zonal ticket pricing.[233] Goodwin was to tell Douglas Jay that he had 'chanced his arm' over the motorways, but felt sure that the party would support him – which it did.

This was the most important victory imaginable for the anti-motorway campaign, and lobbying from Jay was central in the U-turn – it meant that there was now a Plan B in place. Even if the Layfield panel supported the ringways, they could still be stopped because a future Labour GLC would refuse to build them. Mary Jay again; 'You could ask; 'why did we even need a campaign if all we needed to do was win the GLC?' But you needed a campaigning group who could get the facts and arguments in front of their people and get them to change their mind in order to do that. It was sometimes a difficult coalition to keep together because we all knew that we needed a Labour victory at the GLC to stop this. We had an advantage at first because the GLC was Conservative but the ministry was Labour.'

The GLC, meanwhile, desperately decided to try and buy off the pressure in Blackheath. It appointed Colin Buchanan to report on its options, and he came back with a proposal to take Ringway 1 under Blackheath village in a deep bore tunnel at a cost of £15 million. This proposal had been suggested by motorway protesters in Blackheath back in 1962 and rejected then on cost grounds.

But the proposal, gratefully accepted at County Hall, was a double edged sword for the GLC. It would relive the pressure in one of the key epicentres of protest – but if a tunnel was OK for Blackheath, why not for Hampstead or Chiswick? And too much tunnelling would make the current cost estimates look small beer. The planners also considered moving the route south of Blackheath together, presumably on the grounds that the artisans in the terraces of Hither Green would be less articulate than the architects and lawyers of Blackheath.[234]

The treasury watched the Layfield hearings with continuing caution. More than any other government department, it had an acute insight into the panel's thoughts. On 1 August 1972, a treasury civil servant, C J Carey, minuted about a chance meeting with Alistair Sutherland, a Cambridge academic who had done economic consultancy for the treasury and who was an assessor to the Layfield panel.

He gave Carey 'a depressing preview' of the Layfield report which, he warned, would back the ringways. But Sutherland told Carey that the reasons are 'not remotely argued and indeed have not really been explored by the committee. They appear to have gone along with some rather flimsy evidence produced by the GLC which purported to show a three per cent rate of return for urban motorways on certain dubious and optimistic assumptions.' Sutherland said that he hoped treasury economists would have the chance to expose the 'superficial nature of the arguments' in the final report. Sutherland had, said Carey, considered resigning.[235]

Sutherland's own papers show him insisting to the other panel members that 'the GLC prediction for numbers of cars and hence trips is far too high...it would follows that the quantitative output of the transport model cannot be taken seriously as an informer of policy.'[236]

In September 1972, with the hearings essentially over, the GLC attempted another tactical retreat. Richard Brew, who chaired the environmental planning committee, and was now the main spokesman for GLC road building, said that the GLC would shelve the North Cross Route and the southern part of Ringway 2. That meant nothing would happen on these stretches for 20 years. The controversial Ringway 1 stretch under Blackheath would be built in tunnel as Buchanan had suggested.

The following month, Mulley's urban motorways committee reported. Its report – *New Roads in Towns* – admitted that 'major new urban roads may have substantial adverse effects on people living close to them.' It came up with a host of mitigation strategies, centring on planning new roads as an integral part of urban planning as a whole. The report also proposed that indirect costs and benefits should be looked at with as much care as direct cost and movement benefits and the cost of remedial environmental measures should be included as part of the cost of the road itself.'[237] Taken together, it was a condemnation of how roads had been built in the recent past. It threatened a huge increase in the cost of road building in cities.

A November GLC report still thought it feasible to build all the ringways within 15 years at a cost of £1.5 billion. The preferred option now would be to build:
- The complete West Cross Route, with four lanes in each direction
- The South Cross Route. This was held to be 'more acceptable' than Ringway 2 as it would follow a railway line for much of its length
- The North Cross Route from Willesden to Finchley Road, plus the M1 link
- A fully improved Ringway 2 between the M1 and M11

The North Cross Route and the southern section of Ringway 2 would be deprioritised and built later.

The GLC insisted that 'London needs a ring road suitable for lorries in the shortest possible time and changing the priorities of these stretches of Ringway will achieve this.'[238] In fact, this was a blatantly political move. Shelving the

North Cross Route and the southern part of Ringway 2 was aimed squarely at voters in constituencies the Conservatives hoped to retain in the 1973 GLC elections, while they had no chance of winning the inner-city constituencies traversed by the South Cross Route.

In Blackheath, Roland Moyle said the shelving of Ringway 2 in south London was a victory, but told supporters that they must campaign immediately to stop the GLC safeguarding the route, otherwise there would be guaranteed blight for years to come. Putney's Motorway Action Group warned that Ringway 2 had 'only been shelved – not abandoned. Putney has been temporarily reprieved, but large parts of London are still immediately threatened.' At LMAG, solidarity held; a meeting heard that 'representatives present from areas which appeared to benefit from postponement nevertheless agreed that this group must maintain its vigorous opposition to Ringway 1 and Ringway 2 regardless of alterations in timing which could easily be reversed next year.'[239]

Layfield finally reported to the government in December 1972. The five volume report, totalled 1,400 pages and followed 237 days of deliberations. It cost £1 million – £12.3 million in today's money.

The report was critical of much that was in the GLDP. It thought that the GLC had overestimated the growth in traffic, for example; It thought that the estimates of population (a key driver for car buying and hence road use) were 'out of date, based on a dubious methodology, and assumed that the plan would be successful in stemming the decline in population.'

Layfield said the GLC had not paid enough attention to the need to avoid building elevated roads such as Westway, arguing that the extra benefit of building the ringways in cutting, or even in a cut-and-cover tunnel was 'often so substantial as to justify the extra cost.' If a road was built by cut-and-cover, then the disruption and unpleasantness was mostly confined to the actual building period – after construction was ended, the traffic was then channelled underground. It accepted that the GLC had not ignored the environment but added that since the work had been done 'ideas on what are acceptable standards have advanced and we do not think some of the earlier ideas are now generally acceptable' – a clear reference to the *New Roads in Towns* report.

The Layfield report also thought that the GLC could do more to manage traffic demand with more severe restraint than it had proposed. There was too, a need for greater improvements in public transport than the plan included.

Yet the panel still supported the plan on the key issue – the ringways – despite the huge weight of objections.

It thought that growing congestion was an unacceptable situation which would eventually become so bad 'that it would deter many people from using their cars.'[240] Essential service and goods movements would become very slow and expensive and bus services would worsen. Rat-running through residential streets would worsen and the environment would deteriorate further.

All this could not be avoided just by restraining traffic and in any case the degree of restraint needed would be 'draconian.' as well as being unacceptable to the people and damaging the economic life of the capital. 'Clearly,' it concluded, 'some new roads must be built.'[241]

Layfield thought the need was for two rings, one inner and one outer, rather than the three in the GLDP. With much of Ringway 3 – which would become the M25 north of the river – already planned or committed, (see chapter 6) it made sense for that to become the outer ring-road.

That just left the choice between Ringway 2 and the Motorway Box. Layfield came down for the Box, on the basis that it would have 'a high potential' to attract traffic which would otherwise go into central London, and only this would allow environmental improvements in the centre to go ahead.'[242] But the panel did propose to solve the Blackheath issue by building a road from the East Cross Route through the Isle of Dogs and the depressed area of Deptford, whose residents were presumably thought less likely to make such a noise.

Together with a recommendation that roads should be limited to three lanes in each direction, Layfield thought that the proposals would provide 75 per cent of the capacity of the GLC's plans but at only a third of the cost.

Ted Heath's Conservative government anxiously pondered what to do. The Layfield report constituted a ticking timebomb for the Tories; GLC elections were due in April that year, the government was hugely unpopular nationally, anti-motorway feeling in London was high, and a loss of control at County Hall seemed likely.

Generally, such a report would be kept secret for a year or two while the civil servants conducted a detailed analysis and came up with recommendations for ministers. But the scale of opposition to roads put the government in a fix. Delaying publication until after an election meant running the risk of rumours and leaks 'whose effect might be partial or misleading and which would not be effectively countered.' Publishing, on the other hand, 'must be expected to impair the electoral prospects of the government's supporters on the GLC.'

While they pondered, in January 1972, the Commons expenditure committee's report on urban planning weighed into the row, saying that there should be a temporary ceasefire on all urban road schemes not actually at contract stage.

Late in January 1972, Ted Heath bit the bullet and decided to publish the Layfield report as soon as possible.

On 2 February 1973, the cabinet's regional and environmental committee considered whether to back Layfield on the roads or not. The minister in the driving seat was 48 year old Geoffrey Rippon, the environment secretary who represented a constituency (Hexham in Northumberland) hundred of miles away from all the fuss. He told the committee that 'in order to bring more certainly into the protracted debate,' he would back Layfield on Ringway 1. The southern part of Ringway 2 would be abandoned as this was 'politically among the least attractive elements in the road proposals.' (That is, it passed through a swathe of Conservative-held constituencies in outer south London).[243]

This committee could normally take decisions on the part of the cabinet, but in view of the cost of the Motorway Box, it was decided to refer Layfield to the full cabinet.

The decision was leaked to the *Sunday Times*, then its pre-Murdoch heyday as Britain's leading investigative newspaper. The paper called it 'the motor car's greatest victory' and reported that the scheme's main backer was trade and industry secretary Peter Walker 'on the predictable grounds' that new roads were essential to keep transport costs down for business.

The chief opponent was Robert Carr, the home secretary, 'for an intriguing reason.' Carr's number two, as minister of state was Viscount Colville, the man who had been counsel for LMAG at the GLDP inquiry. Before the inquiry he had spent 10 days working from 7.30 to 22.00 in a super tutorial under Michael Thomson in order to master his brief. So paradoxically, said the *Sunday Times*, the home office had the only minister with any ability to dissect the Layfield report.'[244] Carr also represented Carshalton and Wallington – areas where protest against the M23 northern extension was strong.

Rippon's proposal was circulated for comment within other ministries – the treasury, surprisingly, was reasonably content, on the cynical grounds that 'nothing in the statement commits the government to any specific level of expenditure over any specific period of time.'

The *Sunday Times* report launched a leak enquiry, but of course no culprit was ever found. The full cabinet went on to endorse the plan on 18 February.

Campaigners could barely believe the result after all the patient and rigorous effort they had put in at the inquiry. There had been no mass demonstrations or attempts to disrupt the proceedings – instead LMAG had played by the book and submitted huge amounts of detailed evidence from serious and respected experts such as Thomson, Plowden and Pharoah, on the assumption that logic and reason would triumph.

And all to no avail. Layfield had recommended the route which cost the most to build, delivered the worst economic return and had the worst environmental impact.

Tim Pharaoh recalls 'I was gobsmacked – I could only conclude that Layfield had just not understood the issues at all.'[245] Jay (in his autobiography) was similarly baffled: 'I never knew why they had reached such a conclusion. One rumour was that its members got short of time and entrusted the whole transport section to the road engineer on the panel.'[246]

LATA replied quickly,[247] arguing that

- The whole idea of inter-suburban travel demand was 'largely a myth' as the road networks in the GLC's studies were of a form that encouraged inter-suburban journeys to be made
- The panel had totally ignored traffic generation; the way that roads generated their own – new – traffic
- It had based its views on what the demand would be on 30-40 year old plans, when techniques for surveying, forecasting, and assessing travel did not exist

The BRF produced a short document called *A Future for London*. It quoted approvingly from Layfield with no additional commentary from itself, presumably on the basis that it would be superfluous.

At the treasury, the civil servants remained guarded and tentative in their approach. Its internal analysis of Rippon's proposed statement said that in principle they should approve it. Although the cost of Ringway 1 was 'very substantial indeed' and the expenditure committee had wanted a moratorium on all urban motorway spending, J F Slater only went as far as to recommend ministers 'might wish to argue for a less specific commitment about this route, perhaps to the effect that '…the government will need further time to consider the most suitable route for an inner London motorway to relieve congestion in central London.'[248]

An intriguing note in treasury files at the National Archives at Kew is unclear as to its significance. Dated 21 February 1972, it read 'The inner Motorway Box will never be implemented. We are no longer living in an environment when any Government can displace thousands of people from their homes. I am sorry that RE and cabinet should have endorsed another project which is socially and financially out of the question. I understand the chief secretary disagrees.' This would therefore have been the personal view of a more junior minister at the treasury

– possibly Patrick Jenkin. (The chancellor at the time was Anthony Barber with Maurice Macmillan as chief secretary).

Over 30 residents' groups met after the government go-ahead and Jay announced the formation of a 'Save London Campaign' to fight Ringway 1. Its director was Helene Middleweek, who had worked for Shelter and then for the social services department at Camden council. She ran what Douglas Jay called 'a short, sharp, sloganised campaign' from her flat in Chalk Farm, helped by Mark Bass of the Hampstead Motorway Action Group.' (As Helene Hayman she became a Labour MP in 1974 and was the first speaker of the House of Lords in 2006).

Campaign sponsors included the actress Peggy Ashcroft, John Betjeman, the film director Jill Craigie, who was married to Michael Foot, the journalist Simon Jenkin, Des Wilson of Shelter, and Lady Gaitskill.

At the April 1973 GLC elections, Jay had been successful in persuading anti-motorway activists not to stand as independents and risk siphoning off anti-Tory votes. Labour swept back to power, winning 58 seats as against 32 for the Tories. The turnout remained low at 36 per cent, and Labour's victory was, as it had been for the Tories in 1967, partly a reflection of national political feeling.

However these elections were fought for the first time on parliamentary constituency boundaries, and Labour made big gains in areas where the motorway threat was a burning issue. Labour won three out of the four constituencies in Croydon, plus Carshalton, Brentford & Isleworth, Woolwich West,[249] Hampstead, and Norwood, where the victorious Labour candidate was one Ken Livingstone, previously a local councillor in Lambeth and now making his first appearance on the London-wide political stage.

Labour was only 40 votes short of victory in Chislehurst and only 653 votes from unseating Robert Vigars in Kensington – a constituency now merged to include the wealthy south and the Westway blighted north.

At the first meeting after the elections, Goodwin delivered on his pledge and announced that the ringways would be removed from the GLDP, which would then go back to ministers. Most of the planning blight was lifted immediately – although it remained for a little longer between King's Cross and Hackney Wick, in Eltham, Greenwich and the southern part of the West Cross Route. This last safeguarding was finally lifted between 1974 and 1976 and Goodwin said; 'people can rest assured that their dwellings will not be flattened in a crazy quest to feed the voracious appetite of the private car.'

In May came the final *denouement* – the long-awaited inspectors' report into the southern part of the West Cross Route to Chelsea Basin, which ministers had been carefully sitting on.

The two inspectors (K C Jeremiah and R J Soper) roundly condemned it, and Rippon supported them. Although he insisted that he still supported Ringway

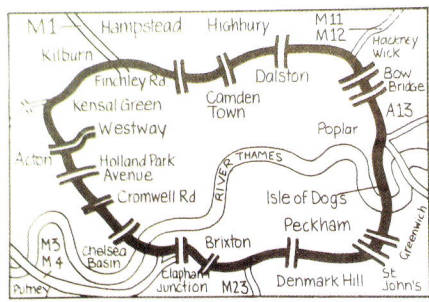

LMAG protest leaflet

1, he said, inexplicably, he would not approve the West Cross Route extension even if the new GLC wanted to proceed. He agreed with his inspectors that the motorway, presented as an interim relief road 'would not be apt for that purpose.' Jeremiah and Soper had said that while the motorway would initially improve conditions, within a comparatively short time traffic on the adjoining secondary roads would return to its present levels.' Just as LMAG had warned in fact.

The inspectors added that their conclusions about traffic build-up 'was largely conceded by the GLC'. Although the GLC had claimed that widening Wandsworth Bridge and the Townmead Road link could be justified on their own merits, the inspectors said that approving them separately ''might seem to anticipate the eventual decision on the other part of the complex.....in the view of the uncertainties about some aspects and the very strong relationship with the West Cross proposals in general we do not recommend approval of these schemes.'[250]

Goodwin asked if the money the government was going to be spending on the ringways could instead be diverted to the Fleet Line tube.[251] The comment was cheeky – but deadly serious at the same time. Vast fortunes had been spent already planning the ringways – the amount of money they would have cost to actually build would have paid for the Fleet Line – and new tube projects – many times over.

One campaigner seems to have been rewarded for his efforts in an unusual way. Jim Clark, chair of the Norbury and District Society, was awarded a papal medal for fighting the ringways. The likely explanation seems to have lay with his parish priest whose church lay right in the path of Ringway 2! [252]

The Labour government backed its friends in County Hall; the inner ringways were not to be revived. Ministers approved the final version of the GLDP in 1976, although Tony Crosland, still the environment secretary, warned that a solution was still needed for the problem of orbital, cross-London, traffic.[253]

Today at Staples Corner where the North Circular crosses the A5. To the right the M1 terminus. Under the Ringway plans it would have continued south under the high North Circular viaduct.

With the death of the inner ringways, the M1 would be going no further south than the North Circular Road. Although the M1 extension from Hendon was designed to end at a roundabout linked to the North Circular, there is no doubt, based on different engineering plans, that the unusual height of the North Circular's east-west flyover at Staples Corner was to allow another north-south flyover to be built under it taking the M1 southwards.[254] But the extension to Ringway 1 was always a GLC project, not a central government one, and Ringway 1 was not going to happen.

However the blight over the northern extension of the M23 continued for years after – this was an MoT project, and in theory the change of power at County Hall didn't affect it. But the men from the ministry couldn't decide what to do in a changing situation.

Layfield's report recognised that with no Ringway 2, the northern terminal of the M23 was unclear again. His solution was simple – continue the M23 further northward to join the South Cross Route; and possibly reprioritise part of Parkway E to provide this link. But of course Ringway 1 was now dead too.

And so the blight in Streatham continued. In November 1974, the area's Tory MP, Bill Shelton,[255] complained; 'Some 200 or 300 houses are affected by it in the eastern linkage alone. Properties are standing empty, and shops are falling into disuse. Those who wish to buy in that area are having problems with mortgages, quite understandably. There are fly-by-night traders. This is all because of the blight and the lack of decision by the government.' But ministers told him that it would be most unwise for the safeguarding of the route – the cause of the blight – to be ended yet.

In February 1976, Tony Crosland set up a working party to decide what to do. In charge would be Sercu – the ministry's south-east roads construction unit, based at Dorking in Surrey. It would have representatives from the GLC, MoT, and Surrey County. Engineering consultancy came from Travers Morgan who had worked on the original proposals. The GLC made it clear from the outset than any extension into Greater London was not acceptable. The planned route remained safeguarded, and so the blight continued, while officials debated what to do.

Protest continued in the suburbs blighted by the plans; the Wallington M23 Action Group called for clear time limits on motorway planning and its leader, Iris Loraine, demanded that the extension be killed off once and for all. The group painted a vivid picture of planning blight in a prosperous suburb; 'bungalows and all types of houses became empty and neglected. There were overgrown gardens of houses with 'sold' notice boards vacant for sometimes two years and purchased by the ministry of the environment – an open invitation to burglars and vagrants...the leasing of properties purchased by the ministry to other ministries or estate agents did not improve matters. Maintenance was seldom done and the value of the housing on or near the route deteriorated.

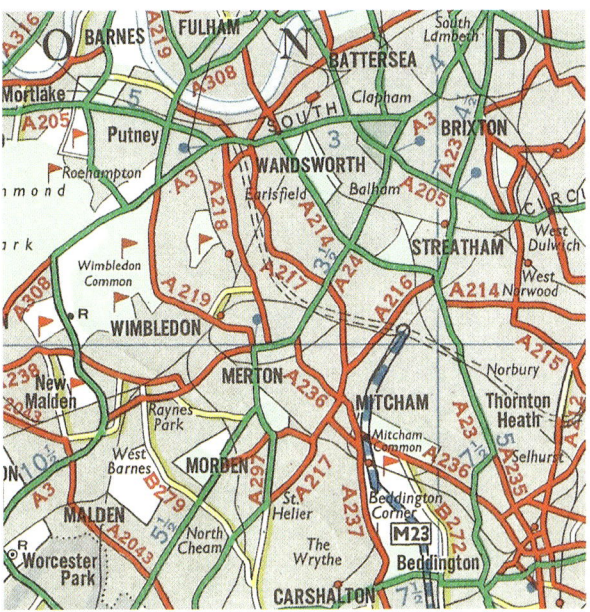

Commercial mapmakers like the AA began to include proposed roads on their maps. This AA map shows the M23 extension and in dotted lines, Ringway 2

Leaseholders sublet for short term and one year periods with contracts option on the government's side. Young couples with two or three children living in unsettled conditions, uncertain of the future for their family life.'

The working party took longer than expected to report – essentially it found that it was having to conduct a mini-transport study in south London. So it was not until the summer of 1978 that it reported, recommending without hesitation that the M23 not proceed north into London. But it did recommend some kind of relief road for the overcrowded A23.

The minister duly accepted the recommendations. But his decision meant holding another inquiry into his proposal to remove it from the plan. There was some opposition to the removal – mainly from business groups such as the CBI, airlines operating from Gatwick, and coach operators.

But some residents' associations objected too – Kingswood District wanted the M23 extension built. It said that the terminus at Hooley caused traffic build up there and led to heavier traffic on other roads into London such as the A217. The comment is instructive – not all residents' associations were opposed to motorways. In 1976, after the working party had been announced, Purley and Woodcote Residents had written to the minister welcoming an extension of the M23. They said it would 'act as a bypass to Purley Cross Roads which is saturated with traffic......the enormous amount of traffic passing through it is quite incompatible with its shopping use, both in safety and environmental grounds.'

They were not wrong of course, Purley really had become a serious traffic bottleneck – but the argument was pure nimbyism – would not the unwanted traffic be equally incompatible with shopping in Streatham? The comment is also instructive in that it shows how difficult it often was to accept that building roads actually made traffic congestion worse – not better. And it shows how the building of one part of a motorway system generated traffic which led inexorably to pressure for more of it to be built.

The 1970s wore on. The crisis-hit Labour government faded into the

Rainy night on the West Cross Route, late 2016

Conservative government. Ministers came and went. And so it was not until May 1980 that the Tory transport minister Norman Fowler killed off the A23 relief road, the final remnant of the M23 extension. The inquiry had approved dropping the scheme; Fowler said it could not be justified due to the cost and 'the serious effects on the environment.'

At this point, it is tempting to consider whether the inner ringways could ever in fact have been built. They had, it is true, had a charmed life, overcoming consistent treasury scepticism and a serious opposition campaign to get at least partial approval from the Layfield Panel, which was then quickly endorsed by the Tory government in 1973.

All the plans had been agreed and were ready. All it needed was a Go button to be pressed and the compulsory purchase orders would have been served, paving the way for communities to collapse while waiting for the demolition to start. Douglas Jay half-suspected that in the end the money would simply not be there. He said that if the protesters had lost, 'London would have been left in the next year or two with half-finished concrete monstrosities, costing hundreds of millions to complete, in the midst of dismembered and derelict residential areas. From all this we were saved by the voters.'[256]

Had the Tories kept control of the GLC that year, the bandwagon would have rolled on. And the Land Compensation Act of 1973 had taken the sting out of the compensation issue for those whose homes were affected by motorways without actually being demolished. However this Act was a double-edged sword; the *Architectural Review* noted acidly that 'at several major inquiries, the white paper has been flourished by the department of the environment as a sort of magic wand to wipe away all undesirable consequences of constructing an urban motorway.'[257]

From now on, homeowners would be treated more fairly, albeit at the cost of a large increase in the cost of construction.

However the oil crisis struck in October 1973 with the Arab-Israeli war and the Arab boycott of the west as punishment for its support for Israel. Petrol prices tripled. The crisis had two major effects:

- It stimulated the search for alternative energy sources to oil, and made conservation into a mainstream issue. With petrol rationing on the cards, and the three-day week of early 1974, suddenly everyone understood about energy shortages
- It brought an end to the long post war boom, triggering a recession which lasted until 1975 and which saw the UK's GDP fall by 3.9 per cent. In this climate, prestige projects became unrealistic; plans to build London's third airport at Foulness were scrapped in the summer of 1974. Six months later, Labour cancelled the Channel Tunnel project too

In February 1974 Ted Heath was defeated at the polls and Harold Wilson returned to Downing Street. Even if the Tories had kept control of the GLC, they now potentially faced opposition in Whitehall.

However Labour came to office with a somewhat schizophrenic attitude to public transport. Although Labour improved financing for British Rail through a new Transport Act, the environment secretary, Tony Crosland, believed that railways disproportionately served the middle class and investment in buses, for example, was a more egalitarian and socialist use of public money. The 1975/76 transport minister, John Gilbert, was a noted pro-roads minister. He was the proud owner of both an Aston Martin convertible and a Mustang and his spell as minister saw him block the eastward extension of the Fleet Line as well as capping railway investment.

It still remains hard to believe that the treasury would have been able or willing to pay its 75 per cent of a cost which would surely have spiralled out of control. Roy Jenkins, a committed opponent of the ringways, was back in cabinet as home secretary where he would certainly have had a big say. Even *The Economist* thought, in the gloom of 1974, that 'if the environment lobby had not won, London's ringways would still have had to be killed because of the cost.'[258]

Projects of this magnitude are, in any case, very vulnerable because of the long lead times for infrastructure schemes, due partly to the complexity of planning law, and partly to the perennial shortage of cash, As a result, major projects usually take decades from inception to completion. So at any stage they are at risk of being killed by the latest financial crisis – as happened to the Channel Tunnel and Foulness Airport.

Even so, the defeat of the ringways was in every sense a historic victory for London and Londoners. The victory had a series of long-term effects which are still in place today;

It revealed the existence and strength of an organised road lobby

The fact that a powerful industry lobby group, funded by some of Britain's largest corporations, was making the running on transport policy and had built massive support in Whitehall was a fact little appreciated in the early 1960s. The fight against the ringways brought the existence and power of this lobby into the open and helped people understand the extent to which transport policy making had been compromised.

It generated a renewed interest in public transport

The London ringways were the first ever defeat for the road lobby. The campaign against them stimulated a renewed interest in public transport in the London Labour Party, which, for most of the 1960s, had enthusiastically backed big road projects. For the first time there was an intellectually coherent case that building roads could not solve traffic congestion as they only stimulated more traffic which in turn, led to demands for more roads. Since the GLC now controlled London Transport, there was a much greater interest in building an integrated transport policy at County Hall. Interestingly, something similar was happening in New York. State governor Nelson Rockefeller was perhaps the first US politician to realise that road building could never solve traffic congestion – he had seen how Robert Moses' superhighways were jam packed on the day they opened. Instead he understood that what was needed was massive investment in the long-neglected subway and railroad systems, And that, in turn, meant getting rid of the previously all-powerful Moses, which Rockefeller finally managed in 1968.

It showed that investing in public transport could be a vote winner

Labour in London – if not always at a national level – began to understand that however much people aspired to owning a car, building motorways was always going to be a massively unpopular policy, even among motorists. It followed, therefore, that a distinctive political position on transport could be a vote winner. After abandoning the inner ringways, the 1973-1977 Labour GLC switched its spending towards public transport; in 1973-74, 72 per cent of GLC transport spending went on roads; by 1975-76, 68 per cent was going to public transport. In 1976 the GLC became the first ever local authority to provide subsidies to BR for urban train services when it stepped in to avoid service cuts on the North London Line.

It made transport the main political issue in London.....
For most of the post-war period, housing was the major political issue in the capital. After the successful fight against the Ringways, transport moved decisively to the top spot. It never really lost that position, and Ken Livingstone's rise to prominence as a national political figure was based entirely on his commitment to cheap public transport and a track record of achievement – such as introducing the congestion charge and, subsequently, getting investment to build London Overground. His policy on roads was in part written by Tim Pharoah, ex LATA and by now an established transport planning consultant. The fact that the mayor has power over transport but not over housing has continued the focus on transport issues among London politicians.

.....and shifted the boundaries of the debate
The political consensus itself had shifted – driven by a new commitment to public as opposed to private transport. A London transport policy based on road building was not going to be sustainable or electorally successful any more. Future Tory leaderships in London, the 1977-1981 regime of Horace Cutler at County Hall, and the mayoralty of Boris Johnson, learned the lesson of the campaign against the motorways, and they made no real attempt to return Tory transport policy to a roads free-for-all. Road improvements might take place, new roads could even be built, but there was no attempt at resurrecting the ringways, to the annoyance of many in the road lobby.[259]

The flamboyant and bow-tied Cutler, who had never publicly supported the ringways, continued Labour's policy of subsidising the North London Line and working closely with BR to improve services. In 1979, his administration used GLC money to help pay BR to restore passenger services from Dalston to Stratford, a key section of what became London Overground.

Johnson, in turn, largely continued Livingstone's transport policies. He retained the congestion charge in central (although not west) London. Although there were fierce differences over the extent to which fares should be subsidised at the 2012 mayoral election, these were now debates conducted within a strong pro-public transport consensus. Johnson also continued Livingstone's plans to get control over London suburban trains; winning in the case of north-east London (the West Anglia routes) and only losing in south-east London because of the opposition of Tory councillors and MPs in Kent. Johnson, a keen cyclist, annoyed business lobbies by arguing for dedicated cycle routes across the capital.

It led to better compensation
The Land Compensation Act of 1973 stemmed directly from the Urban Motorways Committee report *New Roads in Towns*. This called for comprehensive improvement to compensation arrangements so that those where were affected by a road but whose home would not actually be knocked down would be compensated. This compensation, they said, would add 15-20 per cent to building costs and this should be included within government grant.

These recommendations promptly appeared in a 1972 white paper.[260] Now at last there would be compensation for so-called injurious affectation – loss of value inflicted on those whose property is not actually acquired and destroyed but is injured by noise, vibration, or pollution. Henceforth they would get compensation within certain limits, although the Act still didn't permit any relief when a route was merely safeguarded.

This was progress, even though it was partly designed to make road building in cities easier by taking the sting out of the compensation injustice. Of course, paying fair compensation would increase the cost, and therefore the viability, of such projects.

It showed that road building was not inevitable...
This was the first time a major road project had been stopped. The sapping sense of inevitability was suddenly lifted; the destruction of housing and the built environment by road building was not, it turned out, an inevitable part of what we are pleased to call progress. It was now possible to open a discussion as to whether a road was really needed or not, and as part of that discussion, the effect on the environment and public amenity would be a central issue. Road engineers would no longer have unchallenged authority and the issue would, however imperfectly, return to the democratic domain. Discussion of how to manage traffic congestion was now a political question to which there were many possible solutions, it was no longer simply an engineering one to be solved by building more roads, and the 'Predict and Provide' solution was now open to challenge. The campaign against the ringways left behind a mountain of carefully-prepared evidence to prove that road building merely generated more traffic, and that evidence was available to future campaigns. Eventually, as we shall, see, it was finally accepted by ministers.

And showed the power of a single issue campaign...
All sort of people had been mobilised to oppose the ringways. Many of them were natural Conservative voters and were car owners themselves. But being a motorist did not, it turned out, automatically equate with support for unlimited road building. The fact that the campaign had been a limited, single-issue one, was precisely what made it possible to involve large number of people, and future campaigns against road building would see this same coalition in place. In future, Conservatives might become interested in conserving; the battles against driving the M3 through Twyford Down in the 1990s were supported by part of the Conservative Party leadership in Winchester for example. Large-scale road building would inevitably impact on suburbs and rural areas and in that situation a Conservative government could run into very active opposition from its own voters. In future, Tory backbenchers tended to support local opinion when major roads were planned in their constituency and by the 1990s could display a sophisticated understanding of the issues involved.

And stopped London becoming more like Los Angeles
Had the ringways been built, London would have become a very different city. They would have transformed London for the worse, and the renaissance in public transport which happened in the 21st century would never have occurred, as the money would have been eaten up by motorway projects; indeed the quality of public transport would certainly have declined. Having a car could have become as essential to daily life as it is in many US cities.

The road lobby, meanwhile, went away and licked its wounds. By November 1973 the BRF noted bitterly that 'the time would appear to have arrived when for the BRF to advocate directly a motorway or scheme of motorways in a town or city is to raise more opposition than support.'

Still, the road lobby had lost a major battle, but not necessarily the war. It decided upon a new approach; 'to counter this situation it is suggested that the BRF in future should change its approach to urban motorways. It should not advocate them, openly, generally or specifically, but should state that its interest is to assist in the overall development of towns and cities including all forms of transport with every regard for environmental considerations. It would then work with officials in the towns and cities on an unofficial basis on the framing of the overall plan to ensure that eventually it covered adequately the road transport aspect.'[261]

For some time, its focus shifted away from London to the provinces, where the climate of opinion seemed more favourable.

However environmental concerns had been growing even before the 1973 oil crisis, with Teddy Goldsmith founding *The Ecologist* in 1970 and Friends of the Earth starting up in the UK a year later. New road proposals were now going to be judged in the future on environmental grounds too, and inevitably found badly wanting when compared with rail transport.

A new set of anti-roads campaigners drew some other lessons from the defeat of the ringways however – the precise and meticulous opposition presented to the Layfield Panel had not worked. It had been substantially ignored and Layfield had recommended that Ringway 1 go ahead.

From now on, road protest would pay less attention to the formal channels, believing them to be little more than a sham; something rigged to force road projects through by a coalition of civil servants and road lobby interests. Instead, road protest would become much more anarchic and focussed on direct action. In any case a House of Lords decision in 1980[262] endorsed a government statement from 1976 to the effect that 'the merits and foundations of policies, methodologies, design standards and economic assumptions adopted by the government are not matters for argument at an individual inquiry. Any argument about them should take place generally and at national level.'

In other words, objections would not be permitted on the alleged need for a new road. Neither would they be allowed on the grounds of government bias against public transport or that the assumptions used to justify a new road were wrong. John Adams – a frequent expert witness for Friends of the Earth in this period – recalls being banned from challenging assumptions which most motorway opponents thought to be totally flawed. He recalls, 'I understood the logic which said that you couldn't challenge government policy. But you could have a policy which essentially said – build roads to meet forecast demand. But not to be able to challenge the actual forecasts underlying this policy was absurd.'[263]

Activists found that fighting road schemes through the courts were equally unsuccessful. For the some of the activists involved, it was easy to assume that the system was a scam and that only direct action could be successful. They were to win national prominence during a series of battles in the 1980s and 90s.

Others were to draw somewhat more sophisticated conclusions and were to score a major victory against the ghosts of the ringways – the last attempts to build strategic roads in London in the late 1980s.

6 – Round and round the M25

Meanwhile what of the ringways in outer London? They were central government projects from the start, as they were trunk roads built outside of the former LCC area. That meant that the scrapping of the inner ringways had no bearing on their future.

In any case, they had never been as controversial as the inner London motorways. Both LMAG and LATA had backed them on the grounds that they really would divert through traffic – especially heavy lorries – from inner London. Building them didn't involve the mass demolition of houses either, the source of most of the opposition to the inner ringways. Although opponents thought (incorrectly as it turned out) that the outer ringways were less likely to attract the massive traffic that Ringway 1 would, the cheaper construction costs made them a much better proposition financially.

Untangling the history of what became the M25 is complicated because there were different routes planned at various times and the eventual solution was a mixture of them. The two key pieces were
- Abercrombie's E Ring, itself a version of Bressey's North and South Orbital routes
- Abercrombie's D Ring, which became the GLC's Ringway 3

Planning for the outer rings resumed after the Second World War. In December 1945, the transport minister told a deputation from 11 county councils that the orbital route was 'first priority.' [264]

The D Ring / Ringway 3 would start from Dartford and then circle via Swanley, Sanderstead, New Addington, Croydon, Esher, Walton-on-Thames, Sunbury, Northolt, to Ruislip, Pinner and Barnet, It would then go via Waltham Cross, pass across Epping Forest to reach Chigwell, and then return to Dartford.

Along with Ringway 1, this was the other full-scale motorway planned by Abercrombie, who gave it much greater priority than the E Ring, and significant sections of it were eventually built. As well as its orbital function, it was also seen as a way of connecting the M1 with the London docks; Ernest Marples saying it was his 'long term plan' to achieve this link by way of the M10, the South Mimms By-Pass, the D Ring, the Bishops Stortford motorway[265] and the Docks Relief Road.

Opposition to the GLC's ringways had centred overwhelmingly on the two inner rings – 1 and 2 – where housing loss was greatest and environmental impacts worst. But there had been considerable noise about Ringway 3 in north-west London and Layfield admitted that 'the route of this road was the subject of detailed and persuasive criticism at the inquiry.'[266]

In north-west London, the original route of the D Ring was planned to be an upgraded version of existing streets. In 1951, Middlesex County, doing its bit to implement Abercrombie, considered two routes before settling on one through Eastcote, and passing to the west of Bushey to join the proposed M1. Whitehall then vetoed this in 1953, owing to strong local objections, cost, and the extensive demolition of recently-built homes.

So a new route was considered through Harrow and Ealing, mainly following the A132 and the A4090. But when detailed planning started in the early 1960s, it was clear that transforming these roads into a dual three-lane motorway would be a hugely expensive activity requiring what Colin Buchanan, in a report to five borough councils in the area, called 'destruction or disruption of much of the property and uses flanking it.'[267]

So in 1965, the DoT proposed a new (and cheaper) route between Oxhey and Yeading, moving the road further to the west and through the Green Belt, which meant taking it away from the built-up area. The GLC then objected to this, arguing that routing Ringway 3 away from Greater London would mean it would not attract enough traffic and would disturb the Green Belt. It proposed a new route, which promptly blighted homes in its path, especially in the Northolt area, where owner occupiers and council tenants made common cause against it. New protest groups sprang up and before long, GLC members were getting complaints from residents whose home sales had fallen through because of the proposed road.

And once again there were complaints about secrecy. The GLC bore the brunt of these complaints, but Ringway 3 was a Whitehall project, not one of theirs – so information supplied to the GLC in confidence was not shared with residents, mainly on the grounds that residents would see the maps and put two and two together to make five.

In 1968, the GLC backed down and accepted the ministry's route, agreeing – with obvious reluctance – that 'the higher cost of the council's line would inevitably result in much less road for the money which will be available to it in 1983'.[268] Those on that route breathed a huge sigh of relief.

But north-west London objections poured into the Layfield inquiry just the same; the Hillingdon Residents and Tenants objected on the grounds of lost Green Belt land; Northwood Residents objected because Ringway 3 would affect house prices as well as damaging the Green Belt; Ruislip Residents' Association also said it would destroy lots of Green Belt countryside, the Ruislip golf course, the cricket ground as well as residential property.

South of the river, Ringway 3 had the lowest priority of all the ringway schemes. Back in 1947, ministers had decided that there was no justification for the D Ring south and south-east of Sunbury.[269] But Kent County's road engineers went ahead anyway and safeguarded a line for a road between Chelsfield near Orpington, and New Addington on the Kent/Croydon boundary. This route was known as the Croydon-Farnborough link.

However Croydon County wanted to continue this route westwards as far as the M23 motorway. Its first draft development plan, produced to get the town ready for the explosive office growth which kicked off in the late 1950s, and which established Croydon as the poster-child for cheap, decentralised offices, included this link among a raft of hugely expensive road proposals. The road plans didn't go down well in Whitehall, where analysts from the housing ministry called them 'grossly extravagant.'[270] The bean-counters worried that if all towns were to plan on the scale that Croydon had, the total cost would be astronomical and ultimately unaffordable.

So the civil servants removed many schemes – including this link – from Croydon's plan. But the Kent alignment remained in place, and slowly but surely, the D Ring, badly wounded in 1947, came back to life.

Barbara Castle's 1965 announcement approving the M25 specifically stated that the D Ring was going to be needed, the first top-level ministerial endorsement of a route which had definitively come back from the dead, and in that year, the transport department suggested that the GLC 'bear in mind' the possible need for a new road from the Croydon area to Sunbury, as this would influence the design and route of the Croydon-Farnborough link.[271] The GLC took the hint; it reported back in 1966 that the best route for the D Ring would be across the derelict Croydon Airport to where it could interchange with the M23.

At the Kent, end, the Croydon-Farnborough link was generating unease, Orpington was a fast-growing suburb where the safeguarding needed for a future road, whose precise route had not been agreed, was blocking developments. There was another critical question too; exactly what would the link be like? A normal A road? or a motorway? Minutes of a meeting at the ministry in February 1965 noted that Bromley and Orpington wanted to know whether the road would be one for long-distance or local traffic; 'The more stress was laid on its long-distance functions, and the more this influences design standards, the lower frequency of junctions etc, the stronger local opposition in Orpington was likely to be.'[272]

Between Orpington and Croydon, Ringway 3 would have cut through – and depending on the junctions – probably suburbanised an attractive area near to the village of Downe which, even today, is entirely rural.

Despite the GLC's resurrection of Ringway 3 in 1967, the low priority meant that work was still not expected to start until the 1980s, apart from the essential section from the Dartford Tunnel to Swanley. Only in 1969 did the ministry set up a steering group to plan the rest of the route, and in August that year, Richard Marsh appointed Brian Colquhoun, a firm of engineering consultants, to investigate the concept and propose alternative routes for Ringway 3.[273]

However Ringway 3 was going to be no more popular in Surrey than it had been in Northolt and Harrow. A July 1970 article in the *Sutton And Cheam Advertiser* generated enough alarm that a Federation of North Surrey Residents was set up specifically to fight Ringway 3, although it did concede that some motorways and ringways might need to be built. Privately though, Surrey's planning officer, Eric Sibert, said there was 'no possibility whatever of finding a good route for Ringway 3, it is only possible to say which route is least objectionable.'[274] His concerns were aired behind closed doors; officialdom remained as determined as ever to stop details of potential routes leaking out.

Colquhoun's surveyors were not welcomed when plotting potential routes. It is a little-known fact that surveyors planning a potential road had the right under section 254 of the Highways Act 1959 to enter private land and look around to carry out the survey. But when they turned up at Fairtrough Farm at Pratts Bottom in Kent they were told, in no uncertain terms, to get lost, and the same thing happened at another farm nearby.

The Colquhoun team came up with a set of options which could be simplified as a route picking up the Farnborough-Croydon link, passing to the south of Croydon before splitting into an outer route via Walton-on-Thames and an inner one via Kingston. Colquhoun's engineers thought the cost difference between the two was not great, but traffic potential favoured the inner version. Simplified details of the proposals for Ringway 3 appear in the appendix.

But before decisions could be made on a final alignment, Layfield's report proposed that all of Ringway 3 from the M2 in the south-east round to the A1 in the north-west should be struck out of the plan. An important swathe of Green Belt land was thus saved.

One remnant of Ringway 3 can be sampled in west London, however, This is the stretch of The Parkway (A312) running from the A30 to the east of Heathrow, which the GLC widened to dual carriageway as part of Ringway 3 in 1969.

In Hertfordshire, work on the higher priority northern section of Ringway 3 had started with little fuss, even as the fight against the inner ringways reached its height at the 1973 GLC elections. The first stage to be built linked the A1/A6 junction at South Mimms with the A10 at Waltham Cross. The next stage opened from South Mimms westwards to Potters Bar in 1976, and this route became known as the M16.

The progress on Ringway 3 did not mean that the North Orbital Route had been abandoned; quite the contrary. This route had been confirmed in the county development plans for Middlesex, Hertfordshire and Essex in the 1950s, testimony to the continuing power of Bressey and Abercrombie's thinking.[275]

In Hertford County, Ernest Marples approved comprehensive work on the existing A405 between Watford and Hatfield, explicitly as part of the North Orbital Road project, in July 1961.[276]

At the same time, he announced plans to fix the route of the North Orbital from the northern approaches of the Dartford Tunnel to the A12.[277] Repeated parliamentary questions refer to this section as being part of the North Orbital and not the D Ring, indeed, on one occasion Marples was asked if he would change the route of the D Ring so that it connected to the tunnel.[278]

The Watford-Hatfield section still appears on the map today as the North Orbital Road although part is now renumbered as the A414. Few motorists on this road realise that it was once planned to be part of something very much larger.

A brand new section of the North Orbital, starting from the Hunton Bridge junction with the A41, and then running south-west to Maple Cross near Rickmansworth, was approved in principal in 1966, and in detail in 1971 despite some opposition in Chorleywood. It was built to motorway standards, opened five years later in 1976 and later incorporated as part of the M25. From what is now junction 17 (Maple Cross) the A412 still keeps the North Orbital Road title as a relic of the original plan, as it passes through Denham, a few miles east of today's M25.

South of the river, the South Orbital Route made much more progress, and totally overshadowed the D Ring. It was included in local county plans throughout the 1950s which were approved by ministers, but not until August 1966 did Barbara Castle announce that the South Orbital would be built as a full-scale motorway – numbered the M25 – the first we hear of a designation now infamous to all motorists.

However the M25 was not then seen as providing a complete orbital route. Instead, the aim was to build a route for heavy traffic from the Channel ports to avoid London altogether. It would run for 47 miles from Staines in Surrey, where it would join the North Orbital Route, and then relieve the A25 through Surrey before joining the M20 near Wrotham in Kent. The A25 was a narrow route traversing hilly terrain and built up along much of its length making improvements impractical.

It was planned and built in stages, each stage designed to intersect with a radial route. The first was between Godstone and Reigate, where planning started in 1966, and which opened early in 1976. It was followed by Godstone to Wrotham, opened in 1979. At the same time, the section of the Ringway 3 from the A2 at Dartford to the A20 at Swanley was also being built, opening in spring 1977.

Post-Layfield, the strategic objective of building a single London orbital motorway promoted some rethinking in the transport ministry, and civil servants

Church Road...School Road...North Orbital Road???

were contemplating building the ring by linking the M25 in the south with various bits of Ringway 3 and the North Orbital Route to produce a complete circle. The abandonment of Ringway 3 in Middlesex and south of the river led to this thinking being locked down – with the help of some prodding from the BRF which argued that there needed to be a coherent, easy-to-understand London-wide orbital road; in November 1975 John Gilbert, Labour's pro-road transport minister, announced that the M25 would be joined to the M16 on the north side of London to become one complete orbital motorway numbered the M25. It would cross the Thames at Dartford, by a brand new bridge, which opened in 1991.

The complete ring would thus be made up of bits and pieces of various schemes
- Ringway 3 (M16) from Potters Bar, via Waltham Cross and Epping, to Brentwood and under the river to Swanley
- A new linking section, based on Abercrombie's South Orbital, running from the southern part of Ringway 3 at Swanley to Sevenoaks
- The South Orbital from Sevenoaks, via Godstone and Leatherhead to Staines – the core of the original M25
- Another new alignment running from Staines, similar to that of the 1930s North Orbital but on a slightly different route, running to the west of Heathrow, to Maple Cross.
- The North Orbital Road from Maple Cross to the Junction 19 spur
- A completely new linking section from Potters Bar, to the north of Watford, to where it joined the North Orbital road at Junction 19 (Hunton Bridge).

The inner section of Ringway 3 through west and south London was then abandoned, as was the North Orbital route where it ran to the north of the M25. The original Sevenoaks – Wrotham section of the M25 was renamed the M26.

The Labour government which came to power in 1974 soon found itself in the midst of a financial cyclone with huge spending cuts imposed by the IMF. In this climate, road spending could not be exempted – and Labour proposed to cut it by £87 million, but a 1978 white paper[279] laid down that the M25 remained the top priority for motorway building in the UK even in reduced circumstances.

However there was never any public inquiry into the concept and purpose of a London orbital road. There *was* a grand design dating back many decades, but it was implemented piecemeal as and when the money and construction resource became available. And as each section was built planned and built separately, it was subject to a disjointed planning process; each stage was negotiated between the ministry and local councils and was then subject to its own public inquiry. That meant that building a section had to pass the 'what's in it for me?' test, in other words, local councils wanted the road to do something for local transport and communities as well, and for them, the big picture point of the road easily became secondary.

The piecemeal approach meant there were 39 public inquiries lasting over 700 sitting days; some lasted just one day, one lasted 97 sitting days over a period of 13 months. Of the 32 junctions on the completed M25, nine are with radial motorways, another nine with major trunk roads – and 14 are with county roads serving local needs.

It meant that the case for the motorway *as a whole* and what it was really for was never made – generally it was accepted as being an obvious, unquestioned benefit to get heavy lorries out of narrow town and village streets. How this requirement fitted in with a staged approach which, by definition, needed lots of junctions with local roads was not explored, and neither were implications of this approach.

The M25 was hugely popular among local councils and residents who saw it as the only way of getting the increasing number of juggernauts off their roads. And building the M25 *did* work – DoT studies of the Reigate – Godstone section, which opened in 1976, showed that the old A25 lost between 17 and 27 per cent of its traffic.

In parliament, MPs complained not about the M25 being built, or the way it was built – but the delays in building it. Two opposition Tories may be taken as typical, and representative of local opinion.

Robert McCrindle (Brentwood) said 'At the moment from the Dartford Tunnel enormous juggernauts use what in parts is really no more than a suburban road, striking terror into the hearts of residents. In the process the beautiful and attractive villages of Herongate and Ingrave have been almost completely destroyed. If the minister adds to this the existence of two schools, with children spilling out on to the A128 in the heart of Brentwood, I am sure that he will understand why my constituents are impatient for this stretch of motorway to proceed.'[280] He was backed up by Norman Tebbit, then a little known backbencher representing Chingford, who talked of 'lives made miserable and dangerous by heavy traffic.' He demanded that the complete project be built calling it 'monstrous madness' for parts to be built and others not. That, he said, would mean 'traffic would be encouraged along a section of the motorway and would then splurge out again through village and countryside.'

BRF leaflet campaigning for the M25 to be completed

However MPs were being successfully lobbied by the BRF, for whom getting an orbital route built was their top priority in the London area. One-time road lobbyist Andrew Warren recalls 'it wasn't usually that difficult to find people who would support the road....I remember months and months of making exactly the same speech at Rotary Clubs explaining why the M25 was needed. In those days the Rotary Club was like the Tory Party at lunch and the Round Table was like the Tory Party in the evening. So they then fed back to their MPs that this road needed to be built as quickly as possible.'[281]

There *was* some unease. LATA accepted that while some kind of orbital route was needed, it could possibly be smaller than the DoT had planned.[282] It turned out that this option had not been considered. When Carshalton's Tory MP asked for estimates of completing the M25 as a dual carriage road, he was told that no such estimates had been made.[283]

When challenged at local inquiries, ministers argued that building the orbital road was a policy question for national government rather than one which could be discussed at a local inquiry. Looking back, Stephen Plowden calls the refusal to have an inquiry into the entire scheme 'supreme dishonesty' as it meant that 'each section had its own individual inquiry on the implicit assumption that the rest of the motorway would be built.'[284]

LATA had another concern too, by 1978 London's inner city crisis was in full swing, with rapid deindustrialisation, high unemployment and urban violence scarring the inner boroughs. LATA had a full, if inconclusive, correspondence with minsters over the M25, and in December 1978, Plowden wrote to John Horam, the junior transport minister, worrying that a big motorway would increase the accessibility of towns and workplaces in the outer metropolitan area at the expense of those in inner and central London. The M25 would, he said, give anyone living near it much greater employment opportunities; 'in the short term this extension of choice may be desirable to the individuals concerned, but it cannot help the inner city and hence the region generally.'[285]

A similar warning came from John Adams, who was born in Canada. He says; 'I played the north American card,' telling the inquiry into the Epping section of the M16 in 1976 that all the experience of north American cities was that building orbital motorways prompted a migration of jobs and businesses to the periphery.[286]

Professional property opinion backed this kind of argument, In 1981, with only a third of the road built, an influential report argued that the M25 would generate a massive push for office and retail development along the route, to the probable detriment of inner London.[287] This report pointed to the way in which the government's disregard of public transport was itself boosting the trend to decentralisation; fares had risen faster than inflation over the previous five years, which was a disincentive to working in central London if you could find work locally.

It is a curious and remarkable fact that planners and politicians looked to the US when it came to predicting growth in traffic, but not when it came to the social consequences of orbital road building.

While the new road would not demolish many houses, it would run through outstanding areas of the London Green Belt. However the early inquiries saw objectors who accepted the general need for the road caught in a trap. For example in 1967, Banstead council argued that the route should run south of the North Downs in order to protect amenity in its own area. But this would have meant the route severing National Trust land and possibly impacting on the Leith

Hill area – the highest point in south-east England. A 1971 inquiry at Leatherhead saw two rival action groups argue over where the road should go, essentially an argument that the nuisance be moved elsewhere. This prompted the ministry's QC, Douglas Frank, to tell the rival groups that it was 'no use forcing the M25 on other people.'[288]

In 1973 the section of the M16 through Epping Forest ran into the Upshire Preservation Society, led by Joyce Woods, a local magistrate. In February that year, protesters from the area assembled tractors and combine harvesters in Parliament Square before marching down Whitehall, led by a goat, with banners headed 'not Epping likely.'[289]

Counsel for the DoE played the silent majority card at the inquiry, saying that public support for the section was much greater than the opposition to it. John Newey QC said; 'people had to be mobile to keep up their standard of living and lead richer lives'.[290] The inquiry was repeatedly disrupted by John Tyme, a polytechnic lecturer from Sheffield who had become one of the best-known faces of motorway protest and was now making his first appearance in the London area. Tyme believed motorways helped create 'a profligate and wasteful society' and that civil disobedience was the only means of protest given the 'corrupt alliance between the road lobby and the highways mandarins in Marsham Street.'[291]

Tyme insisted that the inquiries were illegal as the 1959 Highways Act required the ministry to adequately describe the 'general effect' of a proposed road, whereas ministry practice had been to issue newspaper advertisements just giving the route. Inspectors invariably overruled this (admittedly technical) argument, and inquiries would be disrupted so that they would be repeatedly adjourned, and then – hopefully – abandoned. Tyme's memoires express disappointment that Epping protesters did not, by and large, agree with his approach and preferred instead to trust the official channels. The protesters did not stop the road – but they did manage to get the Bell Common tunnel under the northern tip of Epping Forest doubled in length.

A little further east, the DoT planners met Lesley Lovelock, the girl who managed to hold up the M25 for four long years. A secretary and amateur artist, she had attended the 1973 inquiry into this section as an objector. The inspector refused to accept objections about the actual need for the road, and so, in objectors' eyes, the inquiry was a meaningless scam. *The Times* reported that 'uproar broke out' for the second day running as the Inspector refused to adjourn the inquiry and 'each time the inspector tried to continue the inquiry the objectors continued to shout, stamp and clap.' police had to remove objectors and one woman was physically carried out.[292]

So she went to court. Then in her early 20s, she argued that two CPOs for land on the section near her home at Cranham were in breach of the Green Belt Act. Entirely acting for herself she pursued the case doggedly through the High Court and the Appeal Court before finally losing in 1980. She had spent over £5,000 of her own money, and the Liberal peer Lord Avebury opened a fighting fund to raise these costs.

The MoT gained something important substantial from the fight however – more legal authority for their contention that objectors at an inquiry could not question the need for the road itself, that being a question for the relevant minister who was answerable to parliament.

The fiercest opposition came over the section between Swanley and Sevenoaks in Kent. An opposition group called DANDAG (Defend Darenth Valley and the

North Downs Action Group) rapidly built up 1,800 members. It was led by David Rae, a steel company executive. It complained that a short cut of just 10 miles would cost £18 million. DANDAG argued that traffic would be mainly local, being drawn on to the M25 through the link to Badgers Mount at the A21/A224. 'It would destroy an area of outstanding natural beauty, ruin the Green Belt, provide incidental short-term relief to some areas before causing an enormous traffic growth throughout the region.'[293]

The plans for this section were laid down in 1973 when locals were asked to comment on three alternative routes. Having no route at all was not part of the consultation. The minister chose his preferred route in 1977, and the inquiry took place a year later. The route rapidly became controversial beyond the locality; an Area of Outstanding Natural Beauty where the Victorian landscape artist Samuel Palmer had painted. DANDAG argued that there was a serious alternative here; not build the link, and send Dartford-bound traffic via the M26 to Wrotham and then the M20. This would require only a small curve building at Wrotham.

For the first time, the Countryside Commission, whose remit was to advise the minister on threats to the countryside, opposed the road, saying the route 'appears to have been chosen without regard to the major landscape planning issue of retaining quiet, unspoilt tracts of countryside.'

As elsewhere, opposition was not unanimous; both the GLC and Kent County supported it in principle, and Badgers Mount residents backed it by 181 votes to 65. There clearly was very substantial support for the idea that only this link would take juggernauts off of local roads.

The inquiry was the first one under new procedures[294] designed to rescue a system which had fallen into disrepute due to the increasing opposition to road building. Inquiries were traditionally held by planning inspectors, usually former road engineers, appointed by the transport department to report on the department's own scheme.

Looked at logically, and from the point of view of government *realpolitik*, this was the exact point of the process, Motorway opponent John Adams of UCL asked rhetorically, 'why should the ministry ever hold an independent inquiry into anything? Why should it willingly allow persons independent of it to have a hand in decisions which lie within its own jurisdiction? The answer appears to be that it never does, except through miscalculation or indifference.'[295]

To try and restore some credibility, some changes were made to the system and the inquiry into Sevenoaks – Swanley was the first to be held by a QC – George Dobry – who, ironically had represented the Conservation Society at the Epping inquiry into the M16.

At the inquiry, Dobry refused to admit objections to the need for the road, on the basis that the inquiry could not debate the need for the road as it was government policy; 'it is government policy to complete the M25 with all possible speed. Only the manner of its completion is open to argument.' [296]

It wasn't until January 1981 that transport minster Ken Clarke released the inspector's report, which recommended that the road be built just as the ministry wanted.

Table Six – M25 opening dates

Junctions	Interchanges and key connections	Distance (miles)	Opening date
1-2	Dartford Tunnel southern approach	1.6	Sept 1986
2-3	Dartford (A2) – Swanley (A20)	3.3	April 1977
3-5	Swanley (A20) – Sevenoaks	8.1	Feb 1986
5	Sevenoaks interchanges (M26. A21)	0.9	July 1980
5-6	Sundridge – Godstone (A22)	9	Nov 1979
6-8	Godstone (A22) – M23 junction – Reigate	4.5	Feb 1976
8-10	Reigate – Leatherhead – Wisley (A3)	8.8	Oct 1985
10-11	Wisley (A3) – Chertsey	5.9	Dec 1983
11-12	Chertsey – Thorpe (M3)	2.4	Oct 1980
11-12	Thorpe (M3) – Egham	2.5	Dec 1976
12-13	Egham – Yeoveney/Staines	0.9	Nov 1981
13/14	Yeoveney/Staines – Poyle (inc airport spur)	2	Aug 1982
14-16	Poyle – Thorney Mill (M4) – Iver Heath (M40)	8	Sept 1985
16-17	Iver Heath (M40) – Maple Cross	4.8	Jan 1985
17-19	Maple Cross – Hunton Bridge (A41)	6	Feb 1976
19-23	Micklefield Green – M1 junction – South Mimms (A1M)	13.5	Aug 1986
23-24	South Mimms (A1M) – Potters Bar	2.7	Sept 1975
24-25	Potters Bar – Waltham Cross (A10)	5.3	June 1981
25-26	Waltham Cross (A10) – Upshire	3.8	Jan 1984
26-27	Upshire – Theydon Garnon (M11)	4.1	Jan 1984
27-28	Theydon Garnon (M11) – Brentwood (A12)	2.9	April 1983
28-29	Brentwood (A12) – North Ockendon (A127)	5.4	April 1983
29-31	North Ockendon (A127) – Dartford tunnel northern approach	4.7	Dec 1982
	Dartford Tunnel (west)	1.4	Nov 1963
	Dartford Tunnel (east)	1.4	May 1980
	Dartford Queen Elizabeth II bridge	1.7	Oct 1991

Source – Department of Transport

The greatest of all the ringways was finally completed on 29 October 1986 when the 13 mile section from Micklefield to South Mimms opened – ahead of schedule – in Hertfordshire. By coincidence, the contractor which completed this last section, Balfour Beatty, had built the very first stretch back in 1973.

It had cost £1 billion to build, with inflation meaning the later sections were disproportionately dear. It needed two million tonnes of concrete and 2.5 million of asphalt, required 49 million cubic metres of spoil removing, and 2.1 million trees and shrubs planting to try to shield the road. And when it was built, its 117 miles made it the longest orbital motorway in the world (a record since beaten by the Berlin orbital). It reaches a summit at a surprising 700 feet above sea level near Reigate in Surrey.

Huge junctions were needed with the radial motorways – junction 7 with the M23 at Merstham has four levels and free-flow connections between the two

Margaret Thatcher 'we can't do without the great car economy'

motorways with the M23 passing over the M25 on a five span steel girder box bridge at a height of 75 feet. The junction with the M4 is another four level interchange with eight bridges and three viaducts.

Margaret Thatcher performed the opening ceremony. For fear of protest it was not a public event, and one reporter thought the occasion 'anticlimactic'.[297] But Mrs Thatcher looked genuinely pleased on a warm autumn morning, happily removing traffic cones and posing for pictures in the middle of an empty motorway. The Iron Lady was visibly in her comfort zone, batting for Britain, surrounded by men who actually got things done, and standing in her electoral heartland, a land apparently made up of entrepreneurial, home-owning, aspirational people who loved their cars and didn't go on strike. At the 1987 election she would win every single constituency in M25-land, a gain from Labour in Thurrock, Essex, making it a clean sweep.

The DoT produced a souvenir brochure to commemorate the occasion, packed full of adverts from the firms which had built the ring, and which was a who's who of the UK's construction and engineering industries.[298] For one leading road engineer, John Salt of Sercu, it all came as a relief, a hand-written memoir of his experiences building the M25 admits; 'at times one wondered if it could ever be completed......but consistency of government resolve, through many administrations, provided the impetus, which, had it been lacking, might have caused abandonment with only limited sections completing.'[299]

There was real public enthusiasm for the completed road; in motorway-free Norfolk, a enterprising coach firm organised guided tours of the new motorway.[300] A *Guardian* reporter who travelled the route after the final cones had been removed saw crowds waving from the overbridges.[301]

Yet the M25 was already a byword for traffic congestion; *The Economist* tartly said that it had taken 70 years to plan it, 12 to build it and just one to find it was inadequate.[302] Aware of the issue, Mrs Thatcher's opening speech condemned what she called 'carping and criticising,' She said; 'Now some people are saying that the road is too small, even that it's a disaster. I must say I can't *stand* those who carp and criticise when they ought to be congratulating Britain on a magnificent achievement and beating the drum for Britain all over the world.'

The Iron Lady insisted that the congestion on the M25 was 'a mark of its success, not of its failure,' adding that widening plans were already under consideration.

Two months previous to the opening, ministers had indeed announced that they would spend £20 million widening the section between junctions 11 and 13 to four lanes using land set aside for central reservations. This stemmed from a recommendation from consultants Brian Colquhoun who had looked into traffic forecasting. When competed, it would join the section between junctions 13 and 15 which had been built from the outset with four lanes.

The congestion – with traffic massively above the forecasts – came as a severe shock, and urgent action was needed. The ministry came under the cosh from the National Audit Office, and then from the Commons public accounts committee, both of which complained that Whitehall should be taking the issue of generated traffic seriously.

Table Seven – M25 traffic; what they planned for – and what they got

Section	Design year forecast traffic	Actual traffic 1992
J14 – J15 (Heathrow spur – M4)	103,000	152,000
J19 – J20 (Hunton Bridge – A41)	59.500	110,000
J10 – J11 (Wisley – Chertsey)	75.900	129,000
J22 – J23 (London Colney – South Mimms)	56,000	114,000
J27 – J28 (Theydon Garnon – Brentwood)	69,000	107,000

Source – Standing Advisory Committee on Trunk Road Assessment

In April 1988, the ministry hired more engineering consultants – Rendel Palmer Tritton (RPT) – to report on what to do. The brief was precise – RPT were 'to concentrate on traffic and engineering solutions to the problems they identify,' and focus on solutions which could be implemented reasonably quickly. They were specifically not required to do a strategic study of M25-land.

While RPT got to work, the M25 clocked up what was its longest ever jam – 22 miles of solid tailback between Reigate and Leatherhead on 17 August 1988.[303]

RPT reported in July 1989, finding that traffic had grown by an average of nine per cent a year since the M25 opened. They calculated that growth to 2007 would be 59-78 per cent on a minimum set of assumptions and 73-93 per cent on a maximum set. The minimum figure assumed that the then high economic growth would revert to the mean and that the boost from motorists transferring to the M25 would have worked its way through. The maximum assumption was to allow for the fact that motorway traffic was growing faster than traffic in general.[304]

But where was all this completely unexpected traffic coming from? The consultants identified six possibilities:
- Reassigned traffic, where drivers switched their route to take advantage of the M25
- Redistributed traffic, involving a change of origin or destination due to the better accessibility offered by the M25
- Modal transfer; a switch in the type of transport, from rail to the M25 for example
- Development traffic, stimulated by new developments in M25-land
- Generated traffic, the phenomenon of journeys which never previously existed now being made possible, This – the central argument against road building – was a very sensitive area – RPT noted cautiously that 'to date the department does not generally recognise that roads may generate traffic for the purposes of economics or provisioning.'
- Changes in travel time, where drivers tried to avoid peak hour jams. RPT had already found the phenomenon of 'peak spreading' where people couldn't drive in the peak hours due to congestion and so they went earlier or later, so spreading the congestion to more hours

They said that 'relative importance of each category of traffic is unknown,' but subsequently they went on to have a bash at it, arguing that reassigned traffic was 'possibly the single most important element of M25 usage.' Redistributed traffic was likely to be next most important. Modal transfer was not significant, and although vast new shopping centres were planned, they did not yet exist and so development traffic was not yet relevant.

Instead, the growth in usage was put down to three factors
- The M25 allowed far more all-motorway trips – Birmingham to Southampton for example
- The higher quality of motorway driving, it turned out that before 1983, traffic levels on motorways were growing in line with traffic generally, post-1983 they rose by around twice the level of all roads
- Drivers making longer but quicker journeys by motorway at the expense of higher fuel costs

When the transport ministry's top civil servant, Sir Alan Bailey, was quizzed at the Commons public accounts committee, he said he could not rule out junction closures as a way of deterring local traffic.[305] But RPT rejected even peak-hour closures, which it said would be difficult to implement. The police had warned that it would just shift the congestion elsewhere.

RPT concluded with three central recommendations
- Widen the entire motorway to four lanes in each direction, initially by narrowing the lanes
- Build a network of link roads, running parallel to the motorway and linking one or more junctions. These would siphon off some of the short-distance local traffic as this would no longer need to use the motorway proper. This really meant parts of the M25 being widened to 14 lanes. RPT reckoned that Junctions 13-14 needed this immediately, and it would be needed on 10 more sections by 1997.
- Introduce access control on slip roads to manage demand

So RPT had delivered a solid engineering report – just as they were asked to. But they still asked out loud whether more capacity could ever defeat congestion on the M25.

In 1990, transport minister Malcolm Rifkind released his M25 Action Plan after consulting on the RPT report.[306] The *Roads for Prosperity* white paper of 1989, billed as the largest road building plan since the Romans, had already jumped the gun by proposing to widen the M25 to four lanes in each direction. A year later, the cost of this was given as £1 billion. Another £1.8 billion would be spent on other improvements.

Government strategy, under fire for the jams on what MPs called 'Britain's largest traffic jam' and 'a sort of circular car lot', was to dig in and praise the M25; Lord Brabazon of Tara claimed that since 1983, the number of heavy lorries in London had been cut by a quarter while the number in central London had nearly halved. Michael Portillio praised it for being 'Europe's longest orbital urban motorway, which had made possible a range of journeys which people could not contemplate before.' This was, of course, precisely the problem.

In June 1992, the ministry went ahead with RPT's key proposal. It announced plans to widen the section between the M3 and the M4 to 14 lanes, by building those three-lane link roads. A public inquiry into this was promised for 1994.

The threat of a 14-lane motorway sparked off massive protests in the affected areas around Egham and Staines. The initial consultation generated 12,000 objections in advance of any inquiry. Roger Higman, a transport campaigner at Friends of the Earth, pointed to the obvious implication; 'if the department is proposing 14 lanes in Staines, it won't be content with just six at Potters Bar or Ashtead.'[307]

Reflecting local opinion. Tory MPs from M25-land lashed into the proposals at a late-night debate in April 1993. They didn't do so on nimby grounds, but instead showed a deep understanding of the way that widening would simply beget yet more congestion. Their comments are worth quoting at length; on the Tory backbenches, if not yet in Whitehall, the high-water mark of Predict and Provide had been passed.

Mark Wolfson (Sevenoaks) called the link roads 'a terrifying prospect,' saying it was a short term solution 'which, over the next 20 years, might deal with the overcrowding, but if, during those 20 years, we continue to make it easy for people to live in Surrey and work in Hertfordshire, more of them will do so. We shall therefore add to the problem.'

Geoffrey Pattie (Chertsey and Walton) asked 'what will happen when we fill up the six new lanes, as we shall? Will we have another six and another six after that?'

Michael Grylls (North West Surrey) said his constituents had accepted the concept and the building of the M25, 'but they had no idea what the noise would be, and nor did the planners or the department. They had no idea what the traffic flow would be, so they could not have known about the noise. Now it will be virtually doubled and that is intolerable.'[308]

Both Grylls and Peter Ainsworth (East Surrey) argued that road pricing was the real solution. Ainsworth also condemned the environmental cost of widening; the destruction of 23 designated sites of special scientific interest, the fact that cars were to blame for 85 per cent of the UK carbon monoxide emissions, 48 per

Junction 13 on the M25 – this aerial view gives a good impression of the exurban sprawl in this part of the south east

cent of nitrogen oxides and for 19 per cent of the greenhouse gas, carbon dioxide.[309]

Whitehall prudently delayed a decision until after the spring 1993 council election. One anonymous Tory MP said 'it is understandable that ministers don't want to get the scheme mixed up with the council elections as so many people are against it.' [310]

Some 23 local authorities – led by Surrey County – had grouped together to fight the scheme. Surrey was a formidable opponent for Whitehall's road machine; a beautiful county, wealthy and prosperous and home to many influential people. Since spring 1993 it had been a hung council, but all parties opposed a 14-lane M25, and all of its MPs were Conservative.

Pragmatically, Surrey was prepared to accept a four lane M25 as they knew they couldn't stop this; the ministry could widen the M25 within its existing boundary without having to call an inquiry. But the link roads were a different matter entirely – and they could be fought.

In July, with the local elections out of the way, MacGregor duly confirmed the link roads.[311]

Surrey's highway officials called an urgent seminar for councillors. Geoff Lamb, the highways director, told them that they would be out of balance with road network, in conflict with regional guidance, would encourage more traffic and longer journeys, worsen pollution and noise and make it easier to promote Heathrow Terminal 5, which Surrey vigorously opposed. Lamb told his councillors that 'a strategy for the 1970s is totally inappropriate for the new century.'[312]

The hard line from the Surrey officials was a sharp turnaround from the 1950s and 1960s when county highway officials were among the strongest proponents of motorway building. Lamb warned that the county had to shift its campaign to a different gear, and Surrey decided to spend £400,000 on getting detailed traffic data to develop alternative options. It commissioned Scott Wilson Kirkpatrick, a firm of engineering consultants, to produce what was claimed to be the UK's largest computer traffic model.

In November 1993, Surrey lost a legal challenge to the link roads. The county argued that the government's stage-by-stage approach prevented the balanced environmental assessment required by EU law.[313] The judge rejected the challenge as premature.

Early in 1995, Surrey revealed preliminary findings from its traffic modelling. This showed that traffic on the M25 could never grow to the levels forecast by the transport department – and used to justify the link roads – because local roads would snarl up with congestion long before.[314] One district council – Runnymede – called for priority lanes for cars with several passengers, motorway pricing, lower speed limits and speed cameras.[315]

Behind the scenes, ministers now had conclusive evidence that building roads could never solve road congestion. As transport secretary, John MacGregor had finally asked the DoT's standing committee on trunk road assessment (SACTRA) to consider whether 'new or improved roads generate extra traffic over and above the growth in traffic which would be expected in the absence of any improvement to the road network.'

In a landmark report, SACTRA[316] said that 'induced traffic can and does occur, probably quite extensively.' And it accepted that 'the M25 experience most probably does, as is popularly thought, serve as an example of a case where 'roads generate traffic.'

It said that for an average road improvement, where forecasting of traffic growth was generally correct, there would be an extra 10 per cent generated traffic in the short term and 20 per cent in the long term.

The transport civil servants had insisted that 'little or no convincing evidence' had been provided to explain just how roads generate traffic' and until such evidence was available, it would be better to continue assuming that any additional traffic stemmed from economic growth. These were arguments decisively rejected by SACTRA.

It got worse for the roadbuilders. The committee warned – crucially – that 'these studies demonstrate convincingly that the economic value of a scheme can be overestimated by the omission of even a small amount of induced traffic.' In plain English – because the ministry had wilfully ignored the fact that roads generate their own traffic, many of the schemes they approved should in fact have failed any reasonable financial test. This meant in turn, that billions of pounds of public money had been wasted on uneconomic road schemes.

The explosive SACTRA report went to ministers in May 1994, and was waiting on the desk of the Ulsterman and physicist Brian Mawhinney, who took over from MacGregor as transport secretary in July that year. Mawhinney broadly accepted SACTRA,[317] and one of his first steps as minister was to order a review of trunk road proposals. Policy slowly began to edge away from industrial-strength road building.

In October, the planned public inquiry into the 14-lane M25 was postponed for a year. In April 1995, the ministry began a cautious back down. Mawhinney announced that the M25 link roads would be scrapped, just days before he was due to meet a delegation from Surrey. Instead, however, the existing carriageway of the M25 would be widened to five lanes in each direction between junctions 12 to 14 and 15 to 16, and six lanes over the most heavily used stretch, between junctions 14 and 15.

The axing of the 14 lane scheme was seen as a victory for Mawhinney – who seemed much less keen on road building than his predecessor – as well as for the environment secretary John Selwyn Gummer. In cabinet, the two were ranged against an alliance of Michael Hesletine and Michael Portillio who wanted the 14 lanes on the grounds that road building benefited the economy – one of the key points of the *Roads For Prosperity* white paper.

Six days before Christmas 1994, the SACTRA report was published – officialdom had finally accepted what protesters had told them all along – that roads really did generate their own traffic.

Labour ended 18 years of Conservative rule in 1997 and, as it had promised, started to review the Tory roads programme. The July 1998 roads[318] review promised a new approach, transport minister Gavin Strang saying that 'simply predicting future levels of traffic and building new roads to accommodate it is no solution.' The £6 billion road programme inherited from the Tories would be scaled down to just £1.4 billion.

However the position on the western part of the M25 was thought to be so acute that more widening was called for between junctions 12 (M3) and 15 (M4) at a cost of £94 million at 1998 prices. But widening between junctions 15 and 16 and junctions 16 and 19 would be scrapped.

Friends of the Earth claimed that the real reason for the widening was the planned fifth terminal at Heathrow which ministers approved in 1999. This was also opposed by Surrey County, and there was some evidence that the road civil

The M25/M23 junction at Merstham. Drivers never get a view of the vastness of this interchange. Note the number of trees – engineers and politicians often pointed to the huge tree planting schemes when challenged by environmentalists

servants wanted to make approval of Terminal 5 conditional on M25 widening, even though Labour's transport minister, John Reid told another M25-land MP, Phillip Hammond, that Terminal 5 was not a deciding factor in the widening, Hammond replied that official denials of any link was something 'which no-one believed locally.'[319]

The 1998 roads review called for another study of the M25, this time to be set fully in its strategic context. This was carried out by Kellogg Brown & Root, a leading US consultancy, and reported in Spring 2002 as the London Orbital Multi-Modal Study (Orbit).[320]

Unlike the 1990 RPT report, Orbit put the motorway squarely in its social context. As a result, it could point unequivocally to root of the constant traffic jams – the growth of a dispersed, car-dependent way of life in the outer suburbs beyond London. Reading Orbit conjures up a true nightmare; the possibility of the exurban sprawls of Los Angeles or Houston being recreated in the densely populated south-east of England.

The Orbit study made it clear that the M25 had become a case study in the law of unexpected consequences. The root of the problem is that the M25 is now doing something very different from what it was built to do. The idea of the outer orbital ringroad was explicitly to divert traffic – especially heavy lorries – away from London and small towns in the South East towards the Midlands and North. That was why it was generally supported by the communities it passed through.

Another aerial view – the M25/M11 junction at Theydon Garnon, Essex

What in fact happened was that the M25 transformed the dynamic of the south-east of England. As Michael Thomson warned back in 1969, the road generated its own traffic because it made journeys possible which were impossible before.

This fact fitted in with the birth of new technology industries, often US-based multinationals, which preferred to locate near to motorway junctions and within easy reach of Heathrow. (US executives expect to be met at an airport and have a short journey to the office). These companies were not generally businesses fleeing high rents in central London, they had, by and large, never been based there in the first place. Instead, they established greenfield campus-type sites designed to be pleasant places to work and with ample free parking, That way, their staff could drive to work, instead of being forced to use what they saw as being expensive and unreliable public transport.

These business parks and offices in M25-land were not just dispersed from the centre of London, they were often on the edges of the towns in M25-land too; that was where the land was cheap and available, and where the space existed for car parking.

The Orbit study came up with more interesting information on how the M25 has helped set up a pattern of life more reminiscent of the USA than of Europe. It found that;

- About half the traffic was going to work
- Many overall trips were very long with over 40 per cent being more

than 100 kms – yet the average use of the M25 was often quite short, with over 40 per cent travelling only one or two junctions
- Average car occupancy for commuting was just 1.15 people per car
- Public transport was a very inconvenient alternative to M25 commuting, quite apart from peak-hour overcrowding on railways
- Britain's culture of job insecurity was itself driving congestion; 'Increasingly,' the team noted, 'jobs are less secure and people are unwilling to move house to be nearer a job which they may have to change in the foreseeable future.' And so they would drive long distances to keep their jobs, and try to live where there were many job opportunities. With many households having two cars, it was unlikely that both partners could both live near their work and so one at least would be forced to drive, possibly for a long distance.

Car prices, the Orbit team noted, had not increased in real terms over a long period (and had actually decreased in very recent years), and the price of fuel in terms of pence per mile had also fallen in real terms.

The planning system was totally ineffective in halting all this car-dependent sprawl. The Orbit team referred (with apparent approval?) to some very pessimistic research the Town and Country Planning Association (TCPA) carried out for the DoE. It observed how throughout the 1970s and 80s the middle classes had been fleeing what they saw as a dirty and crime-ridden capital with poor schools in favour of a nice house in what became M25-land; a nirvana where there were no derelict buildings, post-industrial legacy or unskilled workforces.

The TCPA study concluded that: '. . . if one really wanted to reverse the self-reinforcing trends towards decentralised residential and employment locations, the most effective means of doing so, perhaps the only effective means of doing so, would be to substantially curtail the use of the car.'[321]

John Stewart of ALARM, which fought off roadbuilding schemes in the Thatcher/Major era, points to the fact that while motorways always generated huge opposition, the building of business parks often goes through on the nod, despite their ability to generate traffic as getting there usually demands driving.[322]

The comparisons with the US can be overstated of course. The UK has nothing like the exburban edge cities of the US, places with five million square feet of office space, 600,000 million of shopping, and an environment where there are more jobs than bedrooms on what was empty land only 30 years previously.[323]

The best known business parks in M25-land, although large, are nothing like this size; Stockley Park has 1.5 million square feet of office space and Bedfont Lakes one million. Both are a few miles from Heathrow and boast tenants such as Cicso, IBM, Apple, BP, Canon and Toshiba. Some 8,000 people work at the Stockley Park site which, needless to say, has no direct rail link. Buses to Uxbridge tube or Hayes and Harlington main line station take 20 minutes. But planning restrictions mean neither is likely to expand to US dimensions. Or feature a shopping mall either.

Even so, according to the one property expert, Emma Goodford of Knight Frank, M25-land now has 130 million square feet of office space 'and that's the equivalent, I suppose, of 100 towers at Canary Wharf.'[324]

That 130 million square feet is, then, an impressively large amount. When much of it is accounted for by exburban business parks, it is wasteful of land, and damaging to the environment as it forces unfocused, car-based commuting

Alarm activist John Stewart

because public transport cannot work as well in such a dispersed environment. They thus became the main contributor to the M25 congestion that the ministry – with its myopic refusal to accept the importance of generated traffic – never expected. It was why their traffic estimates were way off, leading to successive demands for widening to produce more capacity.

All this was entirely to be expected, based on the US experience. As early as 1985, traffic snarl-ups in US suburbs caused by the rise of car-dependent edge cities were a hated fact of life. One US academic was able to write a book called *Suburban Gridlock* where he documented in detail how, as far as 20 miles from the downtown cores of Houston, Los Angeles and Washington, peak-hour traffic had gone from free flow to gridlock in just five years along some stretches.'[325] Once again, UK officialdom ignored those bits of the American experience it didn't like.

So we have built up a picture of an orbital ringroad, designed as a through route but which has become a commuter route, with a large percentage of traffic being car drivers making relatively short journeys which were impossible before it was built. It serves offices which would never have been there without the building of the motorway.

There is no serious debate about the accuracy of this picture, and it has left policymakers with a huge dilemma. Labour's then transport secretary, Alistair Darling, accepted this analysis, telling the Commons in 2003 that because of the development which had taken place alongside the M25 over the past 20 years, 'it is increasingly used not just as a through road.'[326]

DoT figures confirm that on some of the most congested sections, it isn't lorry drivers using the great ringway, it is private motorists on their way to and from work in dispersed, low-density M25-land. In the year 2012, for example, HGVs accounted for just nine per cent of the traffic on the dreaded junction 13 – junction 14 section. On the section between junctions 26 and 27 near Potters Bar, it was still only 14.6 per cent.[327]

All this shows the real price for the way the M25 was planned and built piecemeal and with too many junctions, so encouraging short distance traffic movements.

The M25 directly stimulated another huge source of its own traffic – the out-of-town shopping complexes at Thurrock Lakeside in Essex and Bluewater across the river in Kent, relatively depressed areas where planning permission was easier to come by than in the Thames Valley.

The scale of these is huge; Bluewater, opened 1999, gets 27 million visitors a year. Over 7,000 people work there, and with a range of cinemas, it is an entertainment centre too. Lakeside had opened some nine years before and another expansion is underway. This has a 1993 railway station – Chafford Hundred – next to it. But there are only two trains an hour in each direction and the station was mainly aimed at serving a new estate of starter homes where more than half the flats were repossessed in the 1990s housing slump.[328]

But at least Lakeside has a station; the architectural critic and urbanist Owen Hatherley was shocked when he found that 'there is literally no way of turning up and just walking into Bluewater.'[329] The centre is right next to the planned new town and Eurostar station at Ebbsfleet, but it is still unlikely to become a US style edge city – it is in the wrong part of M25-land for prestige office developments.

Both centres are aimed squarely at the motorist, and over 93 per cent of

Bluewater's 'guests'[330] arrive by car. Both sites have parking for 13,000 cars, and with the M25 they have a catchment of millions. Drive east along the A2 on a nice weekend and you can see a subset of these millions, stationary on the M25 above, waiting to go shopping.

By the time of the 1990 RPT report, the impact of these centres was unclear, although the experience of the US was unequivocal as to what would happen. Stephen Joseph of the Campaign for Better Transport[331] points to these centres as a key player in the M25 crisis, saying that 'it was quite unforeseen by its planners, who were using traffic models which did not allow for changes in journey patterns and new developments.'

John Selwyn Gummer, the Tory environment secretary, halted most of the growth of out-of-town shopping centres in 1994, arguing that they damaged established town centres and small businesses, and contributed to an environmentally-damaging rise in car usage. But the other genie had already been let out of the bottle and the trend for new businesses to set up in the western part of the M25 corridor continued unabated. The existing business parks are not going to go away, and absent a huge increase in teleworking, their workers will need the M25 to reach them.

The boom in office development in M25-land meant that the Orbit study seemed trapped. Despite its incisive analysis of the problem, it still concluded that if current trends were to continue, traffic levels would increase and all users, including those essential to the economy, would suffer increasing congestion and unreliable journey times. The only solution, therefore was a further bout of road widening to dual four lanes all around the M25.

However Orbit insisted that any widening had to be part of a broader demand management programme, including area-wide road charging, otherwise the benefit would soon be lost.[332] Orbit pointed to the hard evidence; widening the section between junctions 9 and 10 to four lanes in each direction upped road capacity by 33 per cent, but just one year later, traffic was up by 36 per cent. All the gains of that expensively-built additional road space had been lost.

Exurbia – a view of the Stockley Park business park near Heathrow

The government agreed with the easy part of Orbit – and widening at a cost of £1.6 million entered the Highways Agency's road building programme in 2004. Area-wide road pricing, however, got nowhere beyond a feasibility study.

One of those behind this feasibility study was Stephen Glaister, now of the RAC Foundation. He was prompted to re-read the 1964 Smeed report on road pricing and said 'I was amazed: there was nothing of substance in the draft 2004 document that had not been dealt with in the Smeed Report.' He concluded that 'Smeed's advocacy of road user charging frightened the politicians of the 1960s into putting their heads deeply into the sand, just as did the Road Pricing Feasibility Study in 2004.'[333] Twelve years on, we are no further forward.

The widening – in true M25 tradition – turned out to be another disaster. The £3.4 billion widening project – including a maintenance contract – was not signed until 2009 under the Private Finance Initiative, a controversial scheme where risk is allegedly transferred to the private sector. From the beginning, the Highways Agency wanted to widen the motorway rather than introduce hard-shoulder running, something successfully tried on the continent since 1996. It took five years before plans to trial this were announced, and a further eight years before hard-shoulder running began.

The Commons public accounts committee subsequently exposed some hair-raising bungling in Whitehall. It turned out that in March 2008, the then transport secretary asked for reassurance from the Agency that widening was still the best solution. The agency insisted that savings from hard shoulder running would be more than offset by extra costs, making it £53 million dearer than widening.

But the MPs probed more deeply, and it turned out that those extra maintenance costs of £193 million for hard shoulder running should have been discounted to reflect the fact that they would be spread over the 30-year life of the project. Sticking with widening therefore built on a technical error in the calculation, which concealed the fact that hard shoulder running would have been cheaper.[334]

The committee chair, Margaret Hodge, said that Whitehall's mishandling could cost the taxpayer an extra £1 billion.

The new four lane sections, between the M40 and the A1 at South Mimms, and between the M11 and the Dartford Tunnel were opened in May 2012. The lesson was learned however – extra capacity between junctions 23 to 27 and junctions 5 to 7 was provided by hard-shoulder running – now known as smart motorways – where drivers are directed onto the hard shoulder at especially busy times with variable speed limits enforced. These sections opened in 2004. A further smart motorway section between junctions 25 and 27 was completed in late 2014.

Instead of the hard shoulder there are regularly spaced emergency refuge areas, with an emergency telephone. When a driver has to pull over to the hard shoulder, CCTV allows controllers to close the hard shoulder by displaying a red 'X' on the gantries. Smart motorways provide a cheaper way of expanding capacity, and with less disruption than a traditional road widening scheme. However there may be a price to pay for all this; Edmund King of the AA has already raised safety concerns with the minister over the effect of what he calls 'widening on the cheap.'

In any case, none of it did any good. The leader of Reigate council in Surrey said, after the widening was completed, 'it is now finished and the M25 is just as crowded. It has done nothing to solve the horrendous traffic problems in our borough.'[335]

Today, only the least-used section between Swanley and Sevenoaks, whose construction was accompanied by so much controversy, still keeps its original three lanes in either direction.

Some 13 per cent of all the UK's motorway traffic is now on the M25 even though it only accounts for six per cent of total motorway mileage; jams are so frequent that the M25 has been dubbed the London Orbital Car Park, and one enterprising writer even published a guide to routes which avoided the M25.[336] The AA reports that the most common search term on its online route-finder services is 'avoid M25.'[337]

The road enthusiast website SABRE reckoned that 'we are rapidly going back to where we started, with drivers trying to find other routes around London to avoid the M25. Of particular nastiness is the M4-M40 section, which is crammed with traffic that has been there since the early nineties.'[338]

There have, however, been one or two slight straws in the wind suggesting the the boom in M25-land might have levelled off. In September 2014 Amazon announced that it was relocating staff from Slough to London's uber-cool City fringes.[339] Separately, Steve Norris, the former Tory transport minister, points out that Google has rented a huge amount of space in the King's Cross development 'because the kind of people they want to recruit are the kind of people who don't want to live in Slough or Reading.'

But there is still no obvious solution to the M25 issue. Future widening schemes look highly unlikely and the office development in M25-land is here to stay too, along with the traffic it has generated. So motorists will just have to live with the congestion. Edmund King at the AA says one quick-win improvement would be for accident scenes to be cleared much more quickly than happens at present. But he adds 'it's a funny road, lane discipline on the M25 is nothing like as good as it is on the M1 or the M4, but when when traffic is light, people still drive more slowly. Perhaps it's because there are more junctions, or perhaps it just because its a circle, although why that should matter I'm not sure.'[340]

The M25 was surely inevitable, and probably necessary too. But the piecemeal way it was built, together with official refusal to consider its ability to generate its own traffic, was the direct cause both of its congestion, and the knock-on effects to the environment and quality of life in London's exurb which it largely created.

7 – Ghosts

Although the inner Ringways were officially dead, and the 1977-1981 Tory GLC administration of Horace Cutler made no attempt to revive them, their ghosts continued to haunt London, as the North Circular remained under Whitehall control.

The ghosts walked quietly at first; there were few sightseers and no would-be exorcists. In 1976, the eastern extension of the North Circular was approved with little objection. This part of Ringway 2, safeguarded in 1968, stayed in the final, approved version of the GLDP. The plan was to build a 5.5 mile South Woodford – Barking Relief Road (SWBRR), taking the North Circular along the valley of the River Roding to the A13 in Newham.

On the existing North Circular, the 1961 master plan continued to be executed in carefully separated stages; grade-separated junctions were built at Neasden Lane (1973) and Harrow Road (1975), along with widening to three lanes in each direction, The section through north-west London became, exactly as was intended, a fast pseudo-motorway, offering a clearway from Hanger Lane all the way to Brent Cross. Several Whitehall files in the National Archives actually refer to Ringway 2 in east London as being the M15.[341] It is unknown whether the entire North Circular would ever have been renamed the M15.

In 1977, the M1 reached Staples Corner and the North Circular was carried over both the M1 terminus roundabout and the nearby A5 by a long viaduct, ironing out yet another major bottleneck. Despite the popularity of the Brent Cross centre, the zone around these interchanges is one of the most unpleasant in all of London, with high levels of noise and pollution and a deeply unfriendly environments for cyclists and pedestrians. It gives a good impression of what some of the ringway junctions would have looked and felt like however.

A 1971 plan for a flyover at the A10 Great Cambridge Road roundabout in Edmonton was blocked after locals complained that 480 homes would be knocked down. Scaled down schemes in 1973 and 1980 were scrapped as the latter still needed 100 homes to be demolished. A revised underpass finally opened in 1990.

In 1979, a major extension of the North Circular entered the government's trunk road programme. It became known as the East London River Crossing (ELRC), and it followed the exact alignment of Ringway 2 to Falconwood in south London. This ringway ghost was not silent or stealthy at all; it was a noisy, sinister, chain-clanking spectre, and the fight to lay it became the landmark battle against strategic road building in Britain.

Two radial routes too, were also on the government agenda. The first was the M11 link from Leytonstone to Hackney Wick. Like so many road plans this scheme dated all the way back to the Bressey report via Abercrombie and the GLC's primary road plans in the 1960s. By this time it had become known as the M11 Link road. The M11 was already open to the North Circular and Redbridge Roundabout and the plan was to take this to Hackney Wick where it would join the East Cross Route.

The second was in north London, where the government wanted to widen Archway Road to build a lorry route connecting the M1 to the London Docks. This was an old aspiration; the scheme had entered the trunk road programme in 1962 and five years later, ministry forecasters said that Archway Road would be carrying 180,000 vehicles per day by 1981. The LCC had approved the widening between Archway Roundabout to the Hornsey Lane overbridge (known as Suicide Bridge) in 1963 and it was carried out by the GLC in the early 1970s. But Suicide Bridge marked the boundary of the old LCC area, and so beyond it, responsibility for the road lay with the ministry. Archway Road became one of the most famously disrupted road schemes ever.

In 1979, Margaret Thatcher became prime minister. Road building was now likely to become a much greater priority, and public transport correspondingly less of one. Less then two years later, Labour regained control of the GLC and Ken Livingstone soon became leader on the back of plans for better and cheaper public transport and opposition to strategic road building. The course was set for ideological conflict.

Livingstone's GLC road policy insisted that road schemes must have a benefit greater than their impact, while avoiding ones where environmental or traffic changes were negative, where there was additional risk to cyclists or pedestrians, where through traffic would benefit at the expense of local movement, or where there would be severance of communities, lost jobs through demolition, or delays to buses.

Step one in Livingstone's plan was to understand exactly what schemes the GLC's engineers had been working on, so his key transport lieutenants, Paul Moore, and Dave Wetzel, a former Hounslow councillor and bus driver, called for a complete list. They got it on 19 June 1981 and it listed 163 schemes of varying complexity. Among them was the West London Relief Road, an elevated, four-lane dual-carriageway bypass for Earl's Court Road and Warwick Road. This had been proposed by the GLC road engineers together with Kensington and Hammersmith councils only a year after the Labour GLC scrapped the inner ringways. It was, of course, the unquiet spirit of the West Cross Route, a project which, in the minds of road engineers, had never really died.[342] The report produced for Moore and Wetzel noted that 'no detailed design or consultation has been done and so the level of public support was not yet known.'[343]

Two weeks later, the GLC transport committee scrapped a whole set of road projects, and warned officers that in future, all projects had to meet the new approval criteria. Wetzel recalls today: 'we put in a plan to give a numerical reference to all approved road schemes and made it clear that action would be taken against anyone working on anything which wasn't on this list.' [344]

Eventually, only four major road projects were committed by the GLC;
- The Hayes Bypass, a popular local plan which extended The Parkway further north as dual carriageway
- The north-south route through Tottenham and Enfield
- The Docklands northern relief road
- The Rochester Way Relief Road (successor to the 1960s Dover Radial Route) from the southern end of the East Cross Route eastwards through Eltham. The new team came just in time to make sure that the road – opened in 1988 – was built in cutting rather than elevated as was originally planned.

Wetzel and Moore also moved to end secret road widening plans. The GLC had powers to require a developer to set back new buildings further behind the existing frontage to allow for future road widening. This power was never used, but informally, developers agreed to it to help smooth planning permission. Moore recalls; 'we inherited a whole set of road widening proposals that were never really official, Upper Street in Islington is a good example, and you can

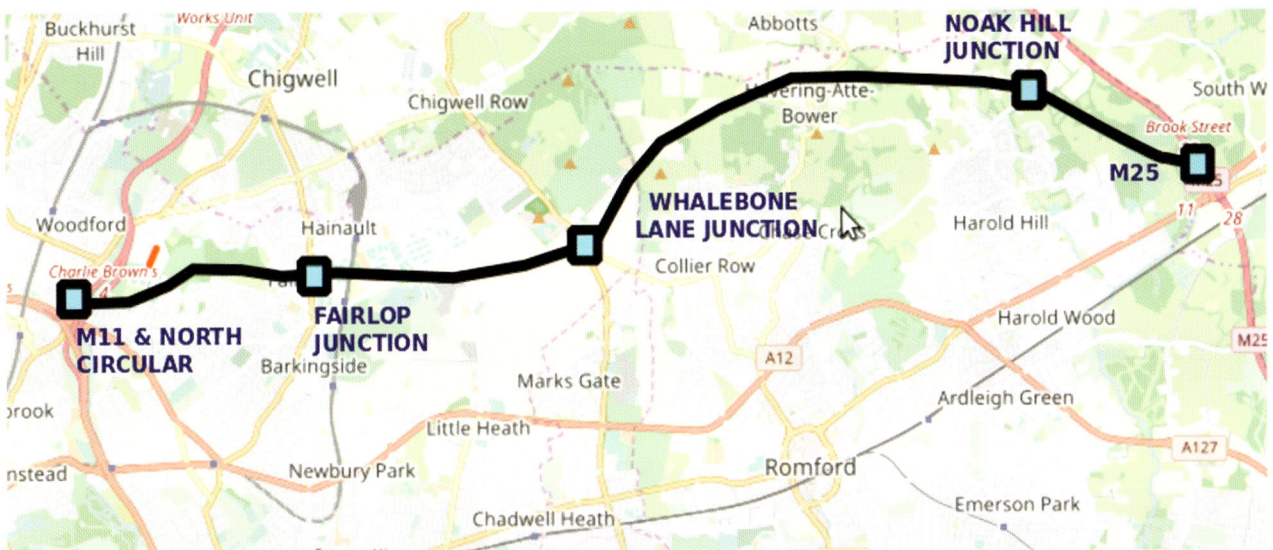

Route of the M12 from South Woodford to Brentwood

see the places where widening was planned by new developments which are set back further from the existing frontages.'

It turned out that there were over 100 secret widening lines of this type, but on 7 October, the transport committee laid down that 'officers shall no longer make safeguarding deals with developers' and that 'no further safeguarding to be approved except by the full committee.'[345]

However the GLC could not stop road programmes controlled by Whitehall; it could object and protest – but nothing more.

With reservations, the GLC had supported the South Woodford – Barking extension of the North Circular. In 1980, the ministry announced its preferred route, bang on the line Ringway 2 would have taken. Some 50 houses would be demolished, but the GLC was also concerned about the environmental damage from a huge viaduct – with its associated interchanges – over the A118 and the railway at Ilford.

The ministry had ruled out a tunnel here as it would add £30-40 million to the cost, and it didn't want an underpass either; its engineers felt that the nearby River Roding represented a flood risk, as well as being a more expensive option.[346] There was a palpable sense of urgency that this road should be built as soon as possible to help regenerate London's collapsing docklands – the last ship was to call at the Royal Group of Docks in 1981 and unemployment was skyrocketing. The argument that road building helped urban regeneration was highly intuitive and frequently asserted – but actually open to question.[347]

But when the GLC's environmental concerns couldn't be resolved, it decided to object in principle at the public inquiry. It was to no avail; construction started in 1984 and the road opened, as a dual carriageway, in 1987.[348]

South Woodford could easily have become London's Spaghetti Junction. Today, the M11 terminates here, although until 1964, it was planned to follow the east side of the heavily-industrialised Lea Valley, to terminate at Temple Mills near Stratford. But the government found that a route down the Roding Valley would save £265 million in today's money. Over 2,000 people objected to the Roding Valley route and the local action group was an active participant in the LMAG struggle against the ringways.[349]

South Woodford would also have been the terminal of the M12 to Brentwood, (Abercrombie's Radial Route 7). This would have started at the western end of the Brentwood bypass before running mainly through farmland to the north of Harold Hill and Collier Row towards and South Woodford. It also tied in with the proposal to build London's third airport at Foulness in east Essex.

The M12 was to have four lanes in each direction between the M11 and Fairlop and three further east. Some 90 homes at Fairlop would be demolished. A GLC report also admitted that houses at the south end of Vicarage Road, Woodbridge Court and Roding Lane North would 'be subject to high levels of traffic noise, visual intrusion and loss of amenity.'[350] The M12 was finally cancelled in 1994 as part of Brian Mawhinney's review of the trunk road programme.

Time was running out for the GLC though. Although the flagship Fares' Fair scheme, London's first attempt at sustainable cheap fares, was struck down by the House of Lords at the behest of Tory-controlled Bromley council, the GLC went ahead with other pro-public transport policies which outraged ministers, who believed that London's economy instead required heavy investment in improved roads.[351]

In 1983, Mrs Thatcher, buoyed by a resounding general election victory, moved to end the opposition to her polices – and the resultant heavy public spending – from the GLC and other metropolitan councils. But rather than fighting to remove Livingstone at the ballot box, Thatcher proposed instead to scrap the GLC and the metropolitan counties entirely. A white paper – *Streamlining the Cities* – duly appeared in October 1983.[352]

A government consultation document discussing the proposed abolition said that 'the GLC has not faced up to the task of modernising and improving its part of the road network and has failed to tackle London's traffic problems effectively.'[353]

The roads lobby in London had been relatively quiescent since the defeat of the inner ringways. Its focus had been on provincial battles where opposition to road building was less organised and where victory was more likely.

The BRF had formed a new softly-softly lobby group – Movement for London – in 1975. Much thought went into how this should work, and its public image, given the stinging defeat they had experienced when the inner ringways were cancelled. The name was carefully chosen, according to BRF internal documents, due to 'the desirability of choosing a title which did not unnecessary encourage antagonism.' The word 'transport' was deliberately avoided since it was thought that the word would make people 'think in terms of buses or trains.'[354]

But the reality was the same – an industry lobby group campaigning for new roads to be built. Its membership was almost identical to that of the BRF's London roads working party and was chaired by Sir Alex Samuels, the man who tried to revive the central London A Ring back in 1954. Secretary was Andrew Warren, who switched from being the BRF London campaign coordinator. Warren had joined the BRF in his twenties and today he recalls having to convince what he called 'dyed in the wool reactionaries' that the ringways would never be built as the money just wouldn't be there. Instead, he thought, the BRF should focus on battles they could win, such as completing an outer orbital road and improving the North Circular.[355]

In early 1983, with the political environment rapidly improving, the BRF produced a new pamphlet *To Keep London Moving,* which contained a whole set of demands for new roadbuilding. On 14 March, a BRF delegation met Nick

Ridley, the environment secretary, and his deputy, Lynda Chalker. The minutes[356] noted that there 'was much common ground between the BRF and the department and that both had an interest in mobilising support at all levels of public opinion.'

The BRF delegation explained that they wanted to see more government intervention, and more roads under direct ministerial control. But despite the obviously cordial atmosphere, Chalker pointed to the 'problem of public antagonism to urban road construction, particularly in London.' Ridley added that it would be better for both the BRF and the government if 'the federation were able to show that they had mobilised the support of a wider, grass roots section of public opinion and that they were not simply a pro-roads lobby. In short they needed to win some friends.'

The Commons transport committee then weighed in by recommending that a new Metropolitan Transport Agency be set up.[357] The government wasn't keen on this; it could end up being rather too democratic. All the London boroughs would need to be represented on it, which would make it unwieldy and, in the words of a candid 14 March 1983 reply from Ridley's transport department, 'would make it very difficult to make decisions on controversial schemes or to carry them through against the opposition of individual boroughs determined to uphold their own local interests.'[358]

The letter added that consultants should be employed to work out, in connection with the boroughs, a '10-15 year road improvement programme within which priorities would be assessed and resources allocated. Particular stretches of road would then be trunked, so that improvement schemes could be carried out.'[359] Trunking meant control would pass from local councils to Whitehall; the 65 miles of trunk roads included the South and North Circulars, the A3 through Wandsworth, The A41 through St John's Wood, the A1 and the A23.

The minister already had powers to turn a normal road into a trunk road, under the 1980 Highways Act, but he faced the irritating drawback of having to tell the citizens six weeks in advance, and then hold an inquiry in case of objections.

The pro-road transport civil servants would also get reserve powers over 305 more miles of road. The bill to enable the switch also vested huge powers in the transport secretary to direct the London boroughs as to how powers they would inherit could, in fact, be exercised.

Opponents of road building were not deceived. West London Traffic Reform, an umbrella organisation representing 24 groups – mainly in rich Chelsea – said that 'the DoT has longed for the day when it could get it hands on London's main roads and implement the old Motorway Box scheme.' Its secretary, Betty Woolf, called the plan 'a midnight coup.'[360]

At Archway Road, meanwhile, inquiry followed inquiry as protesters successfully disrupted proceedings. Blight had set in as properties were acquired prior to demolition. Michael O'Halloran, the local MP, said that 33 shops and 121 other properties were disappearing, leaving 7,000 people with no shopping facilities. His successor as MP for Islington North, Jeremy Corbyn, said 'instead of it being a thriving local community, it will be reduced to a concrete canyon with no shops and no life.'[361]

Over 4,500 people objected, and the campaign got very rough. Among those who joined the protests at the inquiry was Ken Livingstone. The first inquiry in September 1975 ended when the inspector fell ill after proceedings had been disrupted 10 times in eight days. A second attempt was disrupted when police ejected 30 protesters. When the ministry announced a third inquiry under a third inspector, Ralph Rolph, protesters noted that as an inspector he had approved other roads at inquiries. One of the most militant, George Stern,[362] said; 'as far as we are concerned we would be better off with Judge Jeffreys.' [363]

This turned out to be a bit unfair – Rolph asked the ministry to reveal its secret internal figures on traffic growth and analyses of traffic movement – which it steadfastly refused to do. Among the reports which protesters wanted was that relating to an abandoned plan to widen the A1 along Aylmer Road through Hampstead Garden Suburb. In 1977, ministers had refused to publish this as it contained proposals which, if published, would blight peoples' houses. But if Archway Road were widened, the pressure to do the same at Aylmer Road would become irresistible. Rather than reveal this information, the ministry abandoned the inquiry.

Plans to widen the North Circular Road to a dual carriageway from the A1 junction at Henly's Corner to the A1000 in Finchley – a route through Margaret Thatcher's own constituency – were subject to similar disruption. This was another old scheme, originally supported by the Conservative GLC in 1971, but deferred. Determined protesters here forced two inspectors to resign, but unlike at Archway Road, they eventually lost the battle and the road was widened.

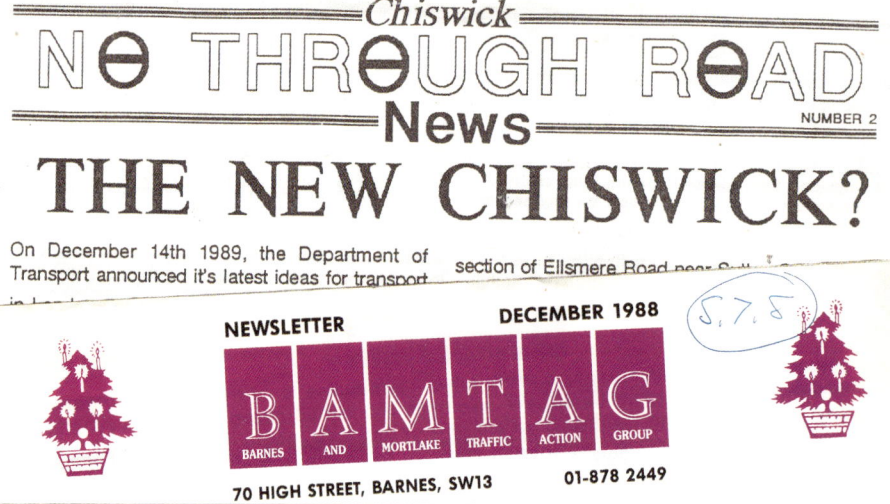

1984 – Local anger at the return of the ringways

COBA – cooking the books

The Archway inquiry was one of several which exposed the extent to which the government's cost-benefit analysis system, used to assess the value of road building, was flawed and had led to billions of pounds being wasted and massive damage being done to the environment.

This system – COBA[364] – then in its ninth incarnation – attempted to compare the cost of the road with the benefits of building it, expressed in the time saved by drivers and the monetary value given to this. It sounds perfectly reasonable.

In fact the system was damagingly broken. COBA9 assumed than 80 percent of the benefit from road building came from savings in driver journey times. There was an undeclared assumption here that people would value these slightly faster journeys despite the destruction that road building meant. In other words, COBA9 specifically excluded the environmental, social or wider economic impacts of a project. One group of anti-road activists said 'COBA is not science but has enough of science in it to sound plausible.'[365]

There were other holes too;
- COBA9 ignored traffic generation, and so its calculations of time savings were being consistently overstated. This meant that – in its own terms, and ignoring environmental damage – many roads built did not make economic sense if honestly assessed
- It assumed that traffic levels would keep on increasing. In reality, they would tail off as congestion kicked in
- COBA9's calculation expressed a financial profit or loss on the project as Net Present Value. But these were assessed not on percentage but on absolute size, so an NPV of £20 million with a return of 15 per cent was preferred to an NPV of £1 million and a return of 45 per cent. The system was thus biased towards big trunk road projects

Even if the COBA figures didn't add up, there was always room for manoeuvre; at the first ELRC inquiry it turned out that the road had a negative value; costs were higher than benefits for drivers. The matter was resolved by deciding that the motorists who would use the road were engaged in important work and so their time had a greater than usual value. A correction of £14.5 million for this factor turned the COBA value into a positive one.[366]

The COBA regime did not apply to railway proposals – they usually had to show a straight financial benefit before the transport department would approve. If COBA had applied instead, many railway projects which were blocked would have shown a positive return.

In 1986, SACTRA roundly criticised the use of COBA to plan urban roads because it ignored traffic generation, the impact of road building on public transport, and did not even consider the cost of maintaining the road in the future. It could no longer, said SACTRA, be justified 'intellectually or in practical terms'.

The problem of forecasting was shown up at Archway Road. In the same year as the SACTRA report, the road was carrying 30,000 cars a day, meaning that the government's forecasters were out by a factor of six. They had obviously based their forecast for traffic growth on the assumption of widening, making their forecasting an entirely circular activity.[367]

In November 1984, Nicholas Ridley followed up the white paper by appointing engineering consultants to carry out a set of assessment studies investigating transport problems across four areas of the capital. There is no doubt that what he wanted was a new master plan for road building across London. Lynda Chalker admitted this when she told the Commons that 'we are considering commissioning a number of assessment studies about the possible options for improvement of London's roads and the local environment over the next 10 to 15 years.'[368] At the same time Ridley abandoned the Archway Road inquiry, subsuming it into one of the new assessment studies.

The chain-smoking, acerbic, Ridley was the driest of dries – he first voted against Conservative government bail-outs of nationalised industries in 1961 and was the architect of the strategy to destroy the miners' union. He had a civil engineering background and a deserved pro-roads reputation – he had attacked the GLC for allegedly letting roads deteriorate while spending money on public transport, tried to stop the GLC prioritising local traffic at Talgarth Road on the A4, and fought a night time ban on heavy lorries. But like the BRF, he tried to follow a softly-softly approach, insisting that there was 'no plan for massive motorway building....sensible traffic management measures, local diversions, improved junctions, and possibly some new lines where it is absolutely essential' could solve congestion.

Opponents were not taken in. One of the militant Archway protesters, Nina Tuckman, said Ridley's schemes were 'clearly the secret manifesto for building motorways all over London which Archway Road campaigners claimed had existed for years.'[369] The GLC, now on its last legs, replied 'I told you so.' On 20 November 1984 Paul Moore said Ridley's statement 'puts into black and white what we have been warning Londoners about for more than a year – if the GLC is abolished, the government will immediately step in with massive road building plans.'

The GLC was not playing idle politics here – it soon came up with hard evidence. In 1985 its researchers looked in detail at traffic statistics for the Blackwall Tunnel, before and after the second tunnel was opened. In a remarkable paper, they found that peak hour traffic had increased by 106 per cent in the morning and by 104 per cent in the evening. No surprise there as capacity had been doubled.

But there had been no significant changes on the other three river crossings. Minor decreases in traffic on Tower Bridge and through the Dartford Tunnel could not account for a doubling of traffic at Blackwall. That meant that the doubled traffic didn't stem from people changing their journey to use Blackwall instead of existing tunnels. There was only a limited bus service through the tunnel, and only one railway (the little-used East London Line) crossing the lower Thames. So it was unlikely that many travellers had abandoned these for car transport.

It therefore looked pretty certain that almost all of the extra traffic using Blackwall during this initial period was generated traffic.[370]

The GLC's researchers duplicated the exact same result across other road corridors, including the Westway and the North Circular. Official refusal to consider this sort of evidence, the fundamental point that you could not solve travel congestion by building roads as they generated their own traffic, made it clear that Ridley and his civil servants were pursuing an ideologically-based transport agenda which had no evidential basis.

Ridley's assessment studies would look at
- West London, including the western end of the South Circular, together with the possibility of a relief road to replace the Earls Court one-way system;
- The main section of the South Circular between Woolwich and the A3 at Wandsworth;
- The area between the A1 in Islington and the A102 in Hackney and Tower Hamlets;
- The corridor through London to the south.

Four consultancy firms were given the work – the assignment came out of the blue to them – this was not work they had previously bid for. The consultants were each given one of the areas and told they had a blank sheet of paper on which to write.

The assessment studies worried British Rail, which had just emerged from a bruising battle with some of the more extreme Thatcherites who wanted to convert railway lines to motorways. This battle saw a serious attempt to close Marylebone station to provide an express busway. One of the advocates of this scheme was Alfred Goldstein, the Travers Morgan senior partner who had served on the 1981 Serpell committee, which recommended decimating Britain's railway network. Goldstein was also a friend of Alan Walters, Mrs Thatcher's adviser, another great proponent of converting railways to roads.

The DoE assured David Kirby at BR said that the studies were not designed to reopen that debate but said that the consultants would be looking at sharing of corridors, especially to build a new version of the West Cross Route. A report from another BR executive – Chris Austin – to the BRB policy unit warned that 'the criteria for the assessment studies are drawn in a way which is very likely to result in a recommendation for highway improvement in the corridors concerned.' Austin was worried that this would benefit the coach operators who were BR's natural competitors.[371]

The coming of the assessment studies generalised the battle against road-building once again. Building of the SWBRR had started the same year, and plans for the inquiry into ELRC were well advanced, but these could still be presented as essentially local schemes with no capital-wide relevance. That changed with the corridors to be considered by the assessment studies; it was now frighteningly easy to draw a map suggesting that the return of the ringways was nigh, affecting, once again, millions of Londoners.

The result was massive protest, coordinated by a group called ALARM – All London Against Road Menace. It soon had over 200 affiliated local groups, and ALARM acted as an umbrella. ALARM was led by John Stewart from south London, still campaigning today against plans to expand Heathrow Airport. Another key activist was Jonathan Bray, now head of the Passenger Transport Executive Group.

Strangely, there were few people involved from the earlier battles against the ringways although the connection to them was repeatedly drawn; John Stewart says activists 'were often people new to campaigning. They benefited from experience from people like Friends of The Earth, and the Highgate group were really influential; they taught people a lot about not trusting inquiries and consultations. And they had great credibility, they had seen off four inspectors and the Archway Road was never widened.'[372] Important support for ALARM came from Transport 2000, which was originally set up by the rail unions in 1972

An ALARM view of the North Circular widening schemes

with backing from British Rail. Friends of the Earth produced useful guides to the road schemes and how to object to them.[373]

In the highly politicised 1980s, this was a very different campaign to its predecessors. There was none of the view that reasoned arguments could change official minds (Blackheath, 1965), no acceptance that some roads *might* need to be built (North Surrey, 1970), or disputes at inquiries over alternative routes (Leatherhead, 1971). There was just militant opposition to all roads, coupled with a positive demand for investment in sustainable public transport.

Bray argued that road building had to be fought by a mass political campaign; having valid and correct arguments wouldn't help in themselves as you could just be ignored by authority. You had to go out and build a movement large enough that it simply couldn't be ignored. ALARM was clear on the tactics needed to fight officialdom; 'you couldn't cooperate with the system – by the time it gets to an inquiry you've already lost it. We made it clear to the groups that there could be no discussion of alternative routes, we agreed on total opposition, and no friendship with officials – they were the enemy.' Equally, he thought that direct action would probably lose as the government couldn't be seen to back down; the battle had to be won politically by starting early so politicians could be made to understand that road building was going to be a vote loser for them.[374]

John Prescott reckoned that the plans would cost £7.3 billion and involve the demolition of 2,470 homes[375] Jeremy Corbyn, whose Islington home was at risk, complained that these costs would be paid by the taxpayers, 'yet a much smaller cost of £2 billion for the Central London rail study would largely be borne by the fare-paying public, either through interest charges to private investment being put into the rail system or by increased fares for those who wish to use the central London rail system when it is developed.'[376]

In July Corbyn presented petitions to the Commons signed by more than 3,000 people in Islington, Over 13,000 signed a petition opposing the Chiswick to Wandsworth plan in the West London assessment study.

Opposition was cross-party, Wandsworth council, the flagship for Tory local government in the late 1980s, released a document,[377] supported by all parties, demanding no major road building, proper enforcement of on-street parking,[378] traffic restraint, and large-scale investment in public transport. One Tory councillor, Peter Bindle, admitted that the road plans could lead to a Tory defeat in the upcoming council elections.[379]

The transport department, meanwhile, had come up with a novel way of minimising the property blight that the studies would cause; it told councils that the planned roads should not appear in property searches unless specially requested with reference to the assessment studies.[380] Property became blighted again, but as these were just discussion options not concrete proposals – no compensation was payable.

ALARM showed a talent for the kind of publicity stunts designed to keep protest in the public eye. On one occasion, ALARM organised a mock valentines day card campaign, saying 'I Love London – you are killing it'. It culminated in Cynthia Payne, the famous madam, turning up at the DoT to give Cecil Parkinson, who had succeeded Ridley as environment minister, a two foot long Valentine's cake with a pink heart sliced by a big black road. *Private Eye* reported that civil servants took it and 'looked forward to sampling it in due course. Then Cecil walked into the room and on sight of the cake, flew into a rage. White with anger, he ordered the offending confection to be removed and destroyed immediately.'[381]

On another occasion ALARM organised a mock funeral march with crosses bearing the names of threatened roads and buildings.'[382]

ALARM insisted that ELRC formed part of a secret government plan. It called it 'a DoT trojan horse, extending the North Circular into south London which will lead to the construction of a south London orbital motorway.'[383] ALARM was convinced that the continuing improvement plans for the North Circular were really a proxy for building an inner M25. But by claiming that individual improvements were merely local solutions to local problems, the DoT hoped to split any opposition and prevent any coordinated protest against the actual concept.

One of the key figures in People Against the River Crossing, chest consultant Dr Barry Gray, referred to the environmental disaster to be inflicted on south London by 'the corpse of a dead, discredited, ringroad scheme of which ELRC is surely a part.'[384]

Then, as now, there was no cross-river road connection between the Blackwall Tunnel and Dartford, but if ELRC could be built, and once all of the North Circular had been improved and widened, it would provide a fast route between the midlands and the channel ports. And unlike the Dartford Tunnel, where a toll had to be paid, using ELRC would be free.

ELRC would start at the A13 where it would join the South Woodford – Barking road. It would run via Beckton and cross the Thames via a new bridge to Thamesmead in Greenwich. It would then continue via a 26 feet viaduct at Plumstead, and carve its way through Oxleas Wood, an area of ancient oak woods which was a Site of Special Scientific Interest, before terminating on the Rochester Way Relief Road at Falconwood. It would need 240 homes demolishing, along with 20 commercial properties and put 50-100 jobs at risk.

The ruin of Oxleas Wood, one of the few remaining areas of ancient deciduous forest in London, made it a key focus of opposition to motorway building at precisely the same time as the assessment studies were taking place. Road planners tended to build roads through open spaces wherever possible, as it was cheaper and generated less opposition than knocking down peoples' homes. But by now, environmental concerns had risen, and Oxleas Wood became a potent symbol of the casual and wanton damage officialdom would do to the environment unless stopped.

The GLC was originally in favour of the ELRC as it promised to be an integral part of plans to revitalise London's derelict docklands. But opinion under Livingstone was rapidly hardening against it.

In September 1985, the public inquiry started, lasting until December 1986. In July 1988, Ridley and Paul Channon, transport secretary, jointly approved the road. Oxleas Wood won a last-minute reprieve however, for the owners of London

A path through Oxleas Wood – not a motorway

City Airport decided that they wanted to operate jet aircraft, and that meant that the ELRC bridge would be too high.

The DoT issued new proposals for an ugly concrete box girder bridge in August 1989. To minimise the protests, it told the 3,000 original objectors that their objections would be disregarded unless they wrote in again.[385] The tactic misfired, 7,200 objections poured in and the case for a brand new inquiry into ELRC looked unanswerable.

Meanwhile, behind the scenes, the assessment studies were beginning to backfire on the ministry. The four consultants met among themselves to discuss the brief and agree a common approach. They agreed that the first step had to be to begin at the beginning – define and understand the actual transport problems instead of starting from an assumption that more roads were needed.

Terry Hill ran the East London area study for Arup, and he recalls going back to the ministry and insisting that if they really had a blank sheet of paper, then the work couldn't be called the East London *Road* Assessment Study – the key word 'road' had to come out as it contained an unverified assumption. Hill, who rose to become chairman of Arup and collect a CBE for his contribution to engineering, has no doubt that the studies were inspired by Margaret Thatcher 'who wanted to build roads and thought that London needed a proper road plan.'

Travers Morgan, in particular, supported Arup in its fight to deliver an open report with no preconceptions. The ministry gave way.

But this clash took place behind closed doors, and the consultants faced great hostility from people convinced that they were planning the return of the ringways. The GLC said that putting engineering consultants in charge of such studies was 'like letting the foxes guard the chicken coop.'[386]

In east London, Hill and his team found that some councils wouldn't even talk to them. He recalls ' I spent months just talking to people in clubs and pubs to find out what their problems were and what they wanted. I had my notebook out and never even drew a line on a map.' Unofficial meetings with council planners had to take place in pubs outside of working hours.

Arup distributed 200,000 questionnaires to homes across the area and had a good response. Hill soon realised that the people factor was going to be central and even recruited a sociologist to the team to try and understand what lay behind the data. He learned something interesting too; 'I found that the people were almost always right – when they said that a particular bus route was unreliable or that a given junction was dangerous, we compared it to the facts and it turned out that they were almost always right.'[387]

In August 1985, while the consultants were busy producing their problem statements – the output for phase one of the studies – a report from the auditor general said that the government wanted to spend £1.5 billion on trunk roads in London. The GLC helpfully suggested where this windfall might be destined; it included the West Cross Route, Eastern Avenue extension, the M23 north towards Streatham, and a vastly upgraded South Circular Road.

Consultations rapidly showed that better public transport was wildly popular and big road programmes were not. Hill says that 'by a factor of two to one people were much more concerned about poor public transport than traffic congestion.' These findings didn't do down at all well with the ministry and there was serious pushback up to permanent secretary level; Hill recalls 'we were being asked whether we had listened too much to the public transport lobby and whether we had not captured the view of the silent majority, that sort of thing. We all stuck

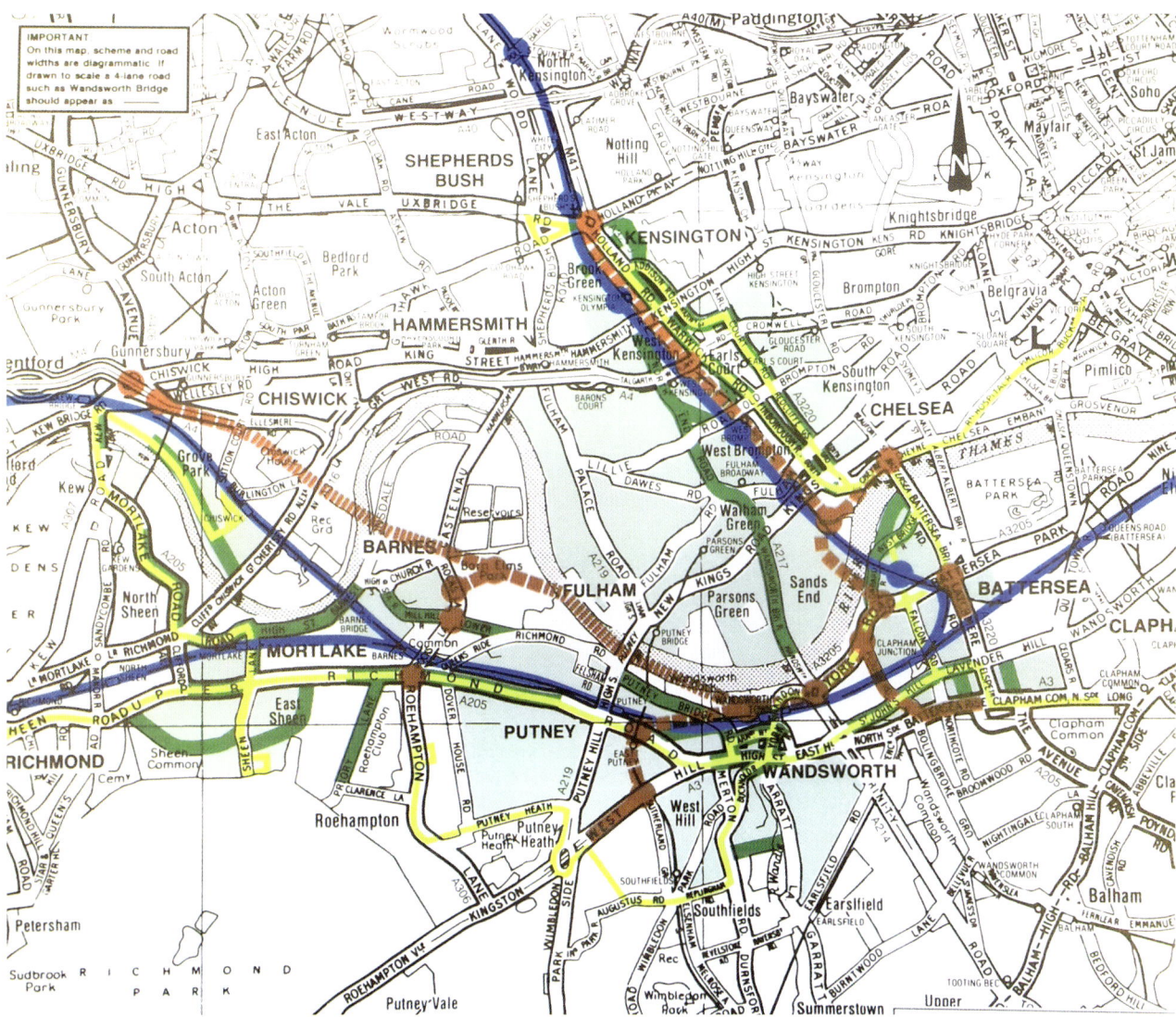

One of the options from the West London Assessment Study. New road options are in hatched brown and the return of the West Cross Route and Ringway 2 are startlingly obvious

to our guns, but it was clear that we would would have to include some options for road schemes in the phase two report.'

The government released the phase one studies late in 1986, studies which only gave ammunition to the opponents of road building. That from Arup revealed that people were more concerned about poor public transport than road congestion, and shot down a traditional argument for orbital ringways – 'the main desire is radial movement to central London – rather than orbitally around it.'[388]

In 1987, announcing the terms of reference for the second – options – stage, Peter Bottomley, the junior transport minister, carefully gave himself space to backtrack. He insisted that he was 'convinced' of the importance of public transport and warned that we would have to accept some limitation on car use in central and inner London, if not planned through parking control or traffic management, then unplanned by congestion.[389]

The complete studies were eventually published in the summer of 1989. They had cost £8.5 million to produce and were a very different product to the GLDP.

However they still laid major road building options down for the minister to consider. The gist was as follows:

South Circular – consultant: Travers Morgan[390]
This started with 14 options, reduced to three for further consideration. They were; road improvements on the South Circular Road itself, a £500 million toll relief road running to the north of the South Circular, through Brixton, Peckham, Lewisham and Eltham. This would cost £500 million, needing the demolition of 1,000 homes, or a £400 million route to the south running through Tooting, Streatham, in tunnel under Crystal Palace before running to Penge and Eltham. 800 homes would be demolished under this option.

Travers recommended the first option – upgrade the existing South Circular with a tunnel at Forest Hill. But they coupled this with a recommendation to extend the Docklands Line Railway to Lewisham, and the East London Line both north and south of the river.

East London – consultant: Ove Arup[391]
Three schemes were singled out to provide economic returns, a £50 million to £100 million traffic management scheme with severe parking restrictions, a £1.5 billion tunnel toll road plan, and a £1 billion road scheme. The toll road plan was intended to take traffic from the A1 through the City to Docklands. It would need tunnels building from King's Cross to Old Street and from Old Street to the Isle of Dogs. Toll roads would connect to this from Tottenham, the M11, the Royal Docks, and the A1 at Highgate Wood.

The alternative route would have cost 3,000 homes as well as £1 billion in cash. It mapped a route from Highgate Wood to Caledonian Road and King's Cross, plus new roads in Stoke Newington, Highbury and Dalston and a by-pass in Hackney.

Ove Arup's East London Study stood out from the others by the attention it gave to public transport. It proposed that a number of railway projects should go ahead, including the long promised Chelsea to Hackney tube; an east-west cross-London rail route; the Jubilee Line Extension (JLE), a Docklands Light Railway extension to Lewisham; and the East London Line extension to Dalston over the disused Broad Street viaduct. Terry Hill notes they they listed the rail schemes in order of return on investment, and the one which was by far the best bet – the Chelsea to Hackney tube – 'is still not in place, while the JLE was built – that's politics for you.'

West London – consultant Sir William Halcrow[392]
This study covered Kensington, Chelsea, Putney, Barnes, Wandsworth and Chiswick. The options it proposed depended on whatever was chosen to enhance the South Circular Road.

These were drastic options. The first – costed at £500 million – planned a road from Chiswick Roundabout to Clapham Common. It would cost £500 million to build, need 600 homes to be demolished, take part of Barnes Common and close the railway between Barnes and Chiswick.

The second option was costed at £1 billion and would take this route to link up with the relief south circular. It would need a four-mile tunnel under Wandsworth from the A3 to Trinity Road and 300 more homes would need to be pulled down. In addition, Halcrow revived the West Cross Route extension south from Holland Park Avenue – now rebranded, sanitised and greenwashed as WEIR – the Western Environmental Improvement Route. It would run to the river where it would split to join Wandsworth and Battersea Bridges. Another option extended this across the river to Battersea. The roundabout at Holland Park Avenue would be replaced by a flyover, and there would be another flyover complex at Cromwell Road

South London – consultant: Mott Hay and Anderson[393]
This gave 'particular support' to two schemes which would link to the proposed south circular relief roads. A £1.2 billion scheme would build a road running parallel to the A23 to the west of Purley to the new south circular with connections from Sutton and Croydon. Alternatively £1.5 billion could be spent building a road direct from the M25 running parallel to the A23 before joining the improved south circular around Streatham.

This study also recommended that the Charing Cross branch of the Northern Line should be extended from Kennington to Streatham and Norwood, as well as the building of a light rail transit system in the Croydon area.

In these studies, then, we see very clearly the ghost of the ringways walking again, with property blight imposed for years, huge demolitions of property required and vast costs to the treasury, which, would, as usual, turn out to be underestimated.

GLC publicity campaigns explicitly made the connection, referring to 'the infamous ringway proposals abandoned in the 1970s following a public outcry.'[394] The actual match between the routes of the ringways and some of the new proposals was remarkable; both options in the Travers Morgan study essentially meant reviving either the South Cross Route, or the southern part of Ringway 2; the Mott Hay & Anderson report was essentially about the northern extension of the M23 and how it would link to the ringways. The Halcrow report again revived the West Cross Route, plus the section of Ringway 2 from south London to Chiswick roundabout.

However the Halcrow study did accept that roads generated traffic. They thought that there would be two per cent more traffic as a result, which was small in terms of environmental impact, although it would be much greater on individual roads. But Halcrow also warned that 'any of the options would be very expensive to implement. None of them shows a positive economic return on investment when evaluated in the narrow context of monetary savings...'

Just before Christmas 1989, the transport secretary, Cecil Parkinson backtracked a bit further. Although he had just published a document stating that it was a 'fundamental part of the government's approach that peoples' aspirations to own and use a car should not be artificially constrained',[395] he now ruled out a slew of options, saying that 'I am prepared to go forward only with the new road schemes that will bring significant overall benefits, taking full account of the environmental effects.'[396] These would go to a final round of consultation until the end of February 1990.

A week later, Robert Atkins, under-secretary of state for transport, took another step backwards. He admitted – in a letter to Stephen Joseph of Transport 2000[397] – that it was 'not possible or desirable to meet forecast levels of demand.'

In March 1990 Parkinson backed down completely and killed the schemes off. He told parliament that there would be no new roads built apart from improvements in access to Croydon and south London from the M25 and Gatwick, and junction improvements and local widening on the South Circular.

This was a huge surprise, and Stewart called it 'a complete cave in.' He thought it partly reflected local council elections due that May, where the Tories were desperate to hold onto Wandsworth council.

The climbdown was carefully justified on the grounds that the ministry had merely asked for proposals from consultants – they were the consultants' proposals and not those of the government. Parkinson, the accountant son of a Lancashire railwayman, was like Mrs Thatcher, no friend of public transport. But he told the Commons that the consultation showed;

- Strong support for improvements to public transport.
- Widespread opposition to most of the major new road schemes suggested by the consultants.
- Support for proposals to slow traffic in residential areas, both to improve safety and to deter rat-running.
- Recognition of the need for better traffic management but concern about the level of traffic and a wish to see higher priority given to buses, cyclists and pedestrians.

Protest – on a London-wide scale and involving all communities and all parties – had fought off the ghost of the ringways. It meant the end of vast-scale attempts to solve London's traffic problems through road building across the city's urban areas.

The assessment studies themselves had an entirely unlooked for effect; by accurately tracking public demand and logging how much road building would cost they showed up public opinion in stark relief. Edmund King, then at the BRF, says he expected the schemes to be canned; 'they were just too big, if they had concentrated on just two or three they might have got them done.' Terry Hill remains clear on the big-picture impact; he says 'the assessment studies killed all major road building in London for a generation.'

Parkinson did however announce a trial-run of a new concept contained in the studies – the red route. This idea was based on the Axe Rouge in Paris where stopping was banned to help speed up through traffic, The first red route pilot covered the A1 from Highgate to the Angel, round the inner ring road to Aldgate, and on to Commercial Road. That left two big projects still ongoing and still to fight, the ELRC and the M11 Link.

The second ELRC inquiry had started in July 1990. To minimise objections, it was held at Stratford in the East End, even though most objectors lived south of the river. The inspectors also refused to hold evening hearings, meaning that many objectors could not attend. The juggernaut rolled; on 27 September 1990 Michael Heseltine and Malcolm Rifkind announced their joint decision to proceed with ELRC.

Protesters gathered support at Greenwich market, politicians were systematically lobbied and a well-presented public transport alternative was drawn-up. Opponents argued that ELRC would be a through road which would not benefit local people in relatively deprived communities.

In October 1991, several members of People Against The River Crossing cycled to Brussels to meet with the EU's environment commissioner, Carlo Ripa di Meana. He agreed that the UK government was breaking EU law by not commissioning environmental impact assessments for ELRC, or the M11 link and the M3 at Twyford Down near Winchester.

The next month, ALARM organised an 'Adopt-a-Tree' scheme to get every tree in Oxleas Wood adopted. As well as bringing in funds and publicity, it would give supporters a real stake in the campaign. And if the bulldozers moved in, activists planned to invite tree adopters to turn up to defend their tree. A 'Beat the Bulldozer' pledge was launched, with the aim of getting 10,000 people to pledge to be there if the bulldozers went in.

ALARM proved astute strategists; they consciously tried to make Oxleas Wood a defining battle for the environment movement, and the Wildlife Trust and the World Wide Fund for Nature both joined an Oxleas Strategy Group. This helped lock them into a campaign that was ultimately run by local people, but which made the best use of the resources and experience of the national campaigns.

During all this, the protests at Twyford Down were all over the TV screens; millions saw essentially non-violent protesters being brutally manhandled by security men working for the government. ALARM strategists had wanted to make a stand at Oxleas Wood precisely because the wood was in London; the catchment area for support – if it did come to mass action – was very wide and TV executives are always interested in stories right on their doorstep.

By 28 June 1993, the government remained intransigent, despite getting a 'Reasoned Opinion' from Brussels, the last stage before the affair was sent to the European Court.

Just seven days later, it backed down. Transport secretary John MacGregor said that while the government was 'fully committed' to a new road link, 'the

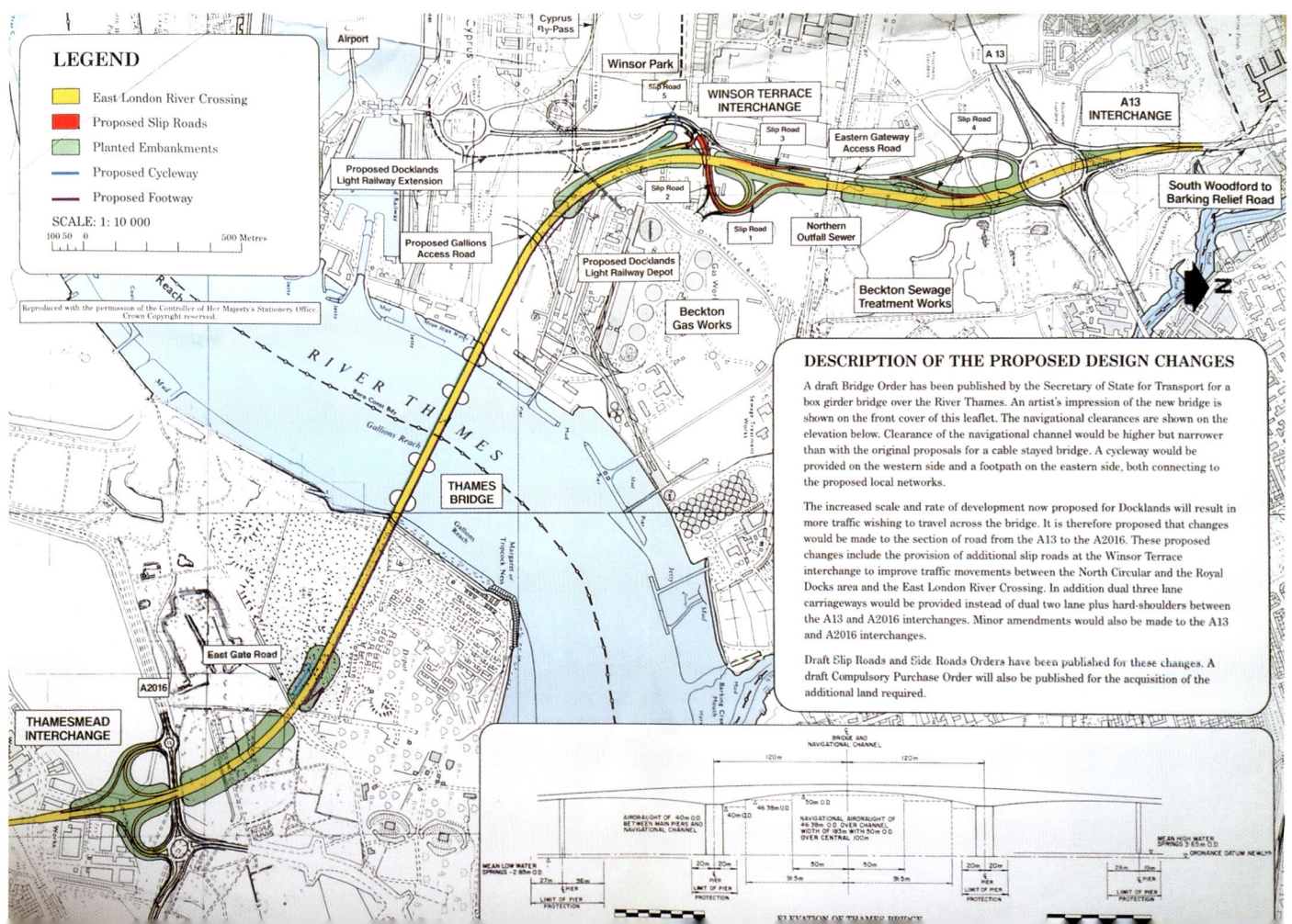

1990 – The official plan for the East London River Crossing

ALARM activist Jonathan Bray

current scheme, designed and chosen some time ago, fails to meet the high environmental standards we now apply to new road schemes.'

Oxleas Wood was saved; Ripa di Meana was among those who attended a huge victory rally in the wood on 31 July.

ALARM activist Jonathan Bray, who led the fight at Oxleas Wood, recalls 'For me the Oxleas campaign had meant hours of hard work in meetings held in draughty halls on dark, rainy nights trying to get the best campaign that I could. For hundreds of local people it had been years of struggle. Was it worth it? Definitely. Oxleas was a turning point. We'd shown how people power could stop roads, a lesson that was quickly learnt right across the country. We'd shown that the environment movement, when it's focused and working in harmony with local communities, could win.' [398]

Protesters lost the other battle – the M11 link – and it was the last piece of the GLC's primary road programme to be actually built in the capital.

The proposed route had been announced in 1981, again on the basis that it would help the regeneration of London's collapsing Docklands, help get industrial traffic off local roads, and stop rat-running through residential streets.

The GLC supported the link in principle, and a GLC/ministry joint working party had been set up to plan the scheme. Like residents, it wanted the route to be tunnelled through Leytonstone to minimise impact. Waltham Forest council supported the road in principle too – it wanted to pedestrianise Leytonstone High Street which had 'become increasingly depressed' as a result of all-day through traffic. There was serious concern from Hackney however, as the road could dump City-bound traffic at Hackney Wick from where it would be thrown on local streets.

Opposition to a tunnel came from the BRF and Movement for London – they argued that a tunnel would be too dear; 'it could only prejudice the completion of many other vital road schemes in other parts of the country.'

The first Link Road Action Group was formed in 1976. For the next 15 years, the residents fought government plans through public inquiries. As elsewhere, planning blight had set in and unwanted property had become home to a community of artists and squatters

The high point of the fight came over the removal of a chestnut tree on George Green, near Wanstead, which attracted national attention. There was mass squatting in houses scheduled for demolition, notably at Claremont Road in Leyton. Usually when property was compulsorily acquired, demolition men destroyed all sanitation to make them uninhabitable. But at Claremont Road, protesters moved in before this happened. One protester recalls; 'The road became well known for the decorations, the street parties, the café, the 'art house', music, theatre and there was even a ghost house. It was something to show to visitors. Because of the street sculptures, no vehicle could be driven along Claremont Road. Opposite the terrace of Victorian houses was the Central Line. It was quiet and a safe place for children to play.'[399]

The protesters were evicted by the police on 28 November 1994 to allow construction to start.

The DoTs figure for demolition was 263, with 500 people displaced. However the No M11 Link Road Campaign reckoned that 500 homes were knocked down with 1,000 people losing their homes. Figures obtained under the Freedom of Information Act showed that the campaign against the road contributed to a 100 per cent increase in costs.[400]

The road finally opened in 1999. It has certainly improved access, but much of it is a bleak brutal canyon with no aesthetic merit. Attempts to build patterns into the brickwork as a way of brightening up the route are a dismal failure and the brickwork is badly stained by years of car exhausts; its four miles always seem longer than they actually are. One protester, Ann Williams, said 'The long-term impact has been a huge increase in air pollution, and it's directly due to the volume of traffic on the link road. That's the most serious aspect of it, apart from the loss of the houses, the trees and a large amount of green space.'[401]

But the government victory at Leytonstone was pyrrhic. Protesters had seen off the assessment studies and ELRC, and since 1991 they had taken ALARM national, to help the dozens of local groups fighting road building In their areas. Oxleas Wood became a powerful symbol of what was possible – Jonathan Bray says; 'before Oxleas we lost every time, after Oxleas, we hardly lost again.'

The achievement of this small group of people was remarkable – unlike the people who stopped the ringways in the 1970s, ALARM and its constituent groups were usually political outsiders. Some were experienced transport campaigners who understood how the system worked, and had no illusions in it. But the majority of those who fought these roads had no campaigning experience at all. And they *were* a small group; PARC had 1,600 paying members, but its regular strategy meetings were attended by only around a dozen people.

An ALARM survey of its own members showed that although 70 per cent were men, most activists were women, and 58 per cent were under 45. They were well educated, with 67 per cent holding a degree, and mainly southern – over half lived in the south, and 22 per cent in London. Overwhelmingly they regarded the environment as the top political issue – hugely ahead of unemployment or education or the NHS. [402]

This coalition had to fight an entrenched and confident Conservative government. The ministers who had defeated the miners seemed unlikely to give in easily to protest over road building, and they showed at Twyford Down that they were prepared to play it tough if necessary and ignore threats of legal action from Brussels. Yet at Oxleas Wood, give in was precisely what they did.

The campaign and the victory helped change official opinion, whose confidence was already slightly jarred by the relentless increase in congestion on the

The eviction of 'Munstonia,' the last squatted house on Fillebrook Road, Leytonstone during the M11 Link protests

M25. The protests against road building had shown how unpopular it really was, and this helped make it a soft target for treasury cutbacks, where the 1994 SACTRA report was to be read with great interest.

The environment department was under pressure to do something to cut CO2 emissions after the 1992 Rio Summit, now that it was clear that cars contributed a huge amount to this pollution.[403] The environment and transport departments now started to disagree with each other.

Road after road started to be cancelled in this climate, and one victory led to another, Calder Valley, Exeter, Birmingham, the M12, Hereford, Salisbury.... the list went on. Some ministry inspectors finally found the courage the challenge the Official Version.......at the inquiry to widen the North Circular across Ealing Common the inspector told the transport department that he didn't believe their assertion that road building did not generate new traffic.[404]

The 1989 *Roads for Prosperity* plan proposed to spend £23 billion on 600 different schemes by the year 2000. By 1998, that number was just 37.

And slowly but surely, the climate of Conservative opinion began to change. In 1992, John Major appointed Steve Norris as parliamentary under-secretary of state for transport and minister for transport in London. Norris was a new type of transport minister. Born in Liverpool, he was a self-made man and he came to the job with a deep interest in, and knowledge of, public transport. He came too, a time when the climate of opinion concerning roads had changed.

'The change of attitude was driven by public opinion – Parkinson only recognised the reality when he killed off the assessment studies – this is democracy – we're only in power because of the last elections and could lose it at the next one,' he says today.

Norris had two obstacles; he had to convince people in his own party that transport did not have to be a political or ideological issue. 'I thought some in the Labour Party also saw it that way and had a public transport good / private transport bad approach, and it was the opposite for us.'

He also had to convince the DoT road branch, stuffed full of road engineers, that the days of Predict and Provide were over and that they had to move to an approach which included public transport and traffic management techniques. Today he remembers the attitude in the road branch as one 'where officials planned a road, crushed the opposition as they would crush the aggregate they used to make it, and then went on to build the road.'

Norris also argued internally for a new dose of realism about what was going to be possible. 'We had £20 billion of approved road schemes which we were delivering at £1.5 billion a year. So the reality was that many of these schemes just would not happen anyway, schemes were constantly being approved, we always had this backlog and the money simply would not be there.'[405]

In 1997 – just weeks before 18 years of Conservative government came to and end, he told BBC that 'I think that protesters were right. They were right and they were there first.'[406]

For road opponents like John Stewart, the arrival of Norris was a breath of fresh air and connections were carefully kept open; 'we saw him as a pragmatic politician who could be an ally.' And historians studying the revival of public transport in London can point to the turning point in 1990 when the Conservatives finally lost the will for mass road building, three years after London Transport hit its symbolic low point with the King's Cross fire. But from 1983, the unexpected happened, after decades of planned decline, London's population bottomed out and started to grow again – and demand for transport was bound to grow with it. If strategic road schemes were definitively off the agenda, then, like it or not, there had to be more investment in public transport.

From 2000, with the restoration of an elected mayor, TfL finally won control of the North Circular, and indeed all other major roads in the capital. And that meant Ken Livingstone inherited a slew of expensive improvement projects from Whitehall which had lain on the table for lack of money.

Livingstone's Mayor's Transport Strategy[407] developed the GLC's 1981 road policy. It laid down that inherited road projects would be assessed against the strategy which required, among other things;

- Improving conditions for pedestrians, cyclists and public transport
- Not increasing the net traffic capacity unless it was essential for regeneration
- Providing a net benefit to the London environment

The Transport Strategy was an emphatic and overdue manifesto for public transport investment. And the North Circular schemes didn't shine when assessed like this – crucially, they breached the rule on not adding substantial new capacity. TfL was also extremely wary about cost overruns – 'there is a history of major civil engineering projects exceeding estimates made at the commissioning of works. As an example, the North Circular Falloden Way contract was tendered at £26 million and there is now a post construction claim totalling £82 million'.[408]

TfL was sitting on three major schemes for the North Circular – one of £266 million to widen the blighted bottleneck at Bounds Green and two costing £183 million to build flyovers or underpasses at Regents Park Road/Finchley Road and Golders Green Road.

That something needed to be done was accepted by everyone; TfL painted a vivid picture of the section between Bounds Green Road and Green Lanes, saying it was 'routed through a densely populated area, predominately residential with commercial and retail facilities and a number of schools.....the resulting congestion, rat-running, severance and inadequate provision for pedestrians, cyclists, and buses is severely detrimental to the local environment and safety.'[409]

But the question, as ever, was money. The Labour government provided a generous financial settlement for TfL in 2004 – money which financed the transformation of the neglected North London Line into London Overground. But it did not provide full funding for the capital programme.

So TfL proposed a smaller scheme where the worst section would be widened to two lanes in each direction. Local councils were unhappy. In Enfield, where rat-running to avoid the congested section was a problem, the council criticised Livingstone's 'failure' to plan for major improvements on the North Circular.'[410] Barnet commented that TfL's plan to sell properties acquired years before would essentially rule out major improvements for years to come. TfL, it turned out, owned no less than 429 properties at Bounds Green, bought for previous widening schemes which were subsequently cancelled. These monuments to failed planning had not had the benefit of 'proper investment and improvement for many years,' and some were essentially derelict. [411] The cut-down scheme finally opened in 2011.

In January 2012, a long-awaited major upgrade of the most important interchange of all – at Henly's Corner where the A1 crosses – was completed ahead of schedule. An underpass here to segregate A1 traffic from North Circular traffic was a long-standing aspiration, but would have been costly, disruptive and, due to the marshy nature of the land, difficult to achieve too.

Yet under Livingstone, ELRC was back on the agenda – rebranded now as the Thames Gateway Bridge. He felt that a new cross-river link would contribute to regeneration in this very depressed area. Although the plan for the full ELRC had been revoked in 1997, an alignment was still safeguarded between Beckton and Thamesmead. [412]

The TGB was to have been a spectacular project, with a span of about 650 metres. There would be four lanes for general traffic, two for public transport, a cycle lane, pedestrian walkways and a DLR crossing. Local road improvements would then be needed at both ends.

TfL proposed charging a toll to cross, but projected revenues of less than £20 million a year would pay less than half the capital cost on a £353 million Private Finance Initiative project to build the bridge.[413] Central government funding would be needed to cover the rest.

The councils at each end – Newham and Greenwich – both supported TGB, but John Prescott, the deputy prime minister, ordered another public inquiry. There were 2,949 objections; among the most devastating came from Friends of the Earth which observed that 49 per cent of homes in Newham and 41 per cent in Greenwich did not even own a car, So who would the bridge really be for? Jacqui Wise, coordinator of the Action Group Against the Bridge, said; 'This was not a local bridge for local people as it was billed. It was never designed to regenerate the area. It was just going to cause worse air and noise pollution.'[414]

FoE quoted a TfL Board member as saying that the scale of the scheme was driven by 'the needs of the car commuter in peak time.' TfL figures showed the benefits of the scheme went mainly to drivers – 94 per cent to cars and goods vehicle and only six per cent to public transport users. [415]

The inquiry heard that 17 million vehicles a year would use the TGB, and according to TfL's environmental statement. by 2016 traffic would grow in in the area by 10-36 per cent, including traffic actually generated by the TGB. Traffic flows would more than double on other roads due to this generated traffic, again according to TfL. There would be heavy jams on the North Circular and the A13 roundabout.

After after 11 months the inspector recommended throwing the scheme out. His conclusions were emphatic;
- If the scheme went ahead, it would generate more traffic
- The whole justification of the TGB was based not on reducing the need to travel, but on increasing it
- The TGB would worsen air quality
- The regeneration model could not be relied upon to any substantial extent to predict changes in employment or population density that might arise from the scheme
- On balance, the scheme would be likely to cause increased congestion[416]

Late in 2008, the new London Mayor, Boris Johnson, confirmed the cancellation of the TGB on the grounds of local opposition, insufficient funding, projected detrimental effects on traffic flow, and concerns over the location and environmental impact.

Epilogue

Today, the M25 is the greatest monument to London's ringway era – the only one which was actually built in its entirety, even if was a mis-mash of various schemes. In the capital, three parts of the inner ringway and associated primary road schemes can be sampled, each of which once enjoyed fully fledged motorway status;
- The East Cross Route, the only part of the Motorway Box to be built in its entirety. It was designated A102 (M)
- The small section of the West Cross Route from the Westway to Holland Park Roundabout (numbered as M41)
- The Westway extension, which became the A40 (M)

All lost their official motorway status in May 2000, and road signs are now trunk road green instead of motorway blue. When Transport for London was set up, these roads had to be reclassified. They were being transferred from the Highways Agency to the mayor: but the Act authorising the transfer did not give the mayor the power to be the highway authority for motorways, So their motorway status had to go, their blue road signs went, and they are now normal A roads, with the West Cross section becoming part of the A3220.

In addition there are the following, none of which ever ranked as motorways.
- The M11 link road to Hackney Wick
- The section of Ringway 2 from South Woodford to the A13
- The Rochester Way Relief Road
- And that part of the Hayes bypass widened as part of Ringway 3

It would seem then, with nothing built since the late 1980s/early 1990s, that large-scale road building in London has ended, with official acceptance that it is a futile answer to traffic congestion. Causes for optimism include the way that public transport has been revolutionised and the way that the central London Congestion Charge is now an accepted part of life. More road space has been given over to cycles and bus lanes, which is partly why central London seems as congested as ever for those motorists who do venture in.

Boris Johnson promised when he ran for re-election in 2012 to set up a working party to take a strategic look at London's roads. It reported a year later.[417] The report was the first such analysis since the GLDP in 1969. It came up with an intelligent list of proposals to better use roads space. But it also warned that investment in roads had badly lagged behind that in public transport while population was rising.

The Roads Task Force fully accepted that traffic generation was a real phenomenon and it proposed several ways that demand could be managed. But it also suggested putting key roads underground – including an orbital tunnel between the North Circular and the inner ring road. To prevent traffic generation, such a tunnel would be tolled.

The plan was accepted and the easier parts are being implemented.

But in May 2014, Boris Johnson publicly supported an Inner Orbital Tunnel and series of 'mini tunnels;' a 22 mile underground motorway with ten access points around London. Burying major roads was clearly influenced by Boston's 'big dig' which buried the chief highway through the city in tunnel. Scheduled to be finished in 1985 at a cost of $2.8 billion, it was actually completed in 2007. Its final cost – $14 billion – made it the most expensive ever US highway project.

Boris Johnson

By early 2015, TfL [418] said it was 'investigating the affordability and feasibility of new road tunnels,' including whether an orbital scheme was feasible. Its update was accompanied by a small schematic map, showing a possible route and junctions. Inevitably there was a close resemblance to the West Cross Route in particular. Even with tolling to curb traffic generation, it seems inconceivable that such a mammoth scheme could survive protest from those living near junctions or drilling sites for what will have to be a deep bore scheme.

Just six months later, the orbital tunnel had been deprioritised in favour of two different schemes, an 18km east-west tunnel linking Hackney Wick to Park Royal, and a second, of 25km to the south from Chiswick to Beckton. With the return of Labour to County Hall in 2016, this has all the marks of a project which will go nowhere fast.

There are more advanced proposals though, in east London, including the Silvertown Tunnel, with a revived Thames Gateway Bridge a lower priority,

The tunnel would provide relief to the Blackwall Tunnel. It would leave the East Cross Route just north of the Blackwall Lane junction, pass under the Thames and emerge at the Silvertown Way / Lower Lea Crossing junction.

There has been substantial local opposition. The No to Silvertown Tunnel campaign claimed it would; 'bring more traffic to Silvertown and the Royal Docks, while it will encourage Kent commuters to drive to Canary Wharf and the City, adding to congestion through Limehouse and Wapping.' [419] Their arguments were a consistent replay of the arguments developed to fight the ringways in the 1960s – building roads only generates more traffic; 'Think of the way the M25 filled up as soon as it was built, and keeps filling up each time it's widened. The building of the second Blackwall Tunnel in the late 1960s saw traffic double within a year.'

The plan went out to public consultation in 2014,[420] Of the 4,300 responses, 84 per cent were in favour.[421] If the tunnel goes ahead, construction could take four years to complete at a cost of around £750 million. The fact that this is seen as a local issue, with no London-wide resonance, means there is a strong chance of

Possible tunnel routes in TfL's Roads Working Party – they seem very familiar from somewhere...

this project going ahead; yet it would be a dearer solution that the TGB/ELRC ghost of Ringway 2. It is almost certain to be tolled however, and that means that tolling will also be needed at Blackwall, inching London a little closer to city-wide road charging. Johnson's successor as mayor, Sadiq Khan, has announced changes to the Silvertown plan to make it greener and more public transport-focused, and also to explore more benefits for local residents who use the tunnel.[422]

In May 2014, the London Chamber of Commerce and Industry called once again for the TGB to be built and received support from Newham council. Even John Stewart says that there might be a case for such a bridge, as long as it were designed for local, short distance traffic and not as a through route, and as long as it formed part of a London-wide traffic management plan.

But long term, there are signs that the great car economy itself may actually have peaked – a phenomenon called Peak Car – and observed in many rich countries including Germany, Japan and the US.[423]

Statistics show that the percentage of those with no car rose in London from 41 per cent in 2002-03 to 44 per cent in 2012/13. In the provinces, car ownership is still rising, reflecting the poor public transport outside London.[424] Car use in the capital, it turns out, peaked as long ago as 1990, when cars accounted for half of all journeys. Today that figure is just 37 per cent.[425]

There is compelling evidence now that in most rich countries, people are beginning to drive less. There are several explanations; the age when young people get their first license is rising, public transport is improving in most big cities, a sixth of Britain's retail spending is now online, and shopping trips have been the type of car use which has clocked up the sharpest decline since the mid 1990s.[426]

Not everyone agrees however, and motoring groups argue that driving will pick up when the economy expands again and the financial squeeze eases on young people.[427] The jury is out, yet in London at least, there is something eerie about Peak Car arriving in 1990 – the year that Cecil Parkinson killed off the London assessment studies.

But if Peak Car is correct, the transport department may be wrong when it continues to predict higher traffic volumes in the future. The rationale for the £15 billion road investment plan announced in 2014 was precisely that traffic was 'expected to grow steadily over the coming decades.'[428] The review paid considerable attention to Peak Car arguments, but concluded that trends working against car use may indeed be having an effect on local roads, but that on strategic routes, traffic was at an all time high.

The ministry argued that falls in car use had been concentrated among men (down 15 per cent), in cities (down 4 per cent) and young people (down 15-25 per cent), while traffic on motorways was up by 15 per cent.[429]

The 2014 proposals concentrated on the strategic network and excluded London, although they did include a major rebuild of the M25/A3 junction as well as a new strategic study of the M25's congested western section.[430]

Terry Hill of Arup predicted that the 1980s assessment studies, envisaged as a way of bringing parts of the ringways back to life, had actually killed off road building in London for a generation. So far the evidence is overwhelmingly on his side. But memories are short – it is now 25 years since Cecil Parkinson killed off the ghost of the ringways. London's population growth is putting extra burdens on transport, and without a London wide traffic-management plan, the prospect of major new roads, while still low, is perhaps not quite zero either.

Appendix – Was your home at risk?

The main source for the detailed routes of Ringways 1 and 2, plus Parkway E, is the GLC's own Background Paper 158 submitted to the Layfield Panel.[431] For Ringway 3 in north-west London, the Brandt-O'Dell report for the MoT,[432] and south of the river Brian Colquhoun's map at Kent County archives.[433]

Ringway 1 – North Cross Route – dual three/four lanes
This would start just to the south of Willesden Junction station, and would run in cutting on the north side of the Overground line crossing under **Kilburn High Road** to meet the M1 link. It then ran between the Midland and Metropolitan lines, passing under **West End Lane** and over **Finchley Road**. An interchange would link the North Cross to Finchley Road.

The rising ground meant that things would then get difficult. The Overground dives under Hampstead in tunnel and so the North Cross Route could not follow it. Instead it would cut through Hampstead, cutting off parts of **Netherhall Gardens**, the eastern end of **Fellows Road** and southern end of **Eton Road**. It would then pass to the south of **Belsize Square**. Much of this section would be built on the cut-and-cover principle

The motorway would then go under **Primrose Hill Road** and over **Adelaide Road** and **Regent's Park Road**. East of there, the 1965 safeguarded route was to the north of **Chalk Farm Road,** but the 1967 route would go in viaduct over BR's Camden goods depot.

Immediately east there would be an interchange with the Camden Town bypass. This would begin from Camden Road and run west in a double-decker structure with the North Cross Route to save land. It would cross **Kentish Town Road** where a slip road from the North Cross and Chalk Farm Road route would join it. It would then descend in cutting on the east side of the railway to Euston before rising to join **Hampstead Road** south of **Mornington Crescent**. It would have run alongside the west of **Oval Road** to pass under the south end of Oval Road, **Gloucester Crescent**, **Parkway** and **Delancey Street**.

Belsize Square NW3; 'the motorway will run alongside the south side of the square'

The North Cross Route, meanwhile, would cross over the railway-strewn lands north of King's Cross to Barnsbury. There might also have been a link road south to King's Cross. BR's 1968 plans to shut St Pancras station also proposed a new coach station which would be linked to the North Cross route by a spur paralleling **York Way.**

The North Cross route would follow the south side of the Overground Line and be partially tunnelled through Highbury in cut-and-cover with **St Paul's Road** being rebuilt on its present alignment over the North Cross route. The southern side of **Mildmay Grove** would be destroyed.

Finally it would rise to cross **Kingsland High Street** on viaduct in order to clear the railway junction at Dalston. A huge intersection with local roads would be built east of the High Street, and the route would stay on viaduct to cross **Dalston Lane** before going back into cutting under **Mare Street,** running to the south of the Overground, until east of **Barnabas Road** where it would rise to connect with the East Cross Route at Hackney Wick.

Ringway 1 – East Cross Route – dual three lanes, dual two lanes through Blackwall tunnel

This route – the only one built in its entirety – began at the Kidbrooke interchange with the South Cross Route and the Dover Radial Route. Running north there is an interchange with **Shooters Hill Road.** Until here the route is officially part of the A2 Rochester Way. Northward it becomes the A102.

The route was then in cutting, passing under **Old Dover Road** and under **Charlton Road** to an interchange with **Woolwich Road.** It is then mainly on the level through the Greenwich peninsula to the Blackwall Tunnel.

On the north side there is a major interchange with **East India Dock Road.** The road is now generally at street level as it traverses a mainly post industrial zone with large council estates. It passes over Limehouse Cut and the District Line to pass under **Bow Road** at the Bow flyover, where the road now becomes the A12. It passes under the Great Eastern main line and **Tredegar Road.** There is a footbridge soon where the East Cross Route severed **Old Ford Road.**

The route crosses the canal towards Hackney Wick, where the road continues as the M11 link, with links to local roads. There would have been an enormous junction here if both the North Cross Route and Eastern Avenue extension had been built.

Ringway 1 – West Cross Route – dual four lanes Holland Park – Chelsea, dual three/four lanes Chelsea – Clapham and Holland Park – Willesden

From the South Cross interchange near Clapham Junction, the West Cross Route rose to cross the Waterloo and Victoria railway lines to follow the east side of the West London line (now part of the Overground), crossing the Thames to a new interchange at Chelsea Basin, then an industrial zone.

Spur roads from here would run to Battersea and Wandsworth Bridges. The former would to go a point in **Cheyne Walk** between **Cremorne Road** and **Battersea Bridge.** The latter required **Townmead Road** widening to dual lanes in each direction and a flyover building to carry this link onto Wandsworth Bridge.

Running north, the route followed the railway, being built partly over it, crossing **Kings Road, Fulham Road** and **Brompton Road.** An interchange would be built at **Cromwell Road,** and the route would then cross over **Kensington High**

Street near Olympia, being built over the railway tracks before joining the interchange at **Holland Park Avenue**. A through road over this roundabout was planned. The section north from here, at ground level, to the junction with Westway is the only part of the West Cross Route actually built.

From here the northward extension would have returned to the eastern side of the West London line, rising to cross over the Great Western railway and the Grand Union Canal, and joining the interchange near Willesden Junction. This linked the West Cross and North Cross Routes with a spur leading towards the A190 west of Gipsy Corner.

Ringway 1 – South Cross Route – dual three/four lanes
From the Kidbrooke interchange with the East Cross Route and the Dover Radial Route the road would have been on the north side of the railway line, passing under **Blackheath Park** in a cut-and-cover tunnel. On leaving the tunnel it passed over the Lewisham-Charlton railway line and then drops into cutting, severing **Pond Road** before passing under **Tranquil Vale** where a short length would be in cut-and-cover.

The route remained on the north side of the railway to Lewisham generally at the same level. There was a interchange with local roads at Lewisham, and continuing towards St Johns the ringway rose to cross the New Cross railway line and remained beside the upper level railway.

From St John's, it followed the Lewisham to Peckham Rye railway at approximately the same level from St John's to **Geoffrey Road**. Here, the railway cutting would be widened on its north side to accommodate the motorway. In the Brockley Cross area, both the existing railway and the motorway were elevated to clear the existing roads.

West of Brockley Cross, the motorway was aligned between the railway and **Drakefell Road** and partly in cutting. At Nunhead the ground falls away and the railway is on embankment, and the motorway followed the same elevation as the railway through to Peckham. From here the route followed the the South London railway. After crossing over **Rye Lane** it met an interchange with local roads west of the shopping centre, and then crossed over to the south side of the railway between Peckham Rye and Denmark Hill stations and went into cutting from **Camberwell Grove** to **Ruskin Park**.

It was then elevated to pass over the Thameslink line at Loughborough Junction and met an interchange with Parkway E at **Loughborough Park**. Ringway 1 remained elevated alongside or over the railway viaducts through Brixton and then regained the south side of the railway and dropped to ground level before rising to clear **Bedford Road** and **Clapham High Street,** where an interchange was planned. It then went into cutting to pass under **Larkhall Rise**. Westward, the ringway remained alongside the railway with an interchange to serve Nine Elms and **Queenstown Road.**

Beyond, there would be a junction. One arm would join the West Cross Route, the other would be a link road to join Ringway 2 at Wandsworth. This would follow the south side of the railway, before crossing part of Clapham Junction station, the Brighton line and the carriage sheds. It then continued elevated alongside the railway line to Putney crossing **Wandsworth Bridge Road** to meet Ringway 2.

Ringway 2. Dual four lanes, A13 – Falconwood, dual three lanes, Falconwood – Dutch House, dual three/four lanes westwards

Starting from the A13 in Newham, the southern part of Ringway 2 would have been elevated and run south between the Beckton Gasworks and the sewage works before crossing the Thames in a dual four lane tunnel. It would have emerged on the south bank near Margaret Ness to join the so-called **Thamesmead Spine Road,** now the A2016. It would then have run almost due south above the Southern Outfall sewer bank, the MoD sports ground. the North Kent line, and **Plumstead Gardens**.

It entered a cutting north of **Plumstead High Street** where it ran to the east of **St Nicholas Gardens**. After underpassing the High Street. The road continued depressed on the west side of **Wickham Lane** between that road and the former GLC Rockmount estate where it would have cut into the foot of the ridge on which high-rise flats had been built.

Opposite **Rutherglen Road**, Ringway 2 curved gently south-west to underpass a diverted **Kings Highway** and was then built in cut-and-cover for a short length under **Rockclliffe Gardens** between the Old and New Woolwich Cemeteries. It then ran on a line to the west of **Camdale Road** having passed the entrance to the Woolwich New Cemetery. It would have passed under the Highmead and Poets' Corner areas in open cutting, continuing below ground level across open ground south-east of Rose Cottage and Hawthorn Cottage Schools. It intersected with **Shooters Hill** at an interchange where the existing A207 would be carried over the motorway on a ground level roundabout.

The ringway continued through Oxleas Wood – no notion of the later controversy in this official description – in open cutting to underpass **Welling Way** and join an interchange with the **A2** and the Dover Radial Route at Falconwood.

From the A2, the ringway continued partially depressed through the north-east part of Eltham Warren Golf Course. For some distance north of **Bexley Road** it was in cut-and-cover where part of the golf course adjoined the former Inner London Education Authority's nature study scheme.

South of Bexley Road it continued depressed below farmland and sports grounds, with a section in cut-and-cover and a further length of cutting before passing under **Footscray Road.**

Ringway 2 would have been built in cut-and-cover across the Royal Blackheath Golf Club. This section finished at the golf course boundary but the route was still in cutting to pass under **Court Road**. West of here the ground falls away quickly and so Ringway 2 would have been elevated across allotments on the southern slope of some steep ground above **Middle Park Avenue**, which the road crossed before crossing the Dartford Loop Line, running parallel with it for a short distance before curing round the the south-west again to cross the proposed **M20** motorway, where there would be an interchange near the Dutch House pub in Mottingham.

From this interchange Ringway 2 was planned to cut into the high ground of Carters Hill above the Quaggy River. It then emerged on the southern slope, crossed under **Mottingham Lane** to enter a short cutting to pass under **Somertrees Avenue**. It continued in cutting under **Baring Road**, rising to cross the railway north of **Grove Park** and over **Verdant Lane**. An interchange would be built with Verdant Lane and **Baring Road.**

From here, Ringway 2 dropped into cut-and-cover tunnel under **Whitefoot Lane** playing fields. It then became elevated to cross **Bromley Road** where there would be a interchange. It continued elevated across Beckenham Hill station before entering a cut-and-cover tunnel through the high ground at **Sedgehill Road**. After a length of open cutting, Ringway 2 passed under **Worsley Bridge Road** where there would be an interchange.

It then crossed over the railway south of Lower Sydenham station and followed the line at about track level before rising to cross the Dover main line east of Kent House station. It then followed the Birkbeck railway line passing over **Beckenham Road** and then dropping to near track level.

It then rose to cross an interchange at **Elmers End Road**, and continued westward to an interchange with the planned Parkway E near **Cambridge Road**.

Ringway 2 then passed under the railway before becoming elevated to cross the line near Goat House Bridge. It then continued in cutting, passing under South Norwood Hill and continuing in cutting to pass north of the shops at South Norwood and Thornton Heath.

An interchange was planned with local roads at **Grange Road**. Near Thornton Heath it followed the railway to Norbury in cutting at about the same level as the track, At the **A23** junction in Norbury, Ringway 2 became elevated at an interchange.

It would continue elevated over **Glencairn Road** to run north west along the alignment of **Ellison Road** before passing under the Victoria – Brighton railway. It would then pass under **Streatham Vale** and cross **Abercairn Road** to a major junction with the M23, whose slip roads would have required further destruction.

Ringway 2 then continued in cutting to pass under the Streatham – Mitcham Junction railway before becoming elevated westwards following the curve of the railway. It would have passed over **Streatham Road**, dropped into cutting to pass under **London Road** and continued in cutting following the Tooting to Haydon's Road line to reach a major interchange with the **A24** at Colliers Wood.

The motorway would be in cutting at Colliers Wood but it would soon have become elevated beside the Tooting to Haydon's Road line until it reached the sewage works, where it rose further to cross over the railway into the Wandle Valley. The motorway then crossed **Plough Lane**, the Waterloo – Exeter main line near Earlsfield, **Penwith Road** and **Kimber Road** to reach the Wandsworth Interchange Area.

Leaving the interchange the route crossed to the north side of the railway line to Putney. It would have been generally at the same level as the railway, in a widened cutting just south-east of Barnes Common.

This section here was one of the least well planned, but the road to join the North Circular at Chiswick roundabout would presumably have followed the railway at the same level as far as **Beauchamp Terrace** (Barnes Common). before cutting northwards towards Chiswick, via a new bridge over the river.

M1 Link – dual 3 lanes

From Staples Corner on the North Circular, the extended M1 would have run under the North Circular Road Viaduct and then south over the railway sidings at Cricklewood, over **Cricklewood Lane** and then along the east side of the St Pancras – Leicester main line. It would have crossed over the railway near **Mill Lane** to reach the North Cross Route interchange. All of this section would have been elevated apart from a short section below ground level between **Minster Road** and Mill Lane.

Ringway 3

Tracking Ringway 3 is easy in the north-east quadrant as this was built as planned and now forms part of the M25. This section begins at Swanley, Kent, goes under the river at Dartford and curves round, via key junctions with the **A13, A12, M11,** and **A10** to a point with the **A1** at South Mimms near Potters Bar.

From here. the M25 takes a north-westerly course using a brand new link to join what was the North Orbital Route west of Watford.

West of South Mimms, Ringway 3 was never built. It would presumably have gone south-easterly toward a new junction with the M1 near Bushey at Caldecote Hill. However the exact alignment seems not to have been planned.

From here, however, the route was planned in detail and the alignment given here is the final route, based on the work of the MoT's consultants Brandt O'Dell. It would have run in cutting between existing properties and below the **A411** before crossing open land west of Bushey Heath and **Oxhey Lane** where an access point would have been provided for Watford. The route would have continued in shallow cutting through **Margeholes** and Sherwoods Wood before passing under the Euston-Birmingham railway and **Prestwick Road**, and then crossing the open space at Oxhey Warren in cutting between housing estates.

It would have continued across **Sandy Lane** and through scrubland between the golf course and the backs of homes on **Westbury Road**. At Moor Park, the route would have used a strip of open land to approach the high ground of Batchworth Heath and thence run north of Mount Vernon hospital.

There would have been an elevated crossing of the Metropolitan line and local roads and it would have crossed below the **A404**. Access to this road would have been from Batchworth Heath, north of the hospital. From here, the route skirts north of Lockwell Wood and then below **Shrubs Road** and **Northwood Road** west of the reservoir, swinging south through Green Belt land towards Bourne Farm and skirting the western edge of Bayhurst Wood.

A spur to the A40 at Denham Roundabout left Ringway 3 at this point.

Ringway 3 itself ran south-east, crossing **Newyears Green Lane**, **Breakspear Road**, and the river Pinn, to the golf course at **Clack Lane**. It crossed above the B466 at the bridge approach near West Ruislip station. It then ran southwards via Ickenham Marsh to cross below the A40 west of RAF Northolt. It continued through open ground to Cuthroat Wood, crossing **Charville Lane** and **Kingshill**

Abercairn Road SW16 – 'a number of houses which will be severely affected should be demolished'

Road, and thence through open space north of Yeading brook to join the **The Parkway,** part of which was widened by the GLC as part of Ringway 3. After **Faggs Road** the route would have ran between Bedfont and Feltham and to the river, where a new bridge would be needed to take Ringway 3 across the Thames to Sunbury.

South of the river, little detailed information exists. Potential lines on maps never became engineers' drawings because a definite route was never agreed and there were various ideas at various times, including a stretch running just to the north of Croydon town centre. Probably the best impression comes from maps produced by the DoT consultants, Brian Colquhoun, in 1971 which can be found in Kent county archives.

This suggests that the outer option would have started at the Sunbury junction with the **M3** to run south-east inbetween Walton-on-Thames and the Queen Elizabeth II reservoir. The route continued to meet the Waterloo – Exeter railway just east of Hersham station, and continued along it past Sandown Park racecourse and Esher station.

It then crossed the railway to run south-east, crossing the **Esher bypass** at an interchange, towards a junction near Chessington South station. From here it ran south-east, and to the east of Horton Mental Hospital. It crossed the Waterloo – Dorking line south of Ewell West station to an interchange with the **A24**, and then a crossing with the Croydon – Sutton line just west of Ewell East station. From here it would have headed south-east past Horton Hospital to follow the Epsom Downs railway for some distance at Banstead where there would be an interchange with the **A217**. As the railway curved away to the north, Ringway 3 continued eastwards, passing two more huge mental hospitals to the north before an interchange with the M23 northern extension at **Woodcote Road**.

It continued eastward along the south side of Croydon airfield, via an interchange with the **A23**, before crossing the Brighton railway north of the stations at Coulsdon, and then crossing the Oxted branch just north of Riddlesdown station. It then curved round the edge of Purley Downs golf club and turned north-east parallel to the **A2022 Addington Road**, passing Selsdon Park Golf Club to the south to a point just to the north-east of New Addington. In this area there would have been an interchange with **Parkway E**. This is a hilly area and substantial engineering works would have been needed here.

From here the route was almost due east, passing between Keston and Downe where there would be an interchange at the **A223** Bromley – Biggin Hill road, north of the High Elms golf course to another interchange with the **A21**. The final stage passed over the Dover main line just north of Chelsfield tunnel before curving north-east back to Swanley.

The inner option would have ran from Cranford, via the valley of the River Crane to cut of the western part of Hounslow Heath before crossing the BR Hounslow Loop over the former Feltham marshalling yard, today a major Royal Mail sorting office.

From here it followed the Crane again to an interchange with the **A316** before crossing Fulwell Golf course, passing through a residential area and meeting the BR Kingston Loop near Teddington, where there would have been an interchange with local roads.

Ringway 3 would have followed the railway, via interchanges at Hampton Wick and in Kingston town centre where much destruction would have been required. The route would have continued alongside the railway past Norbiton before leaving it to turn south and cross the Waterloo – Exeter line just east of Berrylands station.

It then followed the Hogsmill River, at the back of a chain of sports grounds to an interchange with the **A3**. It would have continued through the Hogsmill open space before crossing the BR Chessington Branch west of Malden Manor station. There then followed a difficult stretch through housing at Worcester Park before crossing the Waterloo – Epsom railway just north of Stoneleigh. Shortly after there would be an interchange with the **A24**.

From here the route would have had to cross more residential areas before cutting through historic Nonsuch Park. It would then have crossed the Croydon – Sutton railway between Ewell East and Cheam before passing through East Ewell Village, and the side of the Cuddington Golf Course to join the outer route at Banstead.

Parkway E.
This is the least well-known part of the GLC's motorway plan. It was low priority and so was never planned in detail. The name came directly from the Abercrombie Plan, and never got updated.

This proposed route would have started at the junction with the South Cross Route at **Loughborough Park** and runs generally southwards to New Addington, where it would join Ringway 3.

The route lay to the west of the main rail tracks at Herne Hill sidings and followed the railway on the same side to Gipsy Hill Station. It was near ground-level until it passed through the railway embankment under the Victoria-Dover main line, then it rose to clear **Dulwich Road**.

Parkway E would have been elevated to clear the **South Circular Road** and the Tulse Hill railway junction before it went into cutting near **Knights Hill**. From here it followed the general level of the railway, part in cut and part elevated. The high ridge of Crystal Palace would have been pierced by bored tunnels about half-a-mile long, followed by a short length of cut-and-cover tunnel at Crystal Palace station. The road then followed the railway again through Anerley in cut-and-cover, first on the west and then on the east side of the Crystal Palace to Birkbeck railway as far as the interchange with Ringway 2 near Elmers End.

After passing the Crystal Palace Cemetery near ground level, the road rose to cross low-lying open spaces and the former Addiscombe railway before dropping into cutting from Upper Elmers End to a point near High Broom Wood.

Parkway E was then elevated and followed the boundary between the Croydon and Bromley for about a mile. passing over **Wickham Road**. Running through undulating ground the road was in cutting and then elevated over **Addington Road** and returned to ground-level at Birch Wood.

The M23 Northern extension
This entered Greater London alongside the A23 at Hooley. From then it would have gone north alongside the GLC boundary to curve under **Hollyme Oak Road** and **Portnalls Road** and continue in cutting by Rickman Hill recreation ground. **Rickman Hill Road** would be severed here.

The ground then falls away rapidly and so the M23 would have needed to cross **Chipstead Valley Road** and its schools on a 120 feet high viaduct. On the other side it would then have crossed an area of smallholdings and agricultural land, to cross **Little Woodcote Lane**. Here the Green Belt ended. The M23 would have continued across more smallholdings to cross **Woodcote Road** where there would have been an interchange with Ringway 3. From here it would have ran in a cutting along side the eastern backs of houses on **Sandy Road** avoiding the former Croydon Airport site

It then ran under **Stafford Road,** cut off the south-west corner of Mellows Park, to cut through another residential area and cross the Croydon – Sutton railway. The route then ran in between some allotments and the Banden Hill cemetery to take over a pedestrian walkway on a ridge between **Rookwood Avenue** and **Queen Elizabeth's Walk.**

The route then hit a three level interchange over **Croydon Road** before following the eastern boundary of Beddington Park on a 30 foot high embankment. A fifteenth-century orangery would be embedded in this embankment. It would then continue through the Beddington sewage farm before another interchange with **Croydon Road** and **Carshalton Road.**

The last stretch of the route would have crossed the Croydon – Sutton railway to slice off the western part of Mitcham Common before continuing in cutting to follow the east side of the Victoria – Portsmouth main line, close to **Grove Road, Oakleigh Way** and **Bennets Close** before reaching the junction with Ringway 2.

The GLC's proposed extension of this route would have run generally north eastwards, beside the railway towards Tulse Hill and joining Parkway E near Herne Hill station.

The North and South Orbital Routes
The North Orbital, as planned in 1924, would have started from near Tilbury, with a spur to near Purfleet and the lower Thames Tunnel. The Tilbury section would have taken over the **A128** through Bulphan and Herongate, crossing the **A127** and the **A12** following 2,000 feet of the Shenfield bypass to meet the spur from Purfleet just north of Brentwood.

Much of the North Orbital was designed to follow existing roads, so it would have picked up the **A128** again through Kelvedon Hatch to a point south of Marden Ash, near Ongar. Here it would have crossed the River Roding to run eastwards on a brand new section.

In post-war planning, this section was superseded by Ringway 3, and the North Orbital, which passed through sparsely populated countryside, was a lower priority which would not have its own Thames Crossing, instead joining the D Ring near Navestock. However the bureaucratic mind was often confused. In July 1961 Ernest Marples announced plans to fix the route of the *North Orbital* from the northern approaches of the Dartford Tunnel to the A12. Repeated parliamentary questions refer to this section as being part of the North Orbital and not the D Ring, indeed, on one occasion Marples was asked if he would change the route of the the D Ring so that it connected to the tunnel.[434] By 1967, this section was referred to as part of the D Ring.[435]

The next section seems to have been new, running east by Greenstead and Toot Hill to cross the **B181** and the **B1393** just north of Epping town centre. From there it would have run east northeast via Epping Green towards a junction with the **A10** at Hoddeston. Chris Marshall, an early researcher into the ringway plans, suggested that the **A1170 Dinant Link Road**, a short section of two-lane dual carriageway connecting the A10 bypass to the town centre was in fact built as part of the North Orbital road.[436]

From Hoddeston it would have ran east following the line of the **B158** and then the **A414** to reach the **A1** at Hatfield. Here we meet a part which was actually built and still called the North Orbital Road today. This is now part of the A414 but was built as the A405 and runs past Colney Heath, a junction with the **A1081**, to divide at **Watling Street** south of St Albans. Our route turns south to intersect with the new section of the **M25** at Junction 21A, the M1 at Junction 6, before passing via Leavensdon to join the **A41** between Watford and Kings Langley.

It follows the A41 for a short distance before diverging to the west at Hunton Bridge. This section is a spur of the M25 but was built as the North Orbital Road (still the A405) and runs as far as Junction 17 (Maple Cross). Here the original route – still called the North Orbital – diverges and runs south as the A412, following the reservoirs in the Colne Valley, and crossing the railway just west of Denham station, before ending at the A40. From here it would have gone south-east to the Denham Roundabout before following the A412 and then a stretch of new road past Iver Heath (at this point to the west of the actual M25 alignment) before rejoining the present M25 at Runneymead Bridge.

The New M25 follows the North Orbital route but a short distance away to meet the M4 at junction 15, before passing on the Junction 13 near Staines.

From here the M25 mainly incorporates Bressey's South Orbital Route, envisaged as an entirely new route with no incorporation of existing roads. Its track follows the south orbital route as locked down in the post war period, except for a stretch in Surrey where the route is slightly different.

Near Leatherhead, today's M25 passes to the north of the town whereas Bressey's route would have had it to the south. The two lines converge near Walton-on-the-Hill and cross over each other, this time with the M25 on the more southerly alignment. They cross again near Merstham with the M25 now to the the north before meeting again east of the **A22** near Oxted. The two routes match until near Sevenoaks, there the 1937 route passed slightly to the east of the M25 as built before meeting again at Swanley, to pass to the Dartford Tunnel.

Notes

References to specific documents appear in the relevant place in the text using the following Key: BIS – Bishopsgate Institute; CAM – Camden borough archives; CHI – Chiswick local studies centre; ICE – Institution of Civil Engineers; NA – National Archives; KEN – Kent county archives, Maidstone; LEW – Lewisham borough archives; LMA – London Metropolitan Archives; SUR – Surrey county archives, Woking

Contexts
1. This quote often appears, it seems incorrectly, as 'nothing can stop the great car economy.' The correct – slightly more nuanced – version seems to be this one, from a speech presenting the 1989 Better Environment Awards for Industry. 2 *Hansard* 9 May 1977
3. Marples was speaking at the People and Cities conference, organised by the British Road Federation in 1963
4. Greater London Council, *Tomorrow's London,* 1970

1 – Genesis of an idea
5. Patrick Abercrombie and John Forshaw, – *County of London Plan*, Macmillan for London County Council, 1943
6. The present-day boroughs of Camden, Islington, Hackney, Tower Hamlets, Greenwich, Lewisham, Southwark, Lambeth, Wandsworth, Hammersmith, Kensington, and Westminster, plus the City of London.
7. Patrick Abercrombie, *Greater London Plan, 1944: a report prepared on behalf of the Standing Conference on London Regional Planning*, HMSO, 1945
8. http://duffydesign.com/planning-post-war-london-in-pow-camp/ Stalag Luft III was the camp which featured in *The Great Escape*
9. Report of the Royal Commission into the Means of Locomotion and Transport in London, 1905
10. The Road Fund was set up in 1920 to build and improve roads out of the proceeds of vehicle excise duty. It was one of the few examples of hypothecated taxation in the UK, although that hypothecation only lasted until 1936
11. Local Government Board, *Arterial Roads in Greater London, reports of conferences*, HMSO, 1913-16
12. *The Times* 22 February 1928
13. The relative cheapness of the North Circular reflected the fact that it was mainly built through open country. The towers in the Lea Valley were knocked down as part of road widening activities in the 1980s
14. Speed limits for cars were scrapped in 1931 under the Road Traffic Act 1930. The Road Traffic Act of 1934 reintroduced a limit – this time of 30mph in built up areas
15. *The Times* 6 February 1936
16. NA – MT39/339
17. http://ciht.org.uk/motorway/londonm25.htm
18. Mike Davis, *City of Quartz*, Verso, 1990
19. By 2012, there were 28,7 million private cars in the UK, compared with a population of 63.7 million – a car/people ratio of more than one car per two persons.
20. Ministry of Transport, *Highway Development Survey, Greater London*, HMSO, 1938
21. The concept had been tried out by Robert Moses, in New York. This master road builder once said 'we live in a motorised civilisation.' He was responsible for the network of parkways on Long Island, as well as for roads in New York City designed for the benefit of suburban car owners rather than inner-city residents.
22. *The Age* 7 June 1938

23   Ministry of Transport, *Highway Development Survey, Greater London,* HMSO, 1938
24   Bressey's critical observation was somehow omitted from the GLC's own history of London road planning, which was otherwise highly informative – see Greater London Council Intelligence Unit – *Research report 11, London Road Plans, 1900-1970*
25   *Hansard* 21 June 1939
26   NA – MT106/222
27   That is, the First World War
28   Patrick Abercrombie, *Greater London Plan, 1944: a report prepared on behalf of the Standing Conference on London Regional Planning* – preamble, HMSO, 1945
29   Alan Jackson, *Semi-Detached London*, second edition, Wild Swan Press, 1991
30   Patrick Abercrombie *Greater London Plan, 1944: a report prepared on behalf of the Standing Conference on London Regional Planning* – Preamble, HMSO, 1945
31   *Report of the Select Committee of the House of Lords into the Prevention of Road Accidents,* HMSO, 1938
32   Ministry of Town and Country Planning, *Memorandum on The Report of the Advisory Committee for London Regional Planing,* HMSO, 1947
33   LMA – LCC minutes 17 July 1945
34   NA – MT119/21
35   *Hansard* House of Lords, 3 April 1951
36   London County Council, *Administrative County of London Development Plan – Statement and Analysis*, 1951
37   AN – MT119/21

2 – Lobbyists and Councillors
38   Available on YouTube at the time of writing
39   For the definitive history of Britain's road lobby see Michael Hamer *Wheels Within Wheels, a Study of the Road Lobby*, Routledge, 1987
40   *Hansard* 22 July 1957
41   *Hansard* 4 July 1973
42   The BRF chairman in the 1980s
43   Ian Nairn, *Nairn's London*, Penguin, 1966
44   British Road Federation, *Urban Motorways*, 1956. The alignment Glanville and Baker proposed for the section to Staples Corner was very close to that eventually used. The diagram they used in their paper to illustrate their route also featured Abercrombie's A ring, which in engineers' eyes, had never really died.
45   *Daily Mirror* 12 January 1959
46   *Daily Sketch* 2 March 1960
47   Ministry of Transport, *Report of the Committee on London Roads. Chairman, G R H Nugent*, 1959
48   *Hansard* 17 March 1959
49   *The Times* July 25 1959
50   *Daily Mail* 25 August 1959
51   He was professionally qualified in all three disciplines
52   Colin Buchanan, *Mixed Blessing – the Motor in Britain*, Leonard Hill, 1958
53   *Architects' Journal* 24 December 1959
54   A highly prestigious honour – the Institution's past presidents had included Thomas Telford, Joseph Locke and Robert Stephenson. Isambard Kingdom Brunel died just before he could take up the post
55   Andy Foster, *Birmingham*, Yale University Press, London, p.197
56   People are frequently surprised to learn that Leicester is in fact Britain's tenth largest city
57   British Road Federation, *London needs…..*1960
58   *The Observer* April 24 1960
59   ICE – BRF management committee minutes 19 July 1960
60   London County Council, *Administrative County of London Plan, First Review*, 1960
61   The LCC's perpetual shortage of money often forced it into an alliance with

property developers when it came to central London road improvements. See Oliver Marriott, *The Property Boom*, Hamish Hamilton, 1967
62 Including Konrad Smigielski, who was cited by the London Liberal Party
63 LMA – LCC/CL/HIG/2/8
64 *ibid*
65 LMA – LCC minutes 14 May 1957
66 LMA – LCC minutes 26 January 1960
67 LMA – LCC/CL/HIG/02/145
68 LMA – LCC/MIN/10.300
69 LMA – LCC/CL/HIG/02/147
70 ICE – BRF management committee minutes 24 March 1961
71 ICE – BRF publicity committee minutes 13 June 1961
72 Author's italics
73 London County Council London Statistics 1952-1961 vol 5 (1963)
74 NA – MT 91/910
75 NA – MT169/219
76 LMA – GLC/TD/C/36/022
77 LMA – LCC/MIN/10.301
78 NA – MT106/186
79 Ministry of Transport, *Traffic in towns: a study of the long term problems of traffic in urban areas / reports of the steering group and working group appointed by the Minister of Transport*, 1963.
80 SKM Colin Buchanan, *Traffic in Cities, (Traffic in Towns – a Retrospective)*, 2013
81 T Dan Smith talked of making Newcastle 'the Brasilia of the North' in a reference to the planned from scratch capital of Brazil. His involvement in the Poulson fraud got him six years in jail. He died in 1990, still living in a Newcastle tower block of the kind he encouraged
82 SKM Colin Buchanan, *ibid*
83 London County Council, *London Traffic Survey, Phase One*, 1964
84 Ibid, para 4.00
85 Ibid, para 6.91 and 6.94
86 Greater London Council, *London Traffic Survey Phase Two*, 1966
87 Ibid introduction; the progress of the survey
88 Ibid, p139
89 Greater London Council, *London Transportation Study, Phase Three*

3 Green Light for the Ringways
90 LMA – LCC minutes 24 March 1964
91 LMA – LCC minutes 10 March 1964
92 LMA – LCC minutes 15 December 1964
93 LMA – LCC minutes 15 December 1964. This Crawley/Brighton radial road became the M23
94 Later reduced to 33
95 LMA – GLC minutes 26 January 1965
96 LEW – A01/1/8
97 The underground's Metropolitan and District lines were built this way, the Piccadilly, Northern Lines etc are tubes which required deep tunnelling
98 LEW – A0 1/1/8 – Memo on the LCC's proposals for the Dover Radial Route through Blackheath and district (February 1963)
99 *Kentish Independent* 14 June 1963.
100 *South London Press* 12 June 1963
101 *Architects' Journal* 6 February 1963
102 LMA – GLC minutes 6 April 1965
103 See NA – MT106/437 for the complete Travers Morgan report into the North Cross Route, complete with beautifully produced engineering drawings
104 LMA – GLC minutes 6 April 1965
105 LMA – GLC minutes 25 May 1965

106 *Evening News* 6 June 1967
107 LMA – GLC minutes 19 July 1966
108 *Architects' Journal* 20 April 1966
109 LMA – LCC/CL/HIG/02/146
110 It is common to hear veterans of the struggle against the ringways speculate that the GLC might actually have succeeded if they had not attempted to drive the North Cross Route through wealthy Hampstead
111 *The Times* 11 April 1966
112 LMA – LCC/CL/HIG/02/146
113 Report of the Committee on Housing in Greater London, 1965, Cmd 4609
114 Greater London Council – *London's Housing Needs Up To 1974*
115 *Hansard* 3 March 1970
116 GLDP inquiry, proof of evidence E11/2, par 9.11
117 NA – HLG 159/796 – Buchanan's evidence to GLDP, transcript day 140, pp 40/41
118 LMA – LCC/MIN/10.302
119 LMA – GLC minutes 14 December 1971
120 The legend was given backing by the route of Ronnie Kray's funeral cortege in 1995 which travelled via the flyover when it didn't really need to.
121 NA – MT106/151
122 *Evening News* 5 November 1963
123 LMA – GLC/TD/T/TM/09/004
124 A 1980 GLC report said that Brent Cross had increased traffic in the area by a 4-7 per cent. Surprisingly, 43 per cent of shoppers came by bus as LT had rerouted nine routes to serve the centre. Some 52 per cent came by car, and with increasing car ownership that figure has surely risen since. A huge extension to Brent Cross has now been approved; Barnet council's own estimate that it would generate 29,100 additional vehicles (in a 12-hour weekday period) generated substantial opposition to the scheme.
125 LMA – GLC minutes 10 February 1967
126 NA – MT106/437
127 Pers com
128 LMA – GLC minutes 21 June 1966
129 LMA – GLC minutes 18 July 1967
130 http://www.svpoa.org.uk/history.html
131 LMA – GLC minutes 2 May 1967
132 LMA – GLC minutes 16 June 1967
133 *South London Press* 14 May 1965
134 Brixton Central Area, Proposed redevelopment feasibility study – http://brixton-redevelopment.weebly.com/
135 *The Guardian* 27 April 1995.
136 LMA – GLC/TD/CTD/02/005

4 – Rage against the concrete
137 CAM – A/01244/3/2/1/2
138 LEW – A7/47
139 *The diary of Douglas Jay: from dictation to online resource,* Presented by Mary Jay in an Authorship, Memory & Manuscripts seminar, 20 February 2012, Bodleian Library, Oxford
140 NA – MT106/284
141 Douglas Jay, *Change and Fortune*, Hutchinson, 1980
142 LMA – GLC/DG/PT1/P/5/52
143 ibid
144 ibid
145 LEW – AO1/1/2/1
146 *The Times* 11 March 1969
147 Jay, *ibid*
148 *Sunday Telegraph* 27 August 1965

149 Pers com
150 *Architects' Journal* 21 November 1962
151 LEW – AO1/1/1/1
152 Pers com
153 Pers com
154 *The Observer,* 20 July 1969
155 LEW – A01/1/2/2
156 Pers com
157 ICE – BRF executive committee minutes 23 July 1969
158 NA – MT106/284
159 LEW – A01/1/2/1
160 CAM – A/01244/3/7/2
161 NA – MT106/284
162 *The Guardian* 10 October 2005
163 NA – MT106/284
164 ICE – BRF public affairs committee minutes, 16 May 1972
165 NA – MT106/437
166 NA – MT106/437
167 LMA – GLC minutes, 19 July 1966
168 AN – MT95/910
169 *Leatherhead Advertiser* 26 January 1967. The Aberfan disaster occurred the previous year when a colliery slag heap in south Wales collapsed killing 144 people
170 LMA – GLC/TD//GLDP/08/369/1
171 LMA – GLC press release GLC/DG/PRB/35/009/642 10 December 1969
172 *The Guardian* 30 October 1970
173 The treasury's internal deliberations on the ringways are at NA – T319/2655 and T319/1842
174 NA – PREM13/2997
175 LMA – GLC/TD/CTD/02/026
176 LMA – GLC/TD/CTD/02/005
177 *Hansard* 17 March 1959
178 LMA – GLC/TD/CTD/02/020
179 ICE – BRF London roads working party minutes 8 April 1969
180 LMA – GLC/DG/PRB/35/007/097 GLC press release– February 17 1969
181 LMA – GLC minutes 25/26 March 1969
182 LMA – GLC/DG/PRB/35//007/157 GLC press release 20 March 1969
183 LMA – GLC/DG/PRB/35/007/144 GLC press release 13 March 1969
184 LMA – GLC minutes, 21 November 1967
185 Greater London Council. *Greater London Development Plan, written statement,* para 2.11
186 NA – MT106/284
187 GLDP inquiry background paper B158 – table summary of costs
188 Colin Buchanan and Partners – *North East London; some implications of the Greater London Development Plan* chapter 4 p 57
189 LMA – GLC/DG/PRB/35/007/195A GLC press release 14 April 1969
190 LMA – GLC/DG/PT1/P/5/53
191 *The Economist* 14 March 1969
192 *The Economist* 27 July 1969
193 Stephen Plowden, *Towns Against Traffic*, Andre Deutsch, 1972
194 LMA – LCC/MIN/10.301
195 Pers com
196 British Road Federation, *Motorways in London: a reply to 'Motorways in London', the report by J Michael Thomson,* 1970
197 LMA – GLC/TD/T/TM/01/023
198 *Architects' Journal* 29 October 1969
199 LEW – A0/1/1/2/2
200 LMA – GLC minutes 27 January 1970

201 Pers com
202 Pers com
203 LEW – AO1/1/1/1
204 *Brentford and Chiswick Times* 16 April 1970
205 LMA – GLC minutes 21 July 1970
206 Department of Transport press release, 25 April 1969
207 Institution of Civil Engineers, *Proceedings* March 1968, quoted in *The Guardian* 10 November 2003
208 *The Guardian*, 10 November 2003
209 *The Times* 30 July 1970
210 LMA – GLC/TD/CTD/02/026
211 *The Times* 3 August 1970
212 British Road Federation press release 16 March 1970
213 ICE – BRF Public affairs committee minutes 16 May 1972
214 ICE – BRF Public affairs committee minutes 4 February 1970
215 ICE – BRF Public affairs committee minutes 21 September 1971

5 – Defeat into victory

216 Greater London Council, *Greater London Development Plan, written statement*, 1969
217 NA – HLG 159/1043 – London Amenity and Transport Association, *Transport Strategy in London*, 1970, Layfield Proof of Evidence E12/20
218 NA – HLG159/1043
219 See the author's *A Very Political Railway*, Capital Transport 2014
220 *Roads in London*, BRF evidence to the GLDP inquiry
221 NA – HLG 159/2653
222 Something which was highly popular among some of Mrs Thatcher's advisers at the time
223 See Chris Austin and Richard Faulkner, *Holding the Line*, Ian Allen, 2013
224 *Roads in London*, ibid
225 *The Times* 26 November 1968
226 Pers com
227 Greater London Council, *Movement in London*, P4.19, 1969
228 *The Times* 21 January 1972
229 Michael Thomson – *Motorways in London*, Duckworth, 1969
230 Greater London Council, Background Paper 34, *Secondary Roads Policy*
231 LMA – GLC/TD/CTD/02/020
232 London Labour Party, *A socialist strategy for London*, 1973
233 Greater London regional council of the Labour Party, *Discussion paper on Transport in London*, 1972
234 There is some evidence to back up the frequently asserted idea that unpopular projects are usually sited in poor areas. For example Daniel Aldrich found that areas which had a low level of civil activity in Japan were the best predictor of siting decisions for nuclear power plants, airports and dams. See *Location, location, location: selecting sites for controversial facilities*, Singapore Economic Review 53(1),
235 NA – T319/1842
236 NA – HLG159/36 and HLG159/37
237 Department of the Environment, *New Roads in Towns : report of the Urban Motorways Committee*, HMSO 1972
238 LMA – GLC minutes 14 November 1972
239 CAM – A/01244/3/3/7/1
240 Department of the Environment, *Greater London Development Plan: report of Layfield Panel of Inquiry* para 25.48, 1973
241 Ibid para 25.50,
242 Ibid para 25.55,
243 NA – CAB 128/51, CAB128/52 and CAB129/167/14

244 *Sunday Times* 11 February 1973
245 Pers com
246 Jay *ibid*
247 London Amenity and Transport Association, *The Road Proposals of the Layfield Report: a Critique*, 1973
248 NA – T319/2655.
249 Which included the Eltham, Mottingham and Falconwood areas
250 LEW – AO.1.1.2.2
251 The original name for what became the Jubilee Line
252 CHI – Chiswick Motorway Liaison Committee, newsletter number four
253 Greater London Council *Greater London Development plan: approved by the Secretary of State for the Environment*: 1976
254 NA – MT106/151 and MT106/437
255 Who succeeded Duncan Sandys as MP for Streatham in 1974
256 Jay *ibid*
257 *Architectural Review*, February 1973
258 *The Economist* 25 May 1974
259 For example a 1980 BRF conference on the impact of the M25 saw several speakers demand that the ringways be built. The conference was punctuated with complaints about the 'trendies' of Blackheath who were held responsible for stopping them.
260 White Paper, *Development and Compensation—Putting People First*, Cmnd. 5124
261 ICE – BRF public affairs committee minutes, 1 November 1973
262 *Bushell and Another* v S*ecretary of State for Environment*. The government's guidance for inspectors makes all this crystal clear – see http://www.planning-portal.gov.uk/uploads/pins/advice_for_inspectors/transport_orders.pdf
263 Pers com

6 – Round and round the M25

264 *Hansard* 16 November 1965
265 What became the M11. The Docks Relief Road was another major road project which never happened. It would have started where the M11 was originally intended to terminate – at Temple Mills – and then run past Stratford to Canning Town and the Royal Group of Docks. It had low priority compared with the East Cross Route
266 Department of the Environment, *Greater London Development Plan: report of Layfield Panel of Inqui*ry p42.10, 1973
267 *The D ring in north-west London* – Colin Buchanan and Partners, February 1968
268 LMA – GLC minutes, 19 November 1968
269 NA – HLG71/126
270 NA – MT110/1
271 NA – MT106/224
272 NA – MT106/224
273 For other official discussion on Ringway 3 south of the river see NA – MT120/273, MT120/231, and MT120/232 and KEN – CP/PL/19/24/26 and CP/PL/19/24/27
274 KEN – CP/PL/19/24/27
275 Confusingly, this was sometimes referred to in later years as Ringway 4, a terminology also used, equally confusingly, to the southern part of the D Ring.
276 *Hansard* 12 July 1961
277 The 1920s version of the North Orbital ran to Tilbury Docks with a spur running to Purfleet. After the Second World War, the section to Tilbury was abandoned when the location of the cross river tunnel was moved to the Dartford – Purfleet axis
278 *Hansard* 24 June 1964
279 Department of Transport, White Paper *Policy For Roads: England Cmnd 7132*, 1978

280 *Hansard* 21 January 1975
281 Pers com
282 London Amenity and Transport Association, *Ringways in Outer London*, 1975
283 *Hansard* 15 November 1979
284 Pers com
285 London Amenity and Transport Association, *Ringways in Outer London*, 1975
286 Pers com
287 *M25 London orbital – property market effects*, Nathaniel Lichfield and Partners, Goldstein Leigh Associates. 1981. Nathaniel Lichfield had earlier served on the Mulley committee into urban roads
288 *Surrey Advertiser*, 18 June 1971
289 *Friends of Epping Forest newsletter*, Autumn 2011
290 *The Times* 29 July 1975
291 John Tyme, *Motorways v Democracy*, Macmillan, 1978. Marsham Street was a reference to the environment department's vast London headquarters
292 *The Times* 4 June 1976
293 The records of DANDAG are at the London Metropolitan Archives under LMA/4287/02/326/1 and LMA/4287/02/326/4
294 As laid down by the 1977 Leitch Committee, whose full name was the Advisory Committee on Trunk Road Assessment. It became a standing advisory committee a year later under the chairmanship of professor Tom Williams, who was closely associated with the BRF
295 John Adams, *Transport Planning – Vision and Practice*, Routledge Kegan Paul, 1981
296 Highways Acts 1959 and 1971, M25 Motorway (Swanley to Sevenoaks section) scheme Inspector's report – LMA – 4287/02/326/4
297 *The Independent* 13 March 1994
298 Department of Transport, *The M25 Orbital Motorway*, 1986
299 SUR – 6594/K/1
300 *Daily Telegraph* 10 April 2014
301 *The Guardian* 28 October 2011
302 *The Economist* 23 August 1986
303 Since overtaken by a 37 mile jam in December 1995, but at least on that occasion the traffic was moving….albeit slowly
304 Department of Transport, *M25 Review, Vols 1 and 2* (Rendel Palmer Tritton authors), 1989
305 *Commercial Motor* 19 January 1989
306 Department of Transport, *M25 Action Plan*, 1990
307 *The Guardian*, 26 June 1992
308 Over £24 million was paid in compensation for noise between January 1995 and April 2000 (*Hansard 19 April 2000*). Compensation also had to be paid after widening – between junction 8 and 9, for example, the compensation figures was given as £12.5 million
309 *Hansard* 1 April 1993
310 *Financial Times* 12 March 1993
311 *Hansard* 22 July 1993
312 SUR – CC858/143
313 SUR – CC857/505 – PR327/93/TE
314 SUR – CC857/507 – PR/28/JM/95
315 *Commercial Motor* 27 January 1994
316 Department of Transport, Standing Advisory Committee on Trunk Road Assessment – *Trunk Roads And The Generation of Traffic*, 1994
317 *Hansard* 19 December 1994
318 Department for the Environment, Transport, and the Regions, *A New Deal for Trunk Roads in England*, 1998
319 *Hansard* 29 February 2000
320 Association for European Transport, *The orbit multi-modal study: developing a long term sustainable management strategy for the M25*, 2002

321 Memorandum by Orbit (MMS 51), Select Committee on Transport, Appendices to the Minutes of Evidence, 25 June 2003
322 Pers com
323 Joel Garreau, E*dge Cities – life on the new frontier,* Doubleday, 1991. In the UK, Croydon has occasionally proclaimed itself to be an Edge City, but this is merely an attempt at civic boosterism; the real edge cities of the US are something completely different,
324 http://www.bbc.com/news/magazine-15474473
325 Robert Cervero, *Suburban Gridlock*, Rutgers, 1985
326 *Hansard* 9 July 2003
327 Department for Transport, Traffic Statistics Annual Average Daily Flow
328 *Daily Telegra*ph, 11 December 2002
329 Owen Hatherley, *A New Kind of Blea*k, Verso 2012
330 So-called by management, which enforces restrictions on hoodies and baseball caps.
331 Joseph, who won the OBE for his services to transport, had celebrated his 21st birthday by being carried out of the Archway Road inquiry by the police
332 Area wide road charging would avoid traffic diverting from the M25 onto local roads, as would certainly happen if the road pricing were applied to the M25 alone.
333 Stephen Glaister, T*he Smeed Report at Fifty: will road pricing always be ten years away?* https://www.ucl.ac.uk/transport-institute/pdfs/UCL-smeed-memorial
334 House of Commons. Committee of Public Accounts, *M25 Private Finance Contract, Nineteenth Report of Session 2010–11*
335 *Reigate Independent* 24 September 1997
336 Neil Atkinson, – *M25 Guide: 62 Clearly Marked Routes to Help You Avoid Congestion on the M25, 1997*
337 http://www.ibtimes.co.uk/happy-birthday-m25-25-facts-infamous-motorway-239455
338 http://www.sabre-roads.org.uk/witchypoo/M25.htm
339 *The Guardian 1*1 September 2014
340 Pers com

7 – Ghosts
341 See for example NA – MT106/454, also LMA – GLC/TD/GLDP/08/500/1
342 *The Times* 7 March 1974
343 BIS – Wetzel/44
344 Pers com. Livingstone later appointed both Moore and Wetzel to the board of Transport for London
345 BIS – Wetzel/43
346 LMA – GLC/DG/AE/ROL/24/165
347 According to a report called *The Rush for Roads,* by the Movement Transport Consultancy and commissioned by ALARM, road building failed as a regeneration tool because movement costs were only two per cent of industry costs while increased congestion would then nullify reduced journey times.
348 The original South Woodford to Gants Hill section was then renumbered as the A1400. South of the A13, the route to the Woolwich ferry remains the A1020 and the A117.
349 For the MII see NA – MT106/283 and MT106/286
350 LMA – GLC/DG/PT1/P/5/53
351 Possibly the most significant of these was the introduction of Travelcards in 1983, which at last put London Transport fares on a zonal basis
352 Department of the Environment, *Streamlining the Cities, Cmnd 9063,* 1983
353 NA– AT63/100/2
354 ICE – BRF public affairs committee minutes. 1 November 1975
355 Pers com
356 NA – AT63/100/2

357 House of Commons, fifth report from the transport committee, session 1981-1982, *Transport in London, volume 1*
358 NA – AT63/100/1
359 NA– AT63/100/2
360 BIS – Wetzel/359
361 *Hansard* 11 May 1984
362 Who described himself, incidentally, as a life-long Conservative
363 *The Guardian* 19 April 1977
364 For COmputerised cost Benefit Analysis
365 http://www.roadblock.org.uk/resources/cobabriefing.pdf
366 Dave Black/People Against the River Crossing, *The Fight to Save Oxleas Wood*
367 *New Scientist* 30 October 1986
368 *Hansard* 21 May 1984
369 BIS – Wetzel/288 – Newsletter of the Archway anti widening campaign, winter 1983
370 *The Effects of Strategic Network Changes on Traffic*, Steve Purnell, Jillian Beardwood and John Elliott. Presented to GLC transport committee 10 July 1985, republished in *World Transport Policy & Practice* Vol 5, Number 2, 1999
371 NA – AN170/480
372 Pers com
373 Friends of the Earth, *Roads to Ruin; Stopping the London Road Schemes*, 198? and *London Road Schemes; a Guide to Objecting*, 198?
374 Pers com
375 *Hansar*d 14 December 1989
376 *Hansard* 13 February 1989
377 London Borough of Wandsworth, *Wandsworth's Alternative*, December 1989
378 Which was then in the hands of the Metropolitan Police, not local councils
379 *City Limits*, May 11 1989
380 *The Guardian* 4 January 1989
381 *Private Eye* 2 March 1990.
382 *The Independent*, 16 December 1989
383 *ELRiC News* number 5
384 *Construction Weekly*, 23 August 1989
385 Department of Transport – letter to objectors, 10 January 1990
386 *New Civil Engineer* 7 March 1985
387 Pers com
388 Ove Arup, *Transport related problems, East London Assessment Study update*, December 1986
389 Department of Transport press notice, 21 July 1987
390 Travers Morgan *South Circular assessment study, stage 2 report: options, 1986*
391 Ove Arup and Partners, *East London Assessment Study: report on transport options*, 1989
392 Halcrow, Sir William, *West London Assessment Study stage two: report on options* 1989
393 Mott MacDonald International, *South London Assessment Study, stage 2 report: transport options*, 1989
394 Greater London Council – *Caution! Road Studies At Work*, 1985
395 Department of Transport, *Traffic in London*, 1989
396 *Hansard* 14 December 1989
397 Which became the Campaign for Better Transport
398 http://www.roadblock.org.uk/alarmuk/roadblock.html
399 Maureen Measure http://www.leytonhistorysociety.org.uk/m11_link_road.html
400 http://news.bbc.co.uk/1/hi/uk/4911468.stm
401 http://walthamforestecho.co.uk/the-m11-link-road-20-years-on/
402 *Alarm Bells*, issue 20 July 1997
403 PARC was given Non-Governmental Organisation observer status at the Rio summit

404 *Alarm Bells*, issue 2, November 1991
405 Pers com
406 *BBC Panorama* 7 March 1997
407 Greater London Authority, *Mayor's Transport Strategy Policy 4G.8, p229*, 2001
408 Transport for London, board papers – Major road schemes review, February 2001
409 Transport for London, board papers – February 2005
410 House of Commons transport committee, *Going for gold, Transport for London's 2012 Olympic games, third report of session 2005-2006, volume 2*
411 They have now been refurbished for rent by Notting Hill Housing Trust
412 *Hansard* 21 July 1997
413 Transport for London board papers, 20 November 2002
414 *The Guardian* 6 November 2008
415 Friends of the Earth – *Thames Gateway press briefing*, 7 September 2007
416 Campaign for Better Transport – E*xtracts from the Inspector's Conclusions in the Thames Gateway Bridge Inquiry* http://www.bettertransport.org.uk/sites/default/files/inspector_report_summary.pdf

8 – Epilogue

417 Transport for London – *Roads Task Force report,* 2013
418 Transport for London – *Roads Task Force Progress Report*, April 2015
419 http://www.silvertowntunnel.co.uk/
420 Bias declaration – your author objected to the Silvertown Tunnel on the grounds that it could not solve congestion as it would merely generate more traffic
421 TfL board papers, 4 February 2015
422 TfL board papers, 8 November 2016
423 Astonishingly, Michael Thomson's book actually predicted that something of the kind could happen. He wrote (p168). 'it is possible therefore that by the end of the century the era of motor traffic in cities may have passed its peak.'
424 https://www.gov.uk/government/statistical-data-sets/nts99-travel-by-region-and-area-type-of-residence
425 David Metz, *Local Transport Today*, issues 643–646, March – May 2014. Metz, now at UCL, was a former chief scientist at the Department for Transport
426 http://www.economist.com/node/21563280
427 For essential discussions on Peak Car, see this presentation from Professor Phil Goodwin, also at UCL at *http://www2.uwe.ac.uk/faculties/FET/Research/cts/projects/reports/WC2012_goodwin_peak_car.pdf*. For an opposing view, see *On The Move – Making sense of car and train travel trends in Great Britain*, produced by the RAC Foundation
428 Department for Transport, *Road Investment Strategy – strategic vision*, 2014
429 National Traffic Survey 2002-2012, individual journeys
430 Department for Transport, *Road Investment Strategy – overview*, 2014

Appendix – Was your home at risk?

431 LMA – GLC/TD/GLDP/08/369
432 NA – MT106/290
433 KEN – CP/PL/19/24/27
434 *Hansard* 24 June 1964
435 *Hansard* 15 November 1967
436 http://www.cbrd.co.uk/articles/ringways/ringway4/north.shtml

Bibliography and Image Credits

There are a number of works which were most useful but which do not appear specifically in the notes. They include;
- Baldwin, Sir Peter, Baldwin, Robert, Evans Dewi Ieuan, *The Motorway Achievement* (motorway archive trust) 2007
- Bayliss, David, *Fifty years of motorways: how did we get here and where do we go next?* Transport Research Foundation, 2009
- Caro, Robert, *The Power Broker: Robert Moses and The Fall of New York*, Knopf 1974
- Hall, Peter, *Great Planning Disasters,* University of California Press, 1992
- Hart, Douglas A, *Strategic Planning in London: the rise and fall of the primary road network*, Elsevier, 2013
- Starkie, David, *The Motorway Age.* Pergamon, 1982

Useful Websites
- Chris's British Road Directory, http://www.cbrd.co.uk/ Chris Marshall was one of the first researchers into the ringway plans
- Society for All British Road Enthusiasts http://www.sabre-roads.org.uk/
- The Motorway Archive http://www.ukmotorwayarchive.org/
  This was put together by civil servants and road engineers as an invaluable factual record of motorway building in the UK. This includes much of the information referred to in the book above.

Image Credits

8	OpenStreetMap contributors
10	Estate of Phillip Bear
11	Still from Ministry of Information film The Proud City - A Plan for London
12	HMSO 1944 Greater London Plan
13	Wikimedia Commons
14	OpenStreetMap contributors
20	HMSO 1944 Greater London Plan
22	British Roads Federation
28	Birmingham Museums Trust via Wikimedia Commons
30	Michael Beamish
40	HMSO - traffic in towns
46	OpenStreetMap contributors
51	Google Earth
52	OpenStreetMap contributors
57	Royal Institution of British Architects
59	Wandsworth heritage centre
60	Jonathan Roberts
63	LSE Library's collections, Imagelibrary/204
64	OpenStreetMap contributors
66/7	London Metropolitan Archives/ Historic England
68/9	London Metropolitan Archives
87	OpenStreetMap contributors
97	National Archives via Wikimedia Commons
104	Google Earth
105	Automobile Association
117	British Roads Federation
122	Dutch National Archives / Spaarnestad Photo
125	Pymouss via Wikimedia Commons
128	Google Earth, Infoterra Ltd and Bluesky
129	Google Earth, Infoterra Ltd and Bluesky
130	Jonathan Bray Collection
132	Unisouth via Wikimedia Commons
137	OpenStreetMap contributors
140	Jonathan Bray Collection
144	Jonathan Bray Collection
145	Jonathan Bray Collection and Dudley Miles
147	Crown Copyright Ordnance Survey and Geographia
151	Crown Copyright Ordnance Survey
152	Jonathan Bray Collection
153	Londoninflames via Wikimedia Commons
157	Transport for London
158	Transport for London

Index

A Ring 19, 21-23, 24, 32, 42, 48, 138, 172n
Abercrombie, Patrick 9-11, 18-21, 30, 31, 32, 35, 112, 115 42, 44, 82 167
ALARM
　See All London Against Road Menace
All London Against Road Menace (ALARM) 130, 143-144 145-146, 151-152, 153, 179n
Archway Road 135-136, 139-140, 141-142, 143, 179n

B Ring 19, 20, 24, 46
　See also Motorway Box, Ringway 1
Baker, Allen 31, 172n
Bass, Mark 103
Battersea 19, 45, 47, 58, 64, 65, 75, 77, 149, 161
Baxter, John 88
Bedfont Lakes 130
Beecham, Derrick 86-87, 94
Bendixson, Terence 88
Bennett, Hubert 32, 27, 49, 80
Blackheath 44-45, 46, 58, 59, 64, 98-99, 100, 101, 144, 177n
Blackheath Motorway Action Group (BMAG) 45
Blackwall Tunnel 17, 23, 36, 38, 47, 52, 82, 88, 158
Bluewater 131
Bow 38, 48, 52
Bray, Jonathan 143-144, 152, 153
Brent Cross 53, 135, 174n
Bressey, Charles, Sir 14, 15-16, 17, 18, 19, 23, 31, 35, 38, 42, 80, 115, 135, 169, 172n
Brew, Richard 99
Brian Colquhoun & partners 114, 122
British Road Federation (BRF) 26-27, 28, 29, 31, 32, 35-36, 37, 38, 65, 72, 77, 85, 93-94, 95-96, 102, 111, 116, 138-139, 142, 152, 177n, 259n, 294n
Brixton 19, 45, 56-57, 148
Buchanan, Colin, Sir 32, 40-41, 51, 63, 79, 98, 99, 112,

C Ring 19, 53, 55, 59, 62, 72, 73, 74
　See also Ringway 2
Callaghan, James, MP 45
Camden Town bypass 54
Carr, Robert, MP 101-102
Castle, Barbara, MP 27
Castle, Ted 62, 72, 113, 115
Chalker, Lynda, MP 138-139, 142
Channon, Paul, MP 146
Chelsea 19, 29, 56, 65, 75
Chesham, Lord 29
Chiswick 13, 30, 38, 48, 59, 77, 86, 88, 144
Colville, Viscount 85, 101
Corbyn, Jeremy, MP 139, 144

Cromwell Road Extension 23, 38
Crosland, Anthony, MP 62, 95, 105, 106
Croydon 10, 13 19, 65, 74, 87, 103, 112, 113, 114
Croydon County Council 113
Cutler, Horace, Sir 109, 135

D Ring 19, 20, 42, 47, 53, 77, 112-114, 115
　See also Ringway 3, M16
DANDAG
　See Defend Darenth Valley and North Downs Action Group
Darling, Alistair, MP 131
Dartford 18, 82, 112, 114, 115, 116, 117, 120, 133, 142, 145
Defend Darenth Valley and North Downs Action Group 119-120
Dennington, Evelyn 56, 57, 62
Derwent, Lord 29
Dover Relief Road 44, 45, 136

E Ring 19, 53, 112
　See also North Orbital Route, South Orbital Route, M25, M16
East Cross Route 38, 47, 51-52, 54, 65, 72, 135, 157, 160
East London River Crossing 135, 141, 143, 145, 146, 150,151, 153, 156, 158
　See also Thames Gateway Bridge, Ringway 2
Eastern Avenue Extension 17, 23, 47, 48, 54, 73, 88, 146
Edmonds, Richard 32, 37, 38, 43
ELRC
　See East London River Crossing
Eltham 59, 65, 103, 136, 148
Essex County Council 14

Finchley Road 23, 98
Forshaw, John 9
Freeman Fox 36, 56
Friends of the Earth 111, 127, 143, 144

Garlick, John 72-73, 76, 79
Gilbert, John, MP 107, 116
Glanville, William 31, 32, 73
Goldstein, Alfred 80, 142, 143
Goodwin, Reg, Sir 98, 103, 104
Gray, Barry, Dr 145
Greater London Council (GLC) 5, 39, 44, 46, 47-48, 50-51, 52, 53-54, 55, 56, 58, 59, 62, 63, 72, 73-75, 76-79, 82, 85, 86, 87, 88, 90, 95, 98, 99-100, 101, 103, 104, 105, 107, 108, 109, 113, 114, 120, 135, 136-137, 138, 142, 145, 146, 149, 152

Hackney 15, 17, 24, 38, 42, 43, 47, 52, 65, 73, 79, 88, 103, 135, 143, 148, 152, 157
Hall, Christopher 62, 63

Hampstead 42, 43, 47, 48, 58, 59, 95, 98, 103
Hampstead Motorway Action Group 58, 103
Hammersmith flyover 29, 30, 38
Hay Davison, Ian 45
Heath, Ted MP 87, 101, 107
Hertfordshire County Council 14, 115
Heseltine, Michael, MP 89, 150
Hill, Terry 146-147, 148, 150, 159
Homes Before Roads (HBR) 86, 87
Hunter, David 63, 85
Husbands 39, 40, 43

Jay, Douglas, MP 58-59, 62, 64, 65, 72, 73, 74, 75, 79, 95, 98, 102, 103, 107
Jay, Peggy 58, 90
Jay, Mary 62, 65, 85
Jenkins, Roy 75-76, 108
Johnson, Boris 109, 156, 157
Joseph, Stephen 132, 149, 179n

Kent County Council 113, 120
Khan, Sadiq 159
King, Edmund 27, 133, 134, 150
Kirby, David 143

Lakeside 131
Layfield, Frank, Sir 95, 99, 100-101, 102, 105, 107, 111, 112, 114
Leytonstone 136, 152, 153
    See also M11 link
Livingstone, Ken, MP 103, 109, 136, 138, 139, 145, 155, 156
London Amenity and Transport Association (LATA) 63, 95, 102, 109, 112, 118
London County Council (LCC) 9, 17-18, 20, 21, 23-24, 29, 30, 31, 32, 35, 36, 37-38, 39, 43-44, 45, 46, 49, 58, 64, 91
London Motorway Action Group (LMAG) 59, 62, 63, 64, 65, 72, 74-75, 76, 79, 80, 85, 95, 98, 101, 102, 104, 137
London Orbital Multi Modal Study 128-129, 130, 132
London Transport 34, 62, 78, 154
Lovelock, Lesley 119

M1 28, 31, 40, 43, 47, 88, 99, 105, 112, 135, 164
M11 38, 48, 59, 99, 139
M11 link 135, 151, 152-153, 157
M12 137-138, 152
M15 135
    See also North Circular Road
M16 115, 116, 118, 119
    See also Ringway 3, M25
M23 39, 42, 55, 59, 73-75, 105-107, 114, 121, 146, 163
M25 100, 112-134, 145, 149, 150, 154, 158
    See also M16, North Orbital Route, South Orbital Route
M4 28, 30, 38, 88, 122, 124, 127, 133
M41 157
    See also West Cross Route

MacGregor, John, MP 126, 127, 152
Manzoni, Herbert, Sir 33
Marples, Ernest, MP 5, 29, 31, 40, 41, 63, 72, 112, 115
Marsh, Richard, MP 72, 73, 74, 75, 76, 79, 88, 114
Maunsells 88
Mawhinney, Brian, MP 127, 129, 138
Middlesex County Council 13, 112
Moore, Paul 136, 142, 179n
Morris, Norman, Prof 58, 95
Moses, Robert 34, 108, 171n
Motorway Box
    See Ringway 1
Movement for London 138, 152
Moyle, Roland, MP 45, 59, 64, 86, 87, 100
Mulley, Fred, MP 73, 79, 99

Norris, Stephen 134, 154
North Circular Road 13, 16, 18, 44, 48, 53, 59, 105, 135, 137, 138, 139, 140, 142, 145, 154, 155, 156, 157, 171n, 179n
    See also Ringway 2, C ring
North Cross Route 43, 47, 54, 58, 73, 88, 91, 96, 99, 100, 160
North Orbital Route 13-14, 15, 115, 116, 168, 177n
    See also E ring
Nugent, Richard, Sir 31-32, 35, 76
ORBIT
    See London Orbital Multi Modal Study

Ove Arup 146, 147, 148
Oxleas Wood 145-146, 151-152, 153

PARC
    See People Against River Crossing
Parkinson, Cecil, MP 144, 149, 150, 154, 159
Parkway E 47, 74, 167
People Against River Crossing 145, 150, 153, 181n
Pharoah, Tim 63, 96, 102, 109
Phillips, Jane 47
Phillipson, Robert 77, 85, 95
Plowden, Stephen 80, 86, 95, 102, 112, 118
Plummer, Desmond, Sir 37, 56, 77, 78, 79, 80
Prescott, John 144, 156
Proudlove, J Alan 32

Rayfield, Frank 31
Rendel Palmer Tritton 123-124, 128, 132
Ridley, Nicholas, MP 5, 138-139, 142, 144, 146
Rifkind, Malcolm, MP 124, 150
Ringway 1 75, 78-79, 83, 84, 95, 96, 97-98, 99, 100, 101, 102, 103, 105, 111, 112, 160
    See also B Ring
Ringway 2 53, 83, 87, 88, 99-100, 101, 104, 105, 135, 137, 149, 157, 163
    See also C Ring
Ringway 3 82, 83, 86, 100, 112-114, 115-116, 157, 165

See also D Ring, M16
Ripa de Meana, Carlo 150, 152
Rippon, Geoffrey, MP 101-102, 103
Roads Campaign Council (RCC) 26, 32
Roads Task Force 157
Rochester Way Relief Road 136, 145, 154
   See also Dover Relief Road
Rowland G E 73

SACTRA
   See Standing Advisory Committee on Trunk Road Assessment
Samuels, Alex, Sir 24, 138
Sandys, Duncan, MP 62
Shelton, Bill, MP 105
Silvertown Tunnel 158-159
Sir William Halcrow & Partners 148-149
Smeed committee 62, 133
Smigielski, Konrad 32, 33, 173n
Smith, T Dan 41, 173n
South Circular Road 11, 15, 18, 48, 53, 143, 146, 148, 149, 150
South Cross Route 40, 43, 45, 47, 54, 56-57, 62, 88, 99-100, 105, 149, 160
South Orbital Route 19, 53, 115, 116, 168
   See also E ring, M25
South Woodford – Barking Relief Road 135, 143
   See also East London River Crossing
Staines 17, 115, 116, 124
Standing Advisory Committee on Trunk Road Assessment (SACTRA) 126-127, 141, 154
Staples Corner 31, 43, 105, 135
Stewart, John 130, 143, 150, 154, 159
Stockley Park 130
Stott, Peter 39, 43, 76, 79, 82
Streatham 59, 73, 74, 105-106, 146, 148, 149
Streatham Vale Property Owners Association 55
Surrey County Council 105, 126, 127
Sutherland, Alistair 99

Thames Gateway Bridge (TGB) 156
   See also East London River Crossing
Thamesmead 53, 145, 156
Thatcher, Margaret, MP 5, 45, 122, 136, 138, 140, 143, 146, 150, 171n
Thomas, Mary 62
   See also Mary Jay
Thomson, Michael 62-63, 80-85, 86, 95, 96, 97, 101, 102, 129, 181n
Transport for London (TfL) 155, 156, 157, 158, 179n
Travers Morgan 39, 43, 54, 58, 80, 105, 143, 146, 148, 149
Tyme, John 119

Vigars, Robert 32, 37, 56, 75, 77, 78, 86, 91, 103

Walker, Peter, MP 75, 95, 101
Wallington 59, 74, 102, 105-106
Wandsworth 58, 59, 64, 77, 104, 139, 143, 144, 148, 149, 150
Warren, Andrew 118, 138
West Beckenham 62
West Cross Route 24, 37, 38, 39, 43, 47, 50, 54, 62, 65, 72, 75, 78, 88, 90, 91, 95, 99, 103-104, 136, 143, 146, 149, 157, 160
West London Relief Road 136
   See also Western Environmental Improvement Route
Western Avenue Extension 17, 20, 23
   See also Westway
Western Environmental Improvement Route 149
   See also West Cross Route
Westway 37, 38, 43, 49, 51, 88-91, 100, 103, 157
   See also Western Avenue Extension
Wetzel, David 136, 179n
Whitaker, Ben, MP 58
Williams, Tom, Prof 96, 178n
Wilson, Harold MP 33, 58, 76, 87, 107
Wise, Jacqui 156,